SCHOOLS AND FAMILIES

The Guilford School Practitioner Series

EDITORS

STEPHEN N. ELLIOTT, PhD
University of Wisconsin–Madison

JOSEPH C. WITT, PhD
Louisiana State University, Baton Rouge

Schools and Families

CREATING ESSENTIAL
CONNECTIONS FOR LEARNING

♦♦♦

Sandra L. Christenson
Susan M. Sheridan

♦

THE GUILFORD PRESS
New York   London

Library of Congress Cataloging-in-Publication Data

Christenson, Sandra, 1946–
   Schools and families : creating essential connections for learning / Sandra L.
   Christenson, Susan M. Sheridan.
       p.   cm. — (The Guilford school practitioner series)
   Includes bibliographical references (p.) and index.
   ISBN 1-57230-654-8 (hardcover)
   1. Home and school—United States.   2. Education—Parent participation—
United States.   I. Sheridan, Susan M.   II. Title.   III. Series.

   LC225.3 .C49 2001
   371.19′2—dc21   00-067682

To the many individuals—parents, teachers, psychologists, administrators, and researchers—who strive to create consistency across children's environments, and continuity across school years, for the purpose of fostering conditions for successful adaptation, learning, and development

About the Authors

◆

Sandra L. Christenson, PhD, is a Professor of Educational and Child Psychology at the University of Minnesota and a member of the faculty of the School Psychology Program. Dr. Christenson has published extensively about theory, research, and strategies for engaging students and parents at school and with learning. Her current research is focused on interventions that enhance student engagement with school and learning, and identification of contextual factors that facilitate student engagement and increase the probability for student success in school. She is particularly interested in populations that are most alienated from traditional schooling practices and/or at highest risk for school noncompletion. Her recent investigations involve understanding how students make a personal investment in learning, and ways to promote the role of families in educating students. She is coeditor, with Susan Sheridan, of the APA Division 16 book series entitled, "Applying Psychology to the Schools," and is a recipient of the Lightner Witmer Award from the American Psychological Association for scholarship and early career contributions to the field of school psychology.

Susan M. Sheridan, PhD, is a Professor of Educational (School) Psychology at the University of Nebraska–Lincoln. She received her PhD in Educational Psychology (School Psychology) from the University of Wisconsin–Madison, and her primary research interests are in the areas of home–school partnerships, conjoint behavioral consultation, social skills interventions, and behavioral interventions. She has been the recipient of multiple federal grants; completed several studies; and published books, journal articles, and chapters on these and related topics. Her recent publications include *Conjoint Behavioral Consultation: A Procedural Manual, Educational Partnerships: Serving Students at Risk, The Tough Kid Social Skills Book,* and *Why Don't They Like Me?: Helping Your Child Make and Keep Friends.* She is a recipient of the Lightner Witmer Award from the American Psychological Association for early career accomplishments, the 1995 Outstanding Young Alumnus Award from the University of Wisconsin–Madison School of Education, and the 1996 School Psychologist of the Year from the Utah Association of School Psychologists. She is also the current editor of *School Psychology Review,* the official journal of the National Association of School Psychologists.

Acknowledgments

♦

No book is the result of one individual, and this book is no exception. We not only collaborated in the writing of this book, but found this collaboration to be enjoyable and rewarding. Throughout the writing process we listened to each other, each in turn serving as teacher and learner. We also have learned from the many families and professionals with whom we have been fortunate to work. As school psychology professors, we appreciate the willingness of educators in elementary, middle, and high schools who have opened their doors to us for research and field placement sites for our graduate students. We hope they have learned as much from us as we have from them.

As parents, we personally have experienced the benefits of family–school relationships for our children, who range in age from 5 to 30. In particular, we have experienced firsthand the fact that parents, not teachers, understand the child's school experiences across years and between critical transitions. We would be remiss not to acknowledge the influence of these varied experiences in writing this book. Many vignettes in this book represent lessons we have learned from—and as—parents and educators.

Our heartfelt thanks are extended to our graduate students, who have influenced our thinking and consistently challenged us to address critical issues between families and school personnel. They have been a constant source of stimulation for underscoring the essential nature of and improving the family–school relationship for student success. And, in many cases, they have been our best daily critics. We also acknowledge the individuals who gave graciously of their time to review our manuscript.

We wish to credit the individuals who assisted us throughout the writing phase: Deb Lavoie for her word processing assistance and endless help with communication between us, and Holly Sexton for her clerical assistance and good humor.

We wish to thank those who contributed their skills and expertise in the production phase: our editor, Chris Jennison, and copy editor, Jacquelyn Coggin, at The Guilford Press, as well as our indexer, John Eagle, for his diligence and persistence in the final stage of the book. We acknowledge as well the unwavering support and encouragement of Sharon Panulla, our original editor at The Guilford Press, who encouraged the submission of a proposal on this topic many years ago. Her enthusiasm for and focus on the process of developing family–school relationships were extremely influential in our final product. Most importantly, her patience and sustained belief that this book would be completed were unexcelled. Along with Stephen Elliott and Joseph Witt, series coeditors, she provided the necessary time for our ideas to simmer and coalesce, as well as the continued motivation to complete this book.

Finally, we thank our families for their love, support, and commitment to our work. They provide us with daily doses of joy and wisdom.

Contents

♦

Prologue

♦

Many books exist about families and schools, and working with families has long been an interest of the fields of psychology and education (Lombard, 1979). *Why another book?*

This book is written for professionals who are interested in changing policies and practices related to home–school relationships. A diverse array of professionals who work on behalf of children and families may find it of interest, including school, community, and clinical psychologists, and counselors, social workers, educators, special educators, and administrators. However, it is different than many excellent existing resources for school and community-based professionals. First, this book is not about parent or family involvement. Parent or family involvement is multifaceted and different definitions are not interchangeable (Keith et al., 1993). Parent involvement has been referred to as an undifferentiated, complex construct that is comprised of different parent behaviors (Zellman & Waterman, 1998). Furthermore, parent involvement, by virtue of its label, implies a microsystemic orientation such as the family's role in enhancing school success or the effect of family influences on children's academic and social growth.

Rather, this book is about the interface of two primary socialization environments—family and school—for children's learning. Positive family–school relationships are necessary for socializing and supporting children and adolescents as learners (Bempechat, 1998). This book emphasizes a mesosystemic orientation and is about family–school relationships, and the educational performance and development of children and youth. This book is not about parent involvement. Rather, it is about the goals, contributions, and accountability of families and schools for educational outcomes.

    Second, this book does not describe one model or framework
for working with families. Several books that describe specific
models or frameworks for creating family–school relationships to
enhance children's learning and educational experiences are readily available for school psychologists' reference and use. These resources, including those authored by Canter and Canter (1991),
Fruchter, Gullotta, and White (1992), Swap (1993), Rioux and
Berla (1993), Comer, Haynes, Joyner, and Ben-Avie (1996), Epstein, Coates, Salinas, Sanders, and Simon (1997), Fuller and
Olsen (1998), and the National PTA (2000), provide important content about family–school relationships. Admittedly, these authors,
as well as those who appear in edited books (i.e., Booth & Dunn,
1996; Chavkin, 1993; Christenson & Conoley, 1992; Fine & Carlson, 1992; Ryan, Adams, Gullotta, Weissberg, & Hampton, 1995),
have influenced our thinking. We draw on their work as we describe process variables for connecting in productive, constructive
ways with families.
    In this book, we purposefully make a distinction between ac-
tivities and actions. In the vast literature available on parent involvement, we find the primary emphasis is on activities to be implemented at school to involve parents and families in education.
We prefer thinking about actions that school personnel in general, and school psychologists in particular, can take to work with
families "as partners" over time. The use of the word "actions" implies that there is no one activity or even a best set of activities,
but instead important process-related variables that together suggest unique pathways for the home–school interface. This implies
that attitudes are important for successful implementation. Furthermore, the link between attitudes and actions, and the rationale for implementing specific activities is critical. For example, a
parent volunteer program to assist teachers is, at minimum, a
narrow and perhaps wrong conceptualization of volunteering. The
value of volunteering is that it can be considered and promoted as
concrete evidence of parents saying that education is valuable and
schools saying that parents are essential. Broad volunteering activities provide a chance for two adults to teach the child as well
as model working together for the benefit of students.
    Finally, this book is about the family–student–school context
and, as a result, is about processes important to establishing positive connections between families and school personnel to enhance
children's learning and development in grades K–12. We know
parent/home, school/teacher, student, and community factors in-

fluence the degree to which parents actively participate and are involved in their children's education (Procidano & Fisher, 1992; Smith et al., 1997). We know there is no one preferred model or framework for family–school relationships. Rather, it is necessary to examine assumptions, goals, attitudes, behaviors, and strategies to determine the most appropriate approach (Swap, 1993). Epstein (1995) spoke about the need for the family–school–community action team to "tailor its menu of practices" to the needs of families, schools, and students. We agree. Understanding the unique aspects of the particular family–student–school context, what Pianta and Walsh (1996) have referred to as the invidious triangle, is essential. In addition, understanding the "connects" and "disconnects" (Fantuzzo & Mohr, 2000) for students' learning led us to focus purposely on processes for enhancing connections between families and school personnel.

Our decision to emphasize processes for constructive family–school connections was reinforced by the following comment from a special education director seeking professional staff development in home–school collaboration: "How do we get schools to be family-friendly? I can't tell you how often I hear school personnel bashing parents because they are not involved in their children's education. However, I don't think the schools understand that they play an important role in fostering good home–school collaboration." In this book, we offer an inventory to be used by school personnel to engage in self-assessment of personal attitudes and school practices. It is our belief that this analysis is more important for partnering with families than is implementation of family-involvement activities in isolation. Activities provide good ideas; however, not all good ideas work in every school community. A goal in selecting activities is to achieve a match or goodness of fit for families and schools to enhance students' learning and school experiences.

Therefore, in this book, we describe key elements or conditions necessary for this goodness of fit. They are characterized by four components: approach, attitudes, atmosphere, and actions. Each component represents a theoretically driven and scientifically based area for consideration by school psychologists who are consulting at individual or system levels to develop family–school connections for learners. The components are defined as follows:

- ◆ Approach: *The framework for interaction with families*
- ◆ Attitudes: *The values and perceptions held about family–school relationships*

- Atmosphere: *The climate in schools for families and educators*
- Actions: *Strategies for building shared responsibility*

We offer these four A's as a guide in the development of family–school connections for children's learning. In this book, we provide guidelines to address the following:

- What *approach* will be used to foster positive family–school connections for children's learning? How can the approach be communicated and implemented flexibly to allow for different or unique situations?
- What *attitudes* about family involvement, and among educators, families and students, are evident? How can positive attitudes be enhanced to promote healthy home–school relations?
- In what type of *atmosphere* will families, educators, and students interact? How can the atmosphere facilitate a constructive home–school interface?
- What *actions* will be taken to achieve a balanced, collaborative relationship to address systemwide and individual student concerns? How will these actions address the primary goal of promoting constructive partnerships for children's learning and development?

As we describe these four components, we raise critical issues for the "connects" and "disconnects" for family, students, and school personnel. We challenge the reader to think about the following: What kind of relationship is desired in this family–student–school context? What are the rights of families, students, and school personnel? What are the roles and responsibilities of families, students, and school personnel? What are the resources each brings to enhance educational outcomes and learning experiences for students? With dialogue, not monologue, on these issues, the probability is high that families and school personnel can be partners in education and, consequently, partners in prevention of school failure for children and youth. And we contend that families and schools as partners can occur with traditionally oriented practices and partnership models (e.g., Swap, 1993).

At the beginning of each chapter, we offer questions for readers to consider while reading about approaches, attitudes, atmospheres, and actions. These questions are meant to organize readers' thoughts about important elements that can be realized in their school community. Following each chapter, additional questions for readers serve as a stimulus to recap main points and place them in an applied context. Case studies, vignettes, and activities are presented as actual examples to which school and community professionals may relate. They may also serve as points of discussion for school- or community-based teams, professionals in training, and other readers, to facilitate an active learning process.

Productive family–school relationships can take many forms. Given the influence of context, we suggest that family and school as partners is a concept and not an exact prescription or prescribed set of steps or activities. Working as partners, however, depends on careful consideration of school-based practices for connecting with families vis-à-vis educational and psychological service delivery. Working as partners necessitates careful consideration of how the approach, attitudes, atmosphere, and actions adopted in a school community influence differential educational success for students. The context includes (but is certainly not limited to) what is already in place (i.e., schools' and families' unique strengths, and the existing strengths in the relationship), and what is needed (i.e., the gaps) to maximize educational success opportunities. In this book, we offer a guide for the consideration of families and educators who are creating essential connections to aid in the development of children and youth.

CHAPTER 1

♦♦♦

Family–School Relationships as a Protective Factor

♦

Implicit in two national education goals—Goal 1 and Goal 8—is the notion that family and school are partners in prevention of school failure for children. Family–school relationships have been identified as a primary domain of protective factors for children, particularly those living in high-risk circumstances (Weissberg & Greenberg, 1998). The goal of family involvement with education is not merely to get families involved, but rather to connect important contexts for strengthening children's learning and development. Family–school relationships have been described as a safety net to promote children's learning and school experiences (Christenson, 2000).

Constructing family–school relationships as a means to this end is receiving primary recognition across grade levels. For example, Powell (1992) noted that family involvement during early childhood had moved from the orientation of how to get parents involved to how to support families to promote positive child development. Similarly, the most interesting questions regarding school-age children have moved from how to get parents involved toward what schools can do to promote positive child and family development (Smith et al., 1997). Pianta and Walsh (1996) emphasized the importance of establishing shared meaning across home and school to interrupt the cycle of failure for children. To move from a culture of failure to a culture of success, they argued, we must recognize that "school failure is at its core caused by an inability or an unwillingness to communicate—a relationship problem" (p. 24). In summary, relationships are viewed as a means to foster resilience. According to Wang, Haertl, and Walberg (1997), "Resilience is promoted when the resources in the school, family, and community are united and dedicated to the healthy development and academic success of children" (p. 137).

National Education Goals 1 and 8 explicitly link families and schools, and encourage educators to examine how school policies and practices influence their relationships with families. As we enter the new millennium, the goals, which are presented in Table 1.1, set the expectation that every child will start school ready to learn, and every school will promote partnerships that increase parent participation in facilitating the social, emotional, and academic growth of children (Goals 2000: Educate America Act, Public Law 103-227). With what success have these goals been met by year 2000? According to *The National Education Goals Report: Building a Nation of Learners* (National Education Goals Panel,

TABLE 1.1. National Education Goals 1 and 8

Goal 1: School readiness: "By the year 2000, all children in America will start school ready to learn. The objectives for this goal are that:

◆ All children will have access to high-quality and developmentally appropriate preschool programs that help prepare children for school.
◆ Every parent in the United States will be a child's first teacher and devote time each day to helping such parent's preschool child learn, and parents will have access to the training and support parents need.
◆ Children will receive the nutrition, physical activity experiences, and health care needed to arrive at school with healthy minds and bodies and to maintain the mental alertness necessary to be prepared to learn, and the number of low-birth weight babies will be significantly reduced through enhanced prenatal health systems" (p. 8).

Goal 8: Parent participation: "By the year 2000, every school will promote partnerships that will increase parental involvement and participation in promoting the social, emotional, and academic growth of children. The objectives for this goal are that:

◆ Every state will develop policies to assist local schools and local educational agencies to establish programs for increasing partnerships that respond to the varying needs of parents and the home, including parents of children who are disadvantaged or bilingual, or parents of children with disabilities;
◆ Every school will actively engage parents and families in a partnership which supports the academic work of children at home and shared educational decision making at school; and
◆ Parents and families will help ensure that schools are adequately supported and will hold schools and teachers to high standards of accountability" (p. 36).

Note. From Goals 2000: Educate America Act, Public Law 103-227.

1999), of children enrolled in preschool, the majority of states have reduced the percentages of infants born with one or more health risks and increased the numbers of children with disabilities. Three states—California, Colorado, and Indiana—significantly reduced the percentage of public school principals reporting that lack of parental involvement in their schools was a serious problem. Also, one-third of the states significantly increased the percentage of principals reporting that parent associations in their schools had influenced school policy in one or more areas. Clearly, the data available on implementation efforts for developing family–school partnerships to enhance children's learning and development paint a picture that suggests the intended agenda is unfinished. Promoting successful school experiences for all students is challenging in light of current national reform efforts to raise achievement in relation to high academic standards, end social promotion, and measure student performance using high-stakes testing. Given these challenges, school psychologists play a critical role in promoting successful school experiences for students across grades K–12.

THE ROLE OF POLICY

In the past decade, an interest in family–school relationships has increased immeasurably due to the dramatic changes in the structure and function of families and the consistent, cumulative findings that home environments and out-of-school time contribute to children's learning. In addition, school reform efforts focused only on teacher and school practices have not been overwhelmingly successful in improving student achievement, especially for low-income and nonwhite students (Kellaghan, Sloane, Alvarez, & Bloom, 1993). Because of the recognition that parents play a role in developing children's learning habits, federal policies for family involvement have been established in the National Education Goals (National Education Goals Panel, 1999), and further explicated in the Individuals with Disabilities Education Act (IDEA; U.S. Congress, 1999), and Title 1 (U.S. Department of Education, 1997). Furthermore, position statements from professional organizations that reinforce federal policies have been generated. For example, in April 1999, the delegate assembly of the National Association of School Psychologists (NASP) revised and passed a position statement on home–school collaboration, which appears in Appendix A. The statement underscores that home–school collaboration is a process that guides the development of goals and plans between families and schools. With its emphasis on promoting educationally and psychologically healthy environments for all children and youth, the revision underscores a resilience-based orientation evident in most family involvement models (Christenson, 2000).

School and district policies (e.g., mission statements) and state and federal policies and regulations (e.g., mandated roles for parents in Title 1 and special education) provide a necessary but insufficient framework within which practitioners operate. A commonly held vision across stakeholders, apparent in both written policies and administrative support for parent involvement, is considered key in districtwide reform of parent involvement (Williams & Chavkin, 1989). To have an effect on the actions of families and educators, policies must be visible and known. Davies (1987) has consistently advocated that policies on parent involvement must also be supported by mechanisms for monitoring, enforcing, and providing technical assistance. However, to reach the objectives of the National Education Goals, a relationship between families and schools (what really matters) cannot be mandated. With respect to the change process, Fullan (1996) cautions that we cannot mandate what matters. Viewing policies as essential catalysts, he stated, "If you try to mandate certain things—such as skills, attitudes, behaviors, and beliefs—your attempts to achieve change start to break down. Where change is mandated, policies at best are likely to achieve only superficial compliance" (p. 496). This cautionary remark is far too often violated in design and implementation of family involvement programs.

According to Corrigan and Bishop (1997), family–professional collaboration should no longer be considered an option but rather a professional obligation, because it has been so strongly and consistently supported by research. However, school personnel and families know collaboration works best when individuals are "motivated, not obliged" to work together (Christenson, Rounds, & Franklin, 1992). Conley's (1991) work in school restructuring is particularly relevant. He has defined restructuring efforts (as opposed to reform efforts) as activities that change fundamental assumptions, practices, and relationships, both within the school and the community, in ways that lead to improved student learning outcomes. His focus raises critical questions about how we define family involvement, particularly in terms of roles and responsibilities for students, families, and schools.

One of our assertions is that there is a need for a new social contract between families and schools, one in which students, families, peers, and teachers are placed in an altered relation to one another and to the child's education. U.S. Secretary of Education Richard Riley seems to agree. He recently pointed out, "Parents are the essential link to improving American education, and schools have to do a better job of reaching out to them. Sending a report card home is not enough. Parents want to help their children succeed in school, and often need guidance on how to be most effective" (cited in Skoglund, 1999, p. 1).

THE "WHAT" AND THE "HOW"

In the past 10 years, much significant work has been accomplished in the area of family–school relationships. First, a structure for organizing family–school partnership activities has been developed and widely disseminated for use in schools. Noted researcher Joyce Epstein (1995) has delineated six types of family–school involvement, underscoring that families and schools can connect in many ways, and that families can and do participate both at school and at home. Epstein has moved from traditional definitions for the involvement types. For example, "workshop" means making information about a topic available in a variety of forms, not merely a meeting about a topic held at the school building. Or "help" at home means encouraging, listening, reacting, monitoring and discussing schoolwork, not just "teaching" school subjects.

Sample practices for the six types are illustrated in Table 1.2. Type 1, *parenting,* refers to the school assisting families with parenting skills, helping parents understand child and adolescent development, and helping families provide home conditions that support learning. The development of effective two-way communication about school programs and children's progress between home and school defines Type 2, *communicating. Volunteering,* Type 3, refers to school efforts in recruiting, training, and organizing families to support students and school programs. In Type 4, *enhancing learning at home,* educators are encouraged to work with families. Type 5, *decision making,* refers to involving families in school- and district-level decision making, including decisions for both practices and policies. Epstein's Type 6, *collaborating with the community,* coordinates resources and services to families, students, and schools to enhance students' learning and school experiences. To date, we believe the literature is filled with many ideas for family involvement activities (i.e., the "what").

TABLE 1.2. Sample Practices for Epstein's Six Types of Involvement

Parenting

- Offer information on child development at each age and grade (e.g., workshops, videos, books, tip sheets, computerized messages, bulletin board).
- Explain the relationship between home influences and school performance.
- Establish a lending library for parent education materials.
- Provide parents with information on curricular changes, contents of school records, how to monitor student progress, and so on.
- Develop family support programs, parent education offerings responsive to family preferences, and Café Parent (e.g., parent center).
- Provide home visits at critical transition points (e.g., elementary to middle school) to establish a personal contact, provide information, and address parental questions.
- Develop a media blitz to publicize ways parents support student learning (e.g., "Did You Know?" column in a school newsletter or local newspaper).
- Include tips on how parents with limited budgets can help their children succeed in school.

Communicating

- Offer varied and flexible schedules for appointments (in person or on the phone).
- Establish a "foolproof" contact system between home and school.
- Set the stage for positive communication by getting to know each other (e.g., meet-and-greet events, Doughnuts for Dads).
- Hold an individual interview and joint assessment of the child when he or she first attends the school.
- Hold regular drop-in sessions and office hours for parents.
- Create parent–teacher–student partnership agreements to specify roles and responsibilities.
- Reframe conferences as opportunities for information sharing and problem solving.
- Keep parents in the planning loop by sharing school expectations, discipline policies, course syllabi and homework guidelines; ask for parents' comments.
- Offer back-to-school nights throughout the year to sustain contact between families and educators.

Volunteering

- Survey parents to assess their skills and talents, interests, and needs, and use the results to establish a volunteer program.
- Expect parents to volunteer and offer many options. Parents can complete a *Call Me Once Volunteer Card*, which commits the parent to serve only once a year unless he or she grants you permission to call again.
- Appreciate parents as experts, incorporating into the curriculum the skills from adults in the community.
- Include noncustodial parents on field trips, in special programs, and in-school activities.
- Establish Adopt-a-School, a parent-coordinated effort that arranges for businesses to provide funds and services to the school.

TABLE 1.2 (*continued*)

Volunteering

- Create volunteer opportunities that go beyond traditional tasks, such as Permanent Guest Teachers who, because of their qualifications, "sub" to enable teachers to have time to meet to plan collaborative lessons, to meet with students individually, or to contact families.

Learning at home

- Provide interactive homework activities to increase parent–child communication about schoolwork.
- Send school–home activity packets to parents.
- Provide information on homework policies and how to monitor student performance and progress.
- Sponsor a "Parents Make a Difference" evening, where parents receive an overview of what students will be learning, how they will be assessed, what parents can expect, and how they can assist and make a difference.
- Establish a homework hotline.
- Use home–school assignment books to facilitate communication about ways to encourage learning for children and youth.
- Provide parents with resources (e.g., *MegaSkills*; Rich, 1988) about how to assist their children's learning.

Decision making

- Create parent leaders. Use lay leaders (e.g., parents leading groups).
- Provide training for parents and other advisory council members to help them gain knowledge about educational issues and how to work effectively with schools.
- Ensure that parents' voices are heard on school decisions (e.g., grade-level family representatives on school councils and school improvement teams).
- Develop a family–school team to design ways to address issues that require parent–school input and cooperation for a successful outcome.
- Conduct parent focus groups to increase understanding of critical issues and necessary resources (e.g., improving student success on required tests).

Collaborating with the community

- Furnish local employers with information sheets about the school and parenting/parent involvement ideas.
- Sponsor an annual Give Back Day, where students go into the community to perform needed work or services.
- Participate in school-linked and -coordinated school health efforts (e.g., expanded school health services).
- Work with local churches to sponsor Education Sunday, a workshop to help parents share ideas for providing academic and motivational support to students.
- Develop after school homework/recreational programs.
- Provide information on community resources to address parents concerns.

Much less prevalent are recommendations for processes to enhance home–school relationships (i.e., the "how").

The *National Standards for Parent/Family Involvement Programs* (National PTA, 1998), which were developed by education and parent involvement professionals, are an extension of Epstein's (1995) six types of involvement. As can be seen in Table 1.3, each standard addresses a different type of parent involvement. Accompanying each standard is a set of quality indicators that represents actions to be taken by school personnel to create positive connections for children's learning and development. These indicators appear in Appendix B and can also be obtained from the National PTA (http://www.pta.org). According to the National PTA (2000), "Effectively involving parents requires understanding the four key roles they play in comprehensive and inclusive parent involvement programs" (p. 3). The roles, which are consistent with those identified in the objectives of the National Education Goal 8, are teachers/nurturers, communicators/advisors, supporters/learners, and collaborators/decision makers.

Epstein and others (Comer, 1995; Palanki & Burch, 1995) have contributed significantly to the literature by demonstrating the centrality of a team approach for establishing effective family involvement programs. Specifically, Epstein designed an action team structure to develop schoolwide family–school partnership programs comprised of the six types of involvement (Epstein, 1995). Through a parent–teacher action research team, Davies and his colleagues followed 10 steps to create systemic change that

TABLE 1.3. The National Standards for Parent/Family Involvement Programs

◆ *Communicating*—Communication between home and school is regular, two-way, and meaningful.

◆ *Parenting*—Parenting skills are promoted and supported.

◆ *Student learning*—Parents play an integral role in assisting student learning.

◆ *Volunteering*—Parents are welcome in the school, and their support and assistance are sought.

◆ *School decision making and advocacy*—Parents are full partners in the decisions that affect their children and families.

◆ *Collaborating with community*—Community resources are used to strengthen schools, families, and student learning.

helped school communities identify strategies that work to build family–school–community collaboration for students. Comer and his colleagues used teams to restructure schools. In his model, the School Planning and Management Team sets school-based policies and practices with the ongoing input of families and school personnel for the purpose of encouraging and sustaining children and youth along six developmental pathways.

Clearly, we have important information available about family–school relationships. However, based on our work and comprehensive review of the literature, we contend that our knowledge is stronger for the "what" than the "how." A direction is provided in the objectives of the National Education Goals; quality indicators are available for each standard of comprehensive parent involvement programs, and there are lists of excellent activities for families and educators to consider when designing programs. We have structures for implementing a team process. Thus, important tools for creating connections for children's learning are readily available for school personnel.

Beyond our knowledge that a team approach is important for developing a program, we suggest that less attention is paid to critical process variables for creating constructive connections for children's learning. Our impetus for writing this book is that the literature is clearer about the outcome of constructive family–school relationships (i.e., correlational data described in Chapter 2) than the implementation process. We suggest this is due to the context-specific nature of family–school relationships, complexity of developing intersystem relationships, and communication demands for families and schools. Equally important is the necessity to implement these elements of collaborative practices: (1) equal status among participants (e.g., parents, teachers, students, psychologists, principals), (2) a common goal, and (3) adequate leadership and support (Allport, 1954). Making the family–school relationship a priority for children's learning is a daunting but doable task, one that requires careful consideration of the process used.

In this book, we describe process variables (i.e., the "how") to guide school psychologists who consult at individual or system levels to develop constructive, productive family–school relationships to enhance the academic, social, and behavioral growth of children and adolescents. Before introducing these, we first describe the current state of affairs and critical issues facing families and schools.

CURRENT CONDITIONS

Often, a positive connection exists between families and educators; sometimes the family–school relationship is best described as a troubled terrain. Other times, families and educators are strangers; they "seem like people from a different region of the country, each speaking the same language, but in a unique dialect" (Merseth, Schorr, & Elmore, 1999, p. 6). Regardless of the quality of the interaction between home and school, several things are true. First, there is always a relationship between families and schools (Pianta & Walsh, 1996). Similarly, Doherty and Peskay (1992) caution that parents are always implicated either as active or silent partners; families can provide support or distractions for children's school learning. The desired state is for the family–school relationship to function as a protective factor, albeit, in some situations, it may be a risk factor. Integral to understanding children's school experience is Pianta and Walsh's (1996) notion that discontinuity between family and school with respect to values for education, communication, and support is a risk factor for many children and youth. The role of the student in the family–school relationship is acknowledged. Students are not to be uninvolved; efforts are taken by families and educators to help students see themselves as learners. In fact, the reason for the family–school relationship is to enhance educational experiences by creating a climate for student learning, a culture for student success.

Second, although families and schools are two critical microsystems for children's development, they are each accustomed to operating autonomously. Thus, creating a constructive family–school interface to enhance students' learning and development is a relatively new approach, evident in varied arenas. Educational reform, particularly in the form of standards and high-stakes testing, is occurring nationwide in response to the eight national education goals that have been established as a result of Educate America Act (PL 103-227) signed in 1994. School reform efforts call for the inclusion of families to support learners as they strive to attain specified educational standards (Lewis & Henderson, 1997). Also, in the coordinated school health movement, a family–school relationship characterized by communication, cooperation, coordination, and collaboration is considered an essential support linkage for improving student performance, reducing risk behaviors in adolescence, enhancing healthy development, and achieving high expectations for all students (Marx & Wooley, 1998).

Only recently has it been common in major policy and research reports to recommend family–school–community partnerships as a means to improve student outcomes. For example, the Office of Educational Accountability, housed at the College of Education and Human Development at the University of Minnesota, recently completed a 91-page report on the state results for math, science, and reading. While the results of the tests for students in grades 3, 5, and 8 placed Minnesota at or near the top of state ranks nationally, the breadth and scope of ethnic differences in graduation rates and achievement were noted as being simply intolerable. The study recommended that any turnaround would require a *genuine* family–school–community partnership. The report states, "Responsibility for the differences cannot be laid solely at the feet of schools. It will take a genuine family–school–community partnership to address the problems faced by minority children and their schools. And if it is a true partnership, each partner—the schools, families, and the community—must accept and be willing to be accountable for its share of the responsibility" (Davison, 1998, p. 52). Because of achievement discrepancies for white and nonwhite students, much research in the area of partnerships for students' learning has focused on students from low-income or ethnically diverse backgrounds in urban schools. It is our contention, however, that strong family–school connections are relevant for all students. In fact, we speculate that achievement for average students might be enhanced immeasurably if shared responsibility for students' learning were the societal norm.

In the past decade, partnerships for students' learning and development have frequently been discussed and our content knowledge about the roles for families, schools, and students has increased tenfold, as evidenced by the number of books, journal articles, and conference presentations on the topic. For example, it has been shown that family–school relationships are essential to the programming for children with attention-deficit/hyperactivity disorder (ADHD) (August, Anderson, & Bloomquist, 1992), conduct disorders (Reid & Patterson, 1992; Webster-Stratton, 1993), social skills deficits (Sheridan, Kratochwill, & Elliott, 1990) and homework-completion difficulties (Jayanthi, Sawyer, Nelson, Bursuck, & Epstein, 1995), as well as significant improvement in academic achievement (Hansen, 1986; Heller & Fantuzzo, 1993). Despite these varied arenas, there is still "more rhetoric than reality" about family and school working as *genuine* partners.

Third, family–school relationships are broader and, consequently, not synonymous with parent–teacher relationships. Family may refer to grandparents, older siblings, other relatives, and, in some situations, surrogate parents, such as neighbors. School includes all school personnel and the emotional climate and problem solving that occur among the various professionals interfacing with families on the behalf of children and youth. Hence, family–school relationships focus on the interface of two systems for the purpose of socializing students as learners and enhancing the development of children and youth.

Finally, positive family–school connections take many forms and demand site-specific development (National Association of State Boards of Education, 1992). According to Kagan (1984), strong parent involvement programs are developed with input from families and school personnel on two questions: What forms of parent participation are desirable and feasible? What strategies can be employed to achieve them? The interface between families and school must fit the specific context—or address the needs of parents, teachers, and students. Neither a "one size fits all" approach nor a focus on activities in the absence of nurturing essential attitudes among the partners will work for schools. Historically, our emphasis has been on what we do to involve families (i.e., activities) rather than how we think of the family–school relationship (i.e., attitudes) as a means for socializing and supporting students as learners.

The Importance of Process

It is essential to understand process variables that influence family–school connections that foster children's learning. This area is often thought of as simple; after all, parents and teachers share a vested interest in children and youth. There is common agreement for the notion that effective inclusion of parents and community with education is about (1) supporting, teaching, and enjoying children and youth; (2) working together to promote positive outcomes for children and youth, including school completion, achievement, opportunity to learn, social functioning, and achievement; and (3) creating conditions that support children and adolescents as learners (Christenson, 1995; Epstein, 1995; Rich, 1987). Thus, an effective family–school connection is prevention-oriented and represents a 13-year contract between families and schools to provide a quality education for all students.

The complexity in creating strong family–school connections originates with the historically autonomous functioning of the family and school systems. We argue that there are many issues and considerations for school psychologists and other school professionals when creating constructive connections. Furthermore, perspectives from parents, educators, and students must be actively solicited, valued, and used. In a discussion of the enhanced role for families in the reauthorization of IDEA (U.S. Congress, 1999), Osher (1997) challenged service providers to be attentive to the necessity of family access, voice, and ownership. Too often parent involvement activities are offered without consideration of variables that will influence successful implementation of family involvement activities.

The Status of Relationships

In reality, current, modal family–school relationships would be described differently than the aforementioned commonly articulated definition for effective inclusion of families. For example, parents tend to adopt a reactive rather than a proactive stance with respect to academic support for learning (Bempechat, 1998). They get involved later, most often when children are having difficulty with schoolwork. Furthermore, they are still predominantly passive during individualized educational planning (IEP) meetings (Fine, 1993; Harry, Allen, & McLaughlin, 1995; National Council on Disability, 1995). Also, we know that while teachers can say what they expect of families, they less often articulate what they want to do for families. Parents have less chance to come to school, "hard-to-reach" families may not understand school policies and practices, schools want involvement on their own terms, and educators can be wary of families, often afraid to invite parent assistance to resolve a concern. Additionally, some families do not recognize their role as educators. Delgado-Gaitan (1991) contended that the difference between families who are involved and those who are not is that involved family members recognize that they play a critical role in their child's education.

Educators vary in the kinds of outreach activities in which they engage. Data from the National Center for Education Statistics (1998) suggest that school personnel often do very well at communicating about children's progress (albeit one-way communication), providing information on child development, and making parents aware of volunteer opportunities. In contrast, educators do less well at providing information on how to help children learn at home or with homework, information on community resources, workshops and classes on parenting, and opportunities for parents to be actively involved as decision makers—all of which place a greater emphasis on the interface of home and school for children's school success. Given the two main objectives of National Education Goal 8—support for children's academic work at home and shared decision making at school—there is cause for concern about the identified weaknesses in school practices. Compounding the concern is the finding that teachers in grades K–12 believe it is very hard for children to succeed in school without involved parents (Public Agenda, 1999).

Mutual reluctance has been identified in family–school interactions about schooling issues. Data from the Metropolitan Life Survey of the American Teacher (1987), which included responses from 2,000 parents and 1,000 teachers, showed that although only 8% rated the relationship as poor and 60% felt mutual support, 19% of parents felt awkward talking to school personnel and 55% of teachers felt uneasy or reluctant to approach parents to discuss their child. Repeated in 1997 with some modifications, the views of 1,035 secondary teachers of students in grades 6–12 and 1,036 students in grades 7–12 on varied aspects of family–school partnerships were solicited (Binns, Steinberg, & Amorosi, 1997). Major findings from this survey, summarized in Table 1.4, are provided for two reasons. First, the survey represents a relatively recent picture of family–school partnerships for students' learning. Second, although parent perspectives were not obtained, the results reinforce the complexity of understanding family–school relationships. To illustrate this point, compare the finding "81% of teachers believe their schools do a good job of encouraging parent involvement in educational areas" with the finding "teachers are evenly split over how much say parents should have in policy decisions affecting the classroom" and the finding that "students favor parents having a voice (not the voice) in such decisions." In part, this explains our focus on process variables rather than an exact prescription for creating constructive family–school connections.

Although educators agree philosophically about working as partners with families, they also find themselves trapped by blaming families or viewing "the home as auxiliary, merely providing supplemental support for the work of the school" (Kellaghan et al., 1993, p. 135). In their book, *Contemporary Families: A Handbook*

TABLE 1.4. Findings from the Metropolitan Life Survey

Students' perceptions of parental involvement in education

- ◆ 83% report that their parents are at least somewhat involved.
- ◆ 14% want their parents to become more involved.
- ◆ 25% of students who are getting grades below C report that their parents are not involved.
- ◆ 32% of students who are getting grades below C want their parents to be less involved.
- ◆ 94% of students report that their parents encourage them to do well in school.
- ◆ 84% of students report that their parents are available to help with schoolwork.
- ◆ 45% of students who get class grades lower than C do not receive parental help in finding time and a place to study.
- ◆ 50% of students who get class grades lower than C report that their parents do not help with homework.
- ◆ Students who get mostly A's and B's (87%) report that their parents are available to help with schoolwork, whereas 24% of students who get grades lower than C report that their parents are not available to help with schoolwork.
- ◆ 73% of students say that their parents find the time to talk with them about their school lives; 78% of students who receive mostly A's and B's report this, whereas 49% of students who get grades lower than C report that their parents do *not* find time for conversations about their school lives.
- ◆ 84% of students say they receive parental encouragement to pursue their dreams; 89% of students who receive A's and B's report this, whereas 27% of students who receive grades lower than C's report that their parents do *not* encourage them to pursue their dreams.

Teachers' perceptions of parental involvement in education

- ◆ Teacher perception of the amount of parental support shown for their schools has not changed since 1987.
- ◆ 83% of teachers believe the level of parental involvement in their schools should increase.
- ◆ 95% of inner-city teachers would like parents to become more involved.
- ◆ 78% of teachers are satisfied or somewhat satisfied with the frequency of contact with parents.
- ◆ 63% of all teachers feel that the availability and responsiveness of parents are excellent or good, whereas 40% of inner-city teachers give parent availability and responsiveness ratings of fair and poor.
- ◆ 35% of teachers feel that parental involvement in education should occur both in school and at home. Most students share this view.
- ◆ 52% of all minority teachers believe it is important that parental involvement take place in the school.

Encouraging parental involvement in schools

- ◆ 81% of secondary teachers believe their schools do a good job of encouraging parental involvement.

(continued)

TABLE 1.4 *(continued)*

Encouraging parental involvement in schools (continued)

- 74% of secondary teachers disagree with the notion that schools only contact parents when there is a problem with their child.
- 57% of students believe their schools offer opportunities for meaningful roles to parents.
- 53% of teachers feel that parents should be kept informed rather than actively consulted about changes in subjects taught.
- 79% of students believe parents should have a lot of, or some, say in decisions regarding subjects taught. Students in urban schools are most likely, and students in suburban schools are least likely, to believe parents should have a lot of input in such decisions.
- 55% of teachers believe parents should be kept informed about changes in homework policy, whereas 43% think that parents should be actively consulted.
- Teachers are evenly split over the issue of whether parents should be actively consulted about changes in extracurricular activities.
- 61% of teachers believe parents should be actively consulted about changes in discipline policy. Minority teachers are the most likely to believe parents must be actively consulted about these changes.
- Only 20% of students believe parents should have no say in disciplinary decisions made by school.
- Although a sizable proportion of teachers believe parents need only be kept informed about school policy changes, the majority is in favor of including parents on committees that oversee school policies.
  - 90% of teachers indicate that involving parents on a management team to determine school policies is very or somewhat valuable.
  - 74% of teachers believe involving parents on committees to determine the school curriculum would be very valuable or somewhat valuable.
  - 98% of teachers believe parents volunteering to help at school is very valuable or somewhat valuable.

Some commonly made criticisms of parents

- 54% of teachers report that most or many parents take too little interest in their children's education.
- Half of the teachers feel that most or many parents fail to motivate their children so that they want to learn in school.
- 56% of teachers feel that most or many parents fail to discipline their children.
- Teachers cite uninvolved parents and lack of parental support as the most frequent obstacles for students doing schoolwork at home.
- 85% of students report that their parents are very, or somewhat, helpful when asked to help with schoolwork.
- Minority boys are the most likely to report that their parents are very helpful when asked for assistance with schoolwork.
- 82% of students feel that their parents are very, or somewhat, helpful with problems they are having with teachers or classmates.
- 80% of students feel that their parents are very, or somewhat, helpful when they express a need related to an emotional difficulty.

for School Professionals, Procidano and Fisher (1992) noted that obstacles to school learning are complicated by prevalent tensions and misunderstandings between families and schools. Consider the following possible scenario:

> Parents may not be included in school policy decisions and may be quite unaware of how schools function. They may feel disconnected when excluded from decisions with respect to their children, and in some cases, they may question the agendas of educators. Over time, parents come to rely on educators and blame them when their child is experiencing difficulty. When this happens, educators may form negative attitudes toward specific parents. In fact, what may have happened is that educators did not use parents as a helpful resource; educators simply never sought parent advice or disregarded parent input in their problem solving. The solutions developed by educators for families are perceived as a misfit by parents.

In addition, the magnitude of disagreement between schools and parents has been found to be proportional to the child's difficulties (Victor, Halvorson, & Wampler, 1988). One result of such misunderstandings is mutual reluctance, often exacerbated by social and physical distance between families and school personnel. Conventional opportunities for communication are rare; opportunities for mutual problem solving are rarer. To circumvent finger pointing, mutual support is necessary. Shifting the blame for children's school problems from the school to home or the home to school is not a satisfactory solution (Scott-Jones, 1995a).

However, much more is right than wrong about current family–school relationships. In addition to the findings presented in Table 1.4, we know that when schools' practices change to reach out to all families, irrespective of income and educational levels, families become more involved in their children's educational lives (Dauber & Epstein, 1993). In fact, lower-income parents often become actively involved when their children's school has an inclusive policy that helps them feel valued, encouraged, and supported (Lewis & Henderson, 1997). Student perceptions of parent involvement in education are also relevant. Forty percent of secondary students say their parents are very involved, 43% say they are somewhat involved, and 68% would like their parents' involvement to remain the same. The vast majority of students (94%) report that their parents encourage them to do well in school; 73% report that their parents find the time to talk with them about their school lives, 62% report that their parents help them find the time and place to study, and 84% report that their parents are available to help with schoolwork when needed (Binns et al., 1997). It is noteworthy that students who have trouble academically are less likely to report that their parents provide them with this sort of encouragement and support. Is this in part due to the point at which parents are asked by school personnel to assist their children? Finally, Epstein (personal communication, November 1995) concluded that 20% of families now work as partners with educators; 70% believe they would and could, if provided with adequate information and support; and 10% of families, because of significant personal problems, do not, cannot, and will not. While not "perfect," 90% of families is significant! We appear to have a momentum on which to build and improve school-based practices and to foster shared responsibility for educational outcomes.

CRITICAL ISSUES

Critical issues facing families and school personnel are represented by the three R's: rights, roles and responsibilities, and resources. Strong family–school connections for children's learning and development must move beyond listing barriers to also include discussing and clarifying parents', teachers', and students' *rights, roles and responsibilities,* and *resources.* We contend that, to date, school personnel have not asked the right questions about family–school relationships. We offer the three R's as a guide to begin thinking about essential process variables that highly influence the extent to which the family–school relationship is productive. For example, parents have rights in public schools, but some parents believe they have little to contribute to their children's school performance. Is this, then, an infringement of the rights of teachers who are concerned about equity issues for students and, as a result, take on extra tasks for specific students, tasks that often represent having to parent and teach? Also, mandates such as IDEA, which delineate parents' rights with little or no corresponding focus on parents' roles and responsibilities for enhancing children's performance, stand in stark contrast to Title 1, where home–school contracts signed by parents, teachers and students are required (Macfarlane, 1995). Negotiating and clearly communicating responsibilities among parents, teachers, and students are necessary to address role confusion reflected in the question: Who is responsible for what (e.g., homework)? Parent involvement has consistently been associated with desirable student outcomes

(Henderson & Berla, 1994), and yet the parental role is implied, not explicitly stated, in routine school practices such as student-focused planning meetings between families and school personnel.

With respect to resources, parents have been described as an underutilized resource for enhancing learning (Graue, Weinstein, & Walberg, 1983; Weiss & Edwards, 1992); however, the degree to which low-income, nonwhite parents are viewed as a resource by educators has been questioned (Edwards, 1992). Quite simply, school psychologists interested in developing effective family–school relationships in schools work with others to address these questions: What are the rights of parents, school personnel, and students with respect to the presenting issue/policy? What are viable roles and responsibilities for families, educators, and students in promoting student performance in schools? Do educators view families as resources when they are making policy and program decisions? What resources do parents and teachers provide for ensuring that students are supported and engaged learners?

Although rights, roles and responsibilities, and resources of the key players are important to the kind of family–school relationship established, the centrality of the relationship for children's learning and schooling experiences is highlighted. Emphasizing the relationship over roles, for example, maintains a focus on communication and coordination, and hopefully encourages the partners to think about how they interact (e.g., treatment of each other and what each expects from the other). Epstein and Connors (1995) have said, "Much like partners in business, partners in education must work hard to clarify their mutual interests in the children they share" (p. 140). A critical issue becomes: What kind of relationship do the partners want? The issue is not whether family involvement in education works, or whether family influences on children's learning are known. Rather, the issue is: How are sustaining relationships between parents and educators constructed (Christenson, 2000; Pianta & Walsh, 1996)?

ESSENTIAL PROCESS VARIABLES

In this book, we offer four A's as a heuristic aid to conceptualize the key elements or conditions necessary for optimal school–family relationships: *approach, attitudes, atmosphere,* and *actions.* As you reflect on the current status of family–school relationships and critical issues facing families and educators, consider the various indicators that impact the degree to which positive connections

TABLE 1.5. Conceptualization of Key Elements for Enhancing Positive
Family–School Connections for Children's Learning

Approach: The framework for interaction with families

Consider the extent to which the following conditions are present:

- ◆ Mutually shared goals across home and school for children's learning.
- ◆ Belief that parental involvement in school is paramount.
- ◆ Belief that working together as partners will benefit the child's learning and development, with mutually supported roles and actions to achieve this goal.
- ◆ Recognition of the value of both in- and out-of-school learning opportunities for children's learning and school progress.
- ◆ Recognition that the nature and quality of the family–school relationship influence (positively or negatively) children's school performance.
- ◆ Expectation that families will be involved, and recognition that such involvement can mean different things to different families.
- ◆ Expectation that teachers and school personnel will seek ways to invite parents to share in the educational process for their children, recognizing that this may "look different" to different families.
- ◆ Presence of a mission statement that promotes the importance and expectation of school–family connections for children's learning.

Attitudes: The values and perceptions held about family–school relationships

Consider the extent to which the following conditions are present:

- ◆ Attempts to understand the needs, ideas, opinions, and perspectives of families and educators.
- ◆ A nonblaming, no-fault problem-solving stance in interactions with families.
- ◆ Willingness to share perspectives across home and school.
- ◆ Perception of family involvement as essential (i.e., bringing a critical element to the team that is otherwise unavailable) rather than simply desirable.
- ◆ A positive attitude that focuses on school, family, and child strengths, rather than only on problems or deficits.
- ◆ Willingness to co-construct the whole picture about children by discussing, exploring, and understanding different perspectives.
- ◆ Willingness to listen to and respond to concerns across home and school—viewing different perspectives as a way to better understand students' needs, and viewing parents' and educators' concerns as a way to offer mutual support.
- ◆ Mutual respect across home and school (i.e., respect for family members by school personnel, and respect for school personnel by family members).
- ◆ Understanding that barriers for positive family–school relationships (i.e., constraints of each system) exist for parents and educators.

TABLE 1.5 *(continued)*

Atmosphere: The climate in schools for families and educators

Consider the extent to which the following conditions are present:

- Recognition of the value, and active solicitation, of family input regarding important decisions about their child.
- Use of family and school input to promote positive outcomes for students.
- A welcoming, respectful, inclusive, positive, supportive climate and atmosphere for *all* children and families.
- A variety of communication strategies to reach all parents in a manner that is sensitive or responsive to family background (e.g., language, skills, knowledge level), easy to understand, and "jargon-free."
- A variety of communication strategies to share information and/or monitor children's performance.
- Parental and school trust in each other (including motives, objectives, and communications).
- Mechanisms for listening to and responding to concerns across home and school.
- Meaningful ways and flexible options for parents and students to be involved.
- Opportunities for parents and school personnel to learn from one another (e.g., cross-cultural communication opportunities).

Actions: Strategies for building shared responsibility

Consider the extent to which the following conditions are present:

- Information is provided to families about school policies and practices, parents' and students' rights vis-à-vis education, and ways to foster students' engagement with learning.
- Opportunities or mechanisms are provided for the home and school to plan jointly and collaborate to resolve a shared concern or to improve learning experiences for students.
- A process exists for creating mutually supportive roles for families and educators.
- Supports and resources exist for creating and maintaining partnerships.
- Policies and practices support a coordinated, collaborative approach (i.e., shared responsibility) for home and school.
- Parents and school personnel (i.e., partners) routinely review the availability, accessibility, and flexibility of family–school roles and responsibilities for fostering children's/adolescents' learning and school engagement.

between families and schools exist (or can exist) for children's learning. These are presented in Table 1.5. In subsequent chapters, each element is discussed in detail.

THE CHALLENGE

School psychologists are in an ideal position to facilitate a strong, positive family–school interface for all students. We suggest that schools need a new way of doing business; "break-the-mold" schools need "break-the-mold" parent–educator relationships. We need trust-building opportunities, effective communication, and problem solving that allows for the family–school relationship to include and not control families with respect to children's learning. We need to discuss a vision for children's performance, plan the relationship in advance, chart a common course together, engage in ongoing dialogue, and build trust over time. Barriers, while relatively easy to list, provide a challenge to schools and families. The barrier that presents the greatest challenge is implementing an ecological systems perspective to enhance the school experience, engagement, and productivity of all children and youth. To meet this challenge, a shared understanding of students', parents', and teachers' rights, roles and responsibilities, and resources within a mutually determined type of relationship is required. It necessitates moving discussion toward what schools and families can do to promote positive child/adolescent development with less emphasis on the narrow but commonly asked question of how to get parents involved. It also requires a real commitment and dedication to mutual problem solving, especially when there are problems or concerns for the child. Without this, programs may be terminated prematurely.

Many may be familiar with Ed Young's (1992) book *Seven Blind Mice*. In this story, seven mice independently examined a strange "something" by their pond. Six mice focused on one part of the something, concluding, respectively, that it was a pillar, snake, cliff, spear, fan, or rope. The wise, seventh mouse ran across the top and from end to end of the something, concluding that the parts, collectively, were an elephant. The mouse moral was: *Knowing in part may make a fine tale, but wisdom comes from seeing the whole.* How many family or school tales have you heard? How many have you suggested? Knowledge and wisdom about enhancing children's learning and development, and, consequently, their performance in school come from the opportunity to co-construct the bigger picture about students rather than the inclination to focus on only the part for which one is directly responsible. Actions that change fundamental assumptions, practices, and relationships, both within the school and between the school and community, in ways that lead to improved student learning outcomes offer much promise. And, attention to process variables that ensure strong, constructive family–school connections for children is essential.

Roles for families and school personnel vis-à-vis children's learning and school experiences are assumed. There is always a relationship, whether active or passive, positive or negative. According to Doherty and Peskay (1992), a balanced relationship is one where parents assume responsibilities within their roles as parents (not professional educators), and school personnel assume responsibilities within their roles as instructors (not parent substitutes). According to Bronfenbrenner (1991), the school has the formal responsibility and the family has the informal responsibility for educating youth, and the informal education that takes place in the home is a powerful prerequisite for success in formal education. It is our hope that the four A's described in the remainder of the book expand school psychologists' repertoire for bringing the wisdom needed to foster school engagement and productivity for students in grades K–12. As school psychologists engage in assessment, consultation, and intervention, we hope they will begin to focus on how families *and* schools socialize students as learners. To do so presents an exciting and, fortunately, doable challenge for our field.

QUESTIONS TO CONSIDER

Consider the following questions as a way to discuss the complexity of creating positive family–school relationships. There is not one correct answer to these questions. Their value lies in the opportunity for careful planning about the family–school connection for a specific context.

◆ Are there differences in the definition of family involvement for educators and families?
◆ How can school personnel broaden their perspectives and reach out to all families?
◆ What are the perspectives of parents and educators about the ways educators have shared information on what helps children and adolescents engage in learning and improve their school performance?

- How important to families and educators is family involvement with regard to student success?
- Do educators and families share common beliefs about how families should be involved?
- Which families recognize their role in encouraging and fostering children's learning?
- Under what conditions are families and educators comfortable contacting each other about a student concern?
- How can we manage the time crunch so that educators and family members can share information about and resources for students?
- What are barriers to family involvement, and how can schools, parents, and community members work to overcome them?

CHAPTER 2

♦♦♦

Approach: The Framework for Interaction with Families

♦

In this chapter, we provide the content—theory and research findings—for a framework for interacting with families that recognizes the *significance of families* and the *contributions of schools* to the development and learning of children and youth (Bastiani, 1996). We recognize that this framework requires a paradigm shift. For school personnel, it means extending beyond the mere identification of family, school, community, and peer influences on children's educational performance (i.e., adopting a systems approach), to organizing these influences in a way that accounts for the reciprocal interaction among multiple influences to enhance student learning (i.e., using systems theory). It also means that roles for parents and educators are delineated on an equal basis; therefore, co-roles and options for involvement are critical.

Parents are viewed as essential, not merely desirable or helpful. As noted by Dallin Malmgren (1994), an English high school teacher in Texas, "Making interactions between parents and teachers positive and productive will require a change in perspective on the part of educators" (p. 30). He contends parents can be more useful in the educational process than they are in the educational outcome. "As teachers, we tend to forget that, long before we showed up, most of our students had 'instructors'—Mom and Dad. In many cases, the channel of educational information between parent and student has been clogged over the years. If we can help reopen those lines of communication, our educational impact will soar" (p. 30). No one disputes that enhancing educational outcomes for children and youth is the major goal of schools. However, the centrality of families cannot be ignored if schools are to be optimally successful. And, as we show in this book, involving parents in the process means more than requesting their help with homework.

According to systems theory (Christenson, Abery, & Weinberg, 1986), families play a meaningful role in children's educational success, and the interface of family and school is an element that must be accounted for when examining children's school performance; that is, parents and teachers are educators, but not all education is schooling. In his article "What Do Families Do?" Bronfenbrenner (1991) stated, "The *informal education* that takes place in the family is not merely a pleasant prelude, but rather a powerful prerequisite for success in *formal education* from the primary grades onward" (p. 5, emphasis added). A critical question worth asking is: Have we as educators undervalued the significance of the role of families? Perhaps our traditional conception of the role of families is too narrow. Rather than thinking of parent involvement at school, we must extend our thinking also to include parent involvement at home, as well as the continuity between home and school with respect to the goals of education. Parent involvement at school cannot be equated with parent involvement in schooling and learning. Parents may participate but not come to school.

As you read this chapter, reflect on the extent to which these conditions typify your school community:

- Mutually shared goals across home and school for children's learning.
- Belief that parental involvement in school is paramount.
- Belief that working together as partners will benefit the child's learning and development, with mutually supported roles and actions to achieve this goal.
- Recognition of the value of in- and out-of-school learning opportunities for children's learning and school progress.
- Recognition that the nature and quality of the family–school relationship influence (positively or negatively) children's school performance.
- Expectation that families will be involved, and recognition that such involvement can mean different things to different families.
- Expectation that teachers and school personnel will seek ways to invite parents to share in the educational process for their children, recognizing that this may "look different" to different families.

◆ Presence of a mission statement that promotes the importance and expectation of school–family connections for children's learning.

THE CURRENT CONTEXT

There is always a relationship between families and schools, regardless of the quality (good vs. bad), nature of the contact (positive vs. negative, engaged vs. disengaged), or frequency of contact
(minimal vs. often). It is never the case that no relationship exists
(Doherty & Peskay, 1992; Pianta & Walsh, 1996). What is done
with the relationship and how school psychologists consult with
families and educators to develop constructive relationships are
key.

Furthermore, students are at the center of the relationship.
The fact that family–school relationships occur because children
become students establishes guidelines for appropriate boundaries
with respect to school-based policies and practices with families.
Because the relationship is crucial to the future academic performance and healthy development of children and adolescents, efforts, regardless of the source for the concern, should be stimulated by the question: How can we work together to address concerns
for students? Comer and colleagues (1996) assert that a culture of
failure exists for students when there is limited interaction, mistrust, or discontinuity between family and school. As school psychologists, we are in an ideal position to foster a "culture of success" or to interrupt cycles of failure (Pianta & Walsh, 1996) for
students. As we do, it is understood that students are the main actors in their education, development, and success in school (Epstein, 1995). Working as partners with families will not, by itself,
make students successful learners or high achievers; student commitment across grades K–12 is essential. Enhancing student commitment and engagement with learning is highly influenced, however, by creating what Comer refers to as a healthful climate
between family and school, one where collaboration is the norm
and a system for handling conflicting perspectives exists (Swap,
1993).

Immediate Concerns for Students

Two immediate concerns prevalent in today's society—erosion of
social capital and increased student apathy for schoolwork—

reflect urgency for creating family–school connections for children's learning. The renewed interest in family involvement in education in the last decade is due in part to the dramatic changes in the structure and function of families. These changes raise concern about the ability of many families to provide the conditions that foster children's school progress (Kellaghan et al., 1993). Families differ in their skills, knowledge, resources and available time to promote student engagement at school and with learning. Statistics about children who live in poverty and high-risk situations are repeated in educational, political, and economic arenas. These statistics, albeit highly descriptive of the conditions of many children's lives, may serve to obscure the highly relevant concept of social capital for understanding differential achievement levels.

Coleman (1987) defined "social capital" as the amount of adult–child interaction about academic and personal matters, as well as the social and community support system for families. According to Coleman, social capital in homes is shrinking because of several contextual factors, including single-parent and dual-income families, and a sense of alienation in communities. Furthermore, educational progress and performance depends on input from both home and school. Therefore, school achievement is not maintained or increased if educators simply replace necessary family resources with more school resources—those that provide students with opportunities, demands, and rewards. Rather, academic and developmental outcomes for children are maintained or increased by providing students with attitudes, effort, and conception of self—those qualities from the home that interact with ones provided by the school. Schools can reward and demand, and provide opportunities for children to learn; however, families provide the "building blocks" (i.e., attitudes, effort, conception of self) that make learning possible or the social capital needed by schools to enhance learner outcomes.

Student apathy for learning is a concern, and parents have been identified as integral in fostering children's attitudes toward learning. Elementary and secondary teachers, recognized for excellence in teaching, identified student apathy for learning as a significant concern for students (Educational Communications, 1997). Across several studies of families with varying income and ethnic backgrounds, the presence of three factors in homes has been strongly associated with student achievement: strong, consistent values about the importance of education; willingness to help children and intervene at school; and ability to become involved

(Mitrosmwang & Hawley, 1993). Similarly, Grolnick, Ryan, and Deci (1991) have discussed the process of internalization of family values about education, learning, and effort related to children's motivation to learn, and Bempechat (1998) has demonstrated the power of parents' motivational support for learning outcomes for ethnically and culturally diverse students.

Importance of Continuity for Family Involvement

Educators value family involvement. Teachers, principals, social workers, counselors, and school psychologists recognize that students spend 91% of their time from birth to age 18 outside of school (Ooms & Hara, 1991). Similarly, once students have entered kindergarten, 70% of their waking hours occur outside of school hours (Clark, 1990). Although school personnel recognize the mismatch between how time is spent in- and out-of-school for many students, this discontinuity is less often the focus of family involvement. Rather, educators have responded primarily with a traditionally oriented, institutional response in which the "three big roles" for parents reign: volunteer, fund-raiser, and homework helper. Several excellent models, or frameworks, for involving families in meaningful ways (e.g., Comer et al., 1996; Epstein, 1995; Swap, 1993) exist in the literature and are invaluable resources for school personnel designing programs for their particular family–school context. The models vary according to the degree that they espouse a "traditional" or "partnership" approach.

The degree of continuity across home and school, as experienced by students, will be critical for the approach or specific strategies used to create a constructive family–school relationship. This point is explicated by Phelan and her colleagues, who found that all adolescents feel psychosocial pressures; however, those who experience discontinuity among their home, school, and peer worlds have the most difficulty in making transitions among these different contexts and are most at-risk for poor school performance and mental health concerns (Phelan, Davidson, & Yu, 1998). They suggest that high-risk youth are those for whom there is discontinuity in the interface of systems (family, school, and peer) when continuity is most needed. According to Phelan and her colleagues, students have extreme difficulty in making transitions when they experience borders among these contexts. "Borders" refer to aspects of cultural differences in which the values, beliefs, knowledge, skills, and actions of one group are more valued than those of another. Borders, which occur when culturally different standards are not neutral, are many and varied. For example, Phelan and colleagues describe sociocultural (e.g., ways of operating in schools considered superior to ways at home), socioeconomic (e.g., economic circumstances creating hardship), linguistic (e.g., regarding one group's language as inferior to another's), gender (e.g., treating girls differently than boys), heterosexist (e.g., viewing heterosexuality as the only valid form of sexual expression), and structural (e.g., providing limited access to services for students' learning) borders.

In their Multiple Worlds Study, an ethnographic study involving extensive in-depth interviews, shadowing, and review of cumulative school records with adolescents in urban, desegregated high schools, Phelan and her colleagues identified transition patterns that help to explain the engagement in classrooms and school for culturally diverse students. For example, students who experienced congruent worlds, where similar values, expectations, and ways of behaving were evident among family, school, and peers, made easy and smooth transitions across these environments. These students were usually white, middle-class high achievers; less often less the students from minority backgrounds or academically average students. In contrast, students whose family, school and peer worlds were distinct, and who reported transitions among the worlds to be difficult, were most often students who adapted in some circumstances but not in others. In general, these students performed well in some classes and very poorly in others. Low-achieving students reported experiencing extremely discordant worlds among family, school, and peers. Furthermore, they saw the borders, whether sociocultural, socioeconomic, or linguistic in nature, as insurmountable. With respect to creating constructive family–school relationships, the concept of borders is relevant; in fact, borders are often referred to as barriers for family involvement.

Constructive family–school relationships may be tradition- or partnership-based, and parents play a role in both models. Rather than select one specific model or approach, we find it helpful to examine the family–school context and to reinforce the significance of families for children's learning and schooling. The family–school context can be described in terms of the amount of interaction and information sharing across home and school necessary to promote student success in school. Depending on the needs and characteristics of families, teachers, and students, a school may elect to be more or less tradition or partnership oriented. When there is consistency and continuity across home and school with respect to schooling issues, both approaches have a high probability of creating support linkages for students. However, when discontinuity between home and school exists, it may be necessary to have greater opportunity for "joint steering"; discussing perspectives; clarifying roles, responsibilities and resources; and making shared decisions (Comer et al., 1996). Clearly, a "one size fits all" approach does not work. An indicator of where "the" family–school relationship falls on the continuum can be determined by knowing with whom educators have not connected. As pointed out by Epstein (1995), it is critical for educators to determine how current school practices systematically include or exclude families. School psychologists can help by summarizing under what conditions, and for whom, there are positive connections between families and educators.

Family and School as "Partners"

Thinking of family and school as "partners" does not refer to a specific model or approach. Rather, it refers to a mutual effort toward a shared goal, and as a result implies shared responsibility of families and educators for supporting students as learners. Working as partners is an attitude—not solely an activity to be implemented. Family and school as partners refers to the following defining features, and we contend that they can be implemented under a traditional or partnership approach:

- ◆ A *student-focused philosophy* wherein educators and families cooperate, coordinate, and collaborate to enhance learning opportunities, educational progress, and school success for students in four domains: academic, social, emotional, and behavioral.
- ◆ A belief in shared responsibility for educating and socializing children—both families and educators are *essential* and provide resources for children's learning and progress in school. There are no prescribed roles or activities for families or educators; rather, options for active, realistic participation are created.
- ◆ An emphasis on the quality of the interface and ongoing connection between families and schools. Creating a constructive *relationship* (how families and educators work together in meaningful ways) to execute their respective roles in promoting the academic and social development of children and youth is most important.

♦ A *preventive, solution-oriented* focus in which families and educators strive to create conditions that facilitate student learning, engagement, and development.

   In summary, family and school as partners is a philosophy and way of thinking about forming connections among families and schools to foster positive school and learning experiences for children and youth. By forming "connections," we mean developing an intentional and ongoing relationship between school and family, designed to enhance directly or indirectly children's learning and development, and/or to address the obstacles that impede it (Wynn, Meyer, & Richards-Schuster, 1999). Signs of "disconnects" across family and school will be of particular interest to school psychologists who encourage families and schools working as partners. Also, school psychologists will want to attend to the way school personnel conceptualize roles for families in education. Educators have predominantly taken an institutional approach to child-centered concerns about students' school performance, particularly their achievement. Such an approach results in establishing the school's agenda for family involvement, often resulting in less responsivity to parents' needs. Furthermore, when schools delineate specific roles in the absence of family input, they may be creating a hierarchical (i.e., school knows best), not an equal, balanced relationship with families. This can lead to a less explicit focus on sharing responsibility for children's learning and educational progress.

THEORETICAL BASE FOR FAMILY INVOLVEMENT

Consistent with Coleman (1987), major theoretical approaches for interacting with families emphasize the interface of systems for socializing children and youth. Central to the philosophy embodied in family and school as partners is a belief in shared responsibility for educating and socializing children and youth. From a shared responsibility perspective, the product of education—learning—is not produced by schools, but by students, with the help of parents, educators, peers, and community professionals who support learners (Seeley, 1985). Thus, students learn because of what students do, but students "do" because of a supportive safety net. In Seeley's opinion, the concept of educational partnerships calls for making education a shared responsibility of families, schools, and communities rather than a function delegated to bureaucratic agencies, and it calls for collaborative rather than bureaucratic structures for carrying out this responsibility. The notion of shared responsibility is in direct contrast to delegation of services used more typically by schools and community agencies when interacting with families.

Historically, Bronfenbrenner's (1979) ecological systems theory of child development has provided a strong conceptual framework for focusing on the effect of the interface between home and school for children's development and school performance. Furthermore, his conceptualization has influenced other theoretically driven models of family–school relationships that underscore shared responsibility, such as Epstein's (1987) theory of overlapping spheres of influence and Comer's school development process (Comer et al., 1996), where a positive family–school relationship and shared accountability are viewed as necessities for fostering the progress of children and youth in six developmental areas.

Ecological Systems Theory

According to ecological systems theory (Bronfenbrenner, 1979), an individual is an inseparable part of a small social system comprised of four interrelated systems: microsystem, mesosystem, exosystem, and macrosystem. Visualizing the interrelated systems as the four Russian stacking dolls marketed in many forms in retail stores places the child in the center of multiple and reciprocal influences that are useful in understanding child behavior. Emphasis is placed on understanding the individual as part of separate ecosystems (home or school) and in relation to the child's whole system.

The microsystem describes the relation of the child with the immediate ecosystem and setting (e.g., home *or* classroom). A microsystemic influence focuses on the child's immediate context, such as support for the child's learning in the context of the classroom or the home. In contrast, the mesosystem describes interrelations among major ecosystems in the individual's life (e.g., home *and* school). Thus, a mesosystemic influence focuses on the interface of contexts for children's learning such as the congruence of support for children's learning, across home and school. Events in ecosystems and settings in which an individual does not directly participate, but that impinge upon the immediate microsystems, define exosystem. These are influences from other contexts, such as the effect of the school district's family involvement policy on teacher attitude or behavior, amount of training to work as partners, or parental work demands on time/availability for attending school functions. Finally, the macrosystem is the overall cultural or subcultural patterns of which the other systems are a concrete manifestation. One way to think of macrosystemic influences is to define them as a cultural blueprint. Examples include legislation, such as National Education Goals 1 and 8, and IDEA, societal attitudes toward educational service delivery, and specific economic, social, and political forces.

All levels are important when considering family–school relationships. The macrosystem serves as a foundation and driving force for promoting and articulating overarching agendas and initiatives. The exosystem illustrates the supports and structures from agencies and workplaces outside of the school that allow for meaningful relationships to be formed. The mesosytem represents the interactions and shared responsibilities across home and school that are key to successful relationships. Finally, with respect to the microsystem, the attitudes and actions toward family–school relationships must be sensitive to individuals' immediate settings, including specific school and home environments. This latter point illustrates that ecological systems theory is applicable to understanding the behavior of children and adults. Constructive family–school relationships are contingent on being responsive to the needs of parents and teachers, and demand a sensitivity about the constraints of both home and school systems.

Several characteristics of Bronfenbrenner's taxonomy of contexts offer depth for truly understanding the many faces of family–school relationships (Bronfenbrenner, 1992). With respect to the microsystem, Bronfenbrenner has argued that it is the individual's perception and the meaning of a given situation that exerts the most influence on development. Furthermore, he conjectures that the distinctive characteristics of the environment that support development (e.g., characteristics of the persons with whom the child interacts) must be understood. With respect to the mesosystem, he identified several types of interconnections between home and school: multisetting participation in which the child participates regularly across settings (home, school, child care); intersetting communications in which messages are transmitted to two microsystems for the purpose of providing specific information; and intersetting knowledge in which participants in one setting have information or experience about participants in another setting. With respect to the exosystem, Bronfenbrenner contends that parents' workplaces and quality of social networks, and availability of community resources, greatly influence family behavior. Finally, the macrosystem encompasses the concept of "a cultural repertoire of belief systems" (Bronfenbrenner, 1992, p. 228). To Bronfenbrenner, the belief systems of the significant individuals in a child's world (e.g., value of school) create a context that influences family goals and practices, and, ultimately, child behavior and performance.

Ecological systems theory provides a framework for organizing the reciprocal influences of the various ecosystems of the developing child. When a child is referred, a true systems thinker never debates whether the "cause" is at home or school, or elsewhere. Because each ecosystem is critical, contributing factors, not causes, are most relevant; therefore, systems thinkers choose not to disengage home, school, and other contextual variables. Although systems thinkers observe and interact with individuals, such as a parent, a teacher, or a child, they never lose sight of the entire system in which the individual functions. Efforts are directed to the system as a whole, with the goal of helping the system to work better for the individual.

Based on general systems theory, specific organizational principles govern interactions between the developing child's ecosystems (Christenson et al., 1986). In addition to maintaining balance among individual members in the system and flexibility for the system to adapt to internal and external change, other essential principles applied to family–school relationships include the following:

- *Circular causality.* The system is a group of interrelated individuals; thus, change in one individual affects other individuals and the group as a whole. Causality is circular rather than linear, because every action is also a reaction. School difficulties affect children's behavior within a family and, conversely, family problems influence students' achievement and/or behavior in school.

- *Nonsummativity.* The system as a whole is greater than the sum of its parts; the whole adds the property of relationship to the parts (synergism). Coordinating effort among home, school, and community resources achieves a synergistic relationship, and the notion of synergism further underscores that school–family–community together can achieve more than can any element alone.

- *Equifinality.* According to this principle, the same outcome may result from different antecedents. For example, two families with diverse interactional styles may both have children who are experiencing school success. Simply stated, there is more than one path to the same goal; thus, options for family involvement are not only accepted but also expected from systems theory.

◆ *Multifinality.* This principle suggests that similar initial conditions may lead to dissimilar end states; thus, similar home support for learning strategies may have different effects on children's completion of homework. Therefore, a standard, uniform prescription for parental assistance with homework may achieve the desired goal for some children and families, and not for others.

◆ *Communication.* All behavior is regarded as communication—transmitting interpersonal messages. If home and school operate as two separate worlds, children can become burdened carrying messages between two systems. For example, the role of message bearer for homework assignments, as well as for the family–school relationship, can place a heavy toll on children.

◆ *Rules.* Rules within schools and families serve to organize the respective interactions and function to maintain a stable system by prescribing and limiting an individual's behavior. The rules provide expectations about roles, actions, and consequences that guide either school or family life vis-à-vis the family–school relationship. Difficulties emerge when the rules and values of each ecosystem are not shared and discussed. Parents may jump to conclusions about the school's disciplinary philosophy; educators may stereotype parental attitudes or behaviors. Since rules are essential to maintain the intactness of the system, a set of operating rules for the entire, overarching system of school and family is critical, especially for providing consistency of influence and ensuring generalization of interventions.

Recently, Pianta and Walsh (1996) articulated the contextual-systems model for understanding children's school performance, particularly those at risk for school failure because of discontinuity between home and school. Drawing on principles from general systems theory and Bronfenbrenner's (1979, 1992) multiple influences, they have underscored the role of development. Specifically, they contend that children develop and learn in the context of the family; therefore, shared meaning must be established over time between the child/family system and the school/schooling system.

Co-Roles for Families and Educators

Two pragmatic, explicit examples of a shared responsibility approach for students' learning are illustrative. First, the U.S. Department of Education (Moles, 1993) has described five roles for families *and* school personnel: co-communicators, co-supporters, co-learners, co-teachers, and co-decision makers. Two points are particularly noteworthy about this conceptualization of school–family roles. First, the labels used to describe the roles (e.g., co-communicator) were deliberately selected to facilitate and encourage a shared-responsibility approach for children's learning. Thus, the tone for the relationship is set by the choice of language. Second, the roles are arranged as a pyramid, with co-communicators at the base, followed by co-supporters, co-learners, and co-teachers, with co-decision makers at the top. Each subsequent role requires more active participation, commitment, and skill; thus, they are likely to involve fewer individuals. It is assumed that all families and educators are involved as co-communicators, and fewer are involved as co-decision makers. This conceptualization allows us to avoid thinking about roles for parents or educators in isolation. The focus is on roles within the family–school relationship. Clearly, there are a variety of ways for parents to be involved and different levels of commitment as to how parents want to be involved. This provides a concrete way of thinking of how all families can be involved in a way that is sensitive to their needs or family circumstances.

Specific examples of the co-roles are provided in Table 2.1. Family and school as *co-communicators* address the need to ex-

---

TABLE 2.1. Examples of School and Family Co-Roles

School and family as co-communicators

- ◆ Schoolwide use of assignment books or homework journals, paired with family understanding of procedures.
- ◆ Monthly progress and growth reports with sign-off sheets.
- ◆ Send parent–teacher grams.
- ◆ In the school–family newsletter, provide both family and teacher strategies for addressing student concerns.
- ◆ Provide Our Turn/Your Turn or Our Half/Your Half columns in newsletters.
- ◆ Install parent–teacher homework hotlines for assignments.
- ◆ Share home learning ideas in the school or classroom newsletter.
- ◆ Communicate clearly and frequently the academic and behavior expectations developed by educators, parents, and community members.
- ◆ Hold beginning-of-the-year parent–teacher–student conferences to set academic goals and expectations, and develop learning plans to enhance student support.

(continued)

TABLE 2.1 (*continued*)

School and family as co-communicators (continued)

- Display academic work throughout the school and community.
- Provide grade- or course-level curriculum guides.
- Publicize academic awards, honors, and test results in school and community newspapers.
- Provide forums for two-way communication to address educators' and families' concerns/questions/ideas.
- Provide frequent positive feedback to parents and teachers when children are behaving appropriately or showing improved academic progress.
- Develop a "be on the same page" philosophy by sharing wishes and worries about a child.

School and family as co-supporters

- Develop a computer home-lending program.
- Organize an after school homework center staffed by teachers and parents.
- Organize family field trips to cultural places and events.
- Explore how support activities such as fund-raisers, socials, carnivals, and so on, reinforce the school's academic focus.
- Develop an education hotline to address parental concerns that impact children's education (e.g., attendance policies, graduation standards, special education, enrollment options, alternative schools, discipline and school safety, early childhood education).
- Invite families into the classroom and visit them at home.
- Link families with community resources in times of need.
- Provide extended day care services with enrichment activities.
- Develop parent/community volunteer program.
- Organize student success teams composed of educators, community resource people, and parents to assist students who need additional help and resources to achieve success.
- Organize adult education opportunities on the school campus that help to meet parent needs and raise expectations.
- Provide multiple opportunities for parents to be involved, especially in leadership roles that support the school.
- Invite and encourage adult volunteers to organize after school programs that will provide enriched, safe learning opportunities for students.
- Organize campus and community cleanups.
- Allow school facilities to be used by community service groups.
- Establish a parent/family center where parents can meet, socialize, organize, and learn together.
- Campaign for the positive passage of school referendums.
- Encourage classroom visitations and observations.
- Host more frequent curriculum nights.
- Sponsor home reading programs.
- Provide parents with home learning materials (e.g., checkout system for learning packets).
- Link parent or family workshops to the curriculum.

TABLE 2.1 (*continued*)

School and family as co-learners
- Conduct home visits to acquaint parents with the school's mission and curriculum, and to suggest home learning strategies.
- Organize academic performances that allow students to demonstrate what they are learning at school.
- Hold an interactive forum to discuss graduation standards, the assessment and testing process, and how parents can support the standards being taught at school.
- Develop parent leaders by offering leadership development opportunities.
- Provide workshops on topics determined by parents to be important.
- Provide several back-to-school nights at different times; take attendance and follow up with nonattendees, so that all families have information about school policies and procedures.
- Provide relevant staff development, including effective communication with parents, design of effective homework and home learning activities, ways to involve parents in classroom instruction, and promote the attributes and strengths of the family.

School and family as co-teachers
- Provide an activity sheet on time management.
- Publish newsletter articles on how parents can keep student records and monitor progress.
- Involve parents as teachers and experts in the classroom to share their talents and support the curriculum.
- Assign interactive homework and or provide guidelines on how parents can help students complete the homework.

School and family as co-decision makers
- Involve parents and students in goal-setting conferences.
- Involve the school council in reviewing monitoring procedures, reporting pupil progress, and conducting curriculum reviews.
- Create a family–school team to address mutual concerns.
- Involve the PTSA in planning ways to extend and enhance learning opportunities for students.
- Form an alliance with community resources to extend learning opportunities.
- Involve parents and community in developing the school's mission and goals, and in setting and reviewing school policies and practices.
- Form advisory committees to support each academic area or grade level.
- Establish school committees that give parents and teachers an opportunity to work together on important school issues.
- Create time for parents and teachers to discuss goals and expectations for student performance.

Note. Examples of activities based on the categories of family–school roles by Moles (1993).

change information that enables both to assist children's learning. A variety of techniques, including written, face-to-face, telephone, formal and informal meetings, and videos are used, because a primary goal of communication is to increase shared meaning and understanding about students' performance. Family and school as *co-supporters* address not only the needs of the partners to support the child, but also their need to support each other. For example, families show support to children by providing positive encouragement for learning, and to schools by attending back-to-school nights and student performances. Schools support families by being responsive to their questions and providing a welcoming climate. Teachers support families by calling at the first sign of concern and inviting them to visit the classroom or school.

Family and school as *co-learners* provide opportunities for educators (e.g., administrators, teachers, support personnel) and families to learn about each other and how to work together to support student learning. For example, families want information about school procedures, policies, and practices, whereas school staff need opportunities to increase their effectiveness in communicating with parents. Family and school as *co-teachers* recognize the formal teaching of students in school settings and the ways families support and encourage learning at home and in the community. By working together, teachers and families can create connections and provide mutual support for each other in ways that enhance student learning. Finally, home and school as *co-decision makers, advocates, and advisors* focus on participation in formal organizations and committees, such as the Parent–Teacher–Student Association (PTSA) board, school site council, or Principal Advisory Committee. This continuum is consistent with other interpretations of family–school partnerships (e.g., Epstein, 1995; Henderson & Berla, 1994).

Regardless of educational or income level, or ethnic background, parents want their children to be successful in school; however, they do not know how to assist their children. Parents report they would be willing to spend more time on activities with children if educators gave them more guidance (Epstein, 1986). Nearly ten years later, Epstein (personal communication, November 1995) speculates that only a relatively small percentage of parents, approximately 10%, have personal problems so severe that they cannot work as partners with schools given the proper assistance. She contends that parent educational level and family social class are influential factors only if school personnel do not work to involve all parents. However, parental desire is one thing;

achieving equality when there is little or no provision for parents to be enfranchised as equal partners in the educational process is quite different.

A second example of a shared-responsibility approach is represented by the work of Harry (1992), who has concluded that parent–school discourse must be restructured to enfranchise parents as equal partners. To do so, she challenges professionals to provide official channels for reciprocal rather than one-way discourse, for dialogue rather than monologue. In her book, *Cultural Diversity, Families, and the Special Education System*, Harry (1992) presented an ethnographic study of 12 Puerto Rican American families in a small inner-city school in the northeast region of the United States. Their children received English as a second language (ESL) and special education services for mild disabilities. From her naturalistic observations, record reviews, and in-depth, repeated, informal open-ended interviews, Harry found that the only consistent role offered to families was that of consent-giver. Furthermore, she argued that the legalistic framing of this role tends to convert the notion of consent into a "meaningless ritual of compliance" (p. 186). Based on this study and investigations with parents from other racial and ethnic groups, Harry argued that parent–professional discourse must be restructured, and that it is "up to professionals to provide communication structures that will make dialogue possible and mutual understanding likely" (p. 239).

To accomplish this, she suggests that professionals must provide parents with the opportunity to be actively involved throughout the special education process and, accordingly, describes four possible roles: parents as assessors, presenters of reports, policymakers, and advocates and peer supports. These roles (1) place parents in a meaningful, active role during conferences; (2) enable professionals better to understand parents' intimate knowledge of their children, including the many experiences and cultural aspects that may account for the children's development, learning, and behavioral patterns; (3) signal in a concrete way that parental input is needed and valued; (4) provide opportunity for information sharing across home and school cultures; and (5) provide natural support networks to parents. Although these roles were developed for use in special education, Harry indicates that they are appropriate for mainstream parents wherever an alteration in balance of power between parents and professionals is needed. Parents whose cultural backgrounds place them at a distinct disadvantage in dealing with school systems by creating sociocultural borders (Phelan et al., 1998) are clearly relevant. One way to equalize the balance of power is to create meaningful roles for parents and educators that allow them to co-construct the bigger picture about the conditions of the child's life vis-à-vis learning and development. In this way, parents and educators are co-teachers and co-learners, an approach also advocated by Comer and colleagues (Comer et al., 1996).

EMPIRICAL BASE FOR FAMILY INVOLVEMENT

Conclusions of Family Involvement Studies

Over recent decades, the considerable amount of research on family–school relationships has led to several commonly accepted conclusions. A caveat is in order, however, namely, that most research illustrates a systems approach; much less research has emphasized the reciprocal interaction that characterizes systems theory. Nonetheless, important databased conclusions to guide practices in schools can be made.

1. *Definitions for parent involvement have broadened.* Parent involvement refers to participation at school and at home. In fact, because of work demands and situational family barriers (e.g., transportation, day care), more parents are available to participate at home. This is a broader definition of parent involvement than recognized by some educators, who tend to use a traditional definition that includes narrowly conceived activities such as fund-raising and attendance at school functions. New definitions, particularly in urban settings, replace "parent" with "family," because the most significant adults in the lives of many children may be siblings, relatives, or even neighbors who provide child care (Davies, 1991). Options for involvement have moved beyond the "big three" (volunteer, homework helper, fund-raiser) to include roles for parents as teachers, decision makers, advocates, and supporters (Henderson & Berla, 1994). Admittedly, traditional roles for parents are provided without much risk, whereas the nontraditional roles introduce more risk for school personnel.

Although the majority of research has been conducted with lower-income families or in reference to students at risk for educational failure, the goal of family–school partnerships is to enhance the school success of all students. Indicators of student success in school are broader than achievement and include classroom and school participation, attendance, graduation from high school, and fewer discipline referrals and suspensions. The focus on success for all students is very important, since the possibility exists that achievement for average students would be elevated significantly if collaboration between families and schools were the norm. This, of course, is one of the goals of the federal program, Partnership for Family Involvement in Education, which is implementing a five-step, strategic planning process, including the following:

- Awareness—increasing communitywide understanding of the need to strengthen and promote family involvement.
- Commitment—developing shared commitments by families, schools, and communities to act jointly.
- Capacity building—developing the capacity of families, schools, and communities to work together.
- Knowledge development—identifying and developing knowledge of the use of programs and practices that successfully connect families, schools, and communities.
- Performance improvement—supporting the development of appropriate performance benchmarks that assess progress toward greater family involvement through family, school, and community partnerships.

Finally, recognition of the fact that families and schools have a 13-year contract has increased efforts for students in grades K–12.

The burgeoning interest in family involvement in education is evident from many directions and sources. For example, there is an available critical mass for greater family involvement in learning across grade levels. For example, 40% of parents believe they are not devoting enough time to their children's education; teachers ranked strengthening parents' roles in their children's learning as the issue that should receive the highest priority in public education policy in the 1990s; 72% of students ages 10–13 and 48% of students ages 14–17 said they would like to talk to their parents about schoolwork; and 89% of business executives identified lack of parent involvement as the biggest obstacle to school reform (*Strong Families, Strong Schools*, 1994). In a survey conducted by Connors and Epstein (1994), 82% of high schoolers agreed that parent involvement was needed at the high school level. Eighty percent of parents indicated they wanted to be more involved; more than 50% of students indicated they wanted their parents involved. Only 32% of the teachers, however, felt it was their responsibility to involve parents.

2. *We know that home environmental influences are positive*

*correlates of students' academic achievement and school perfor-
mance.* In a keynote address at the 1995 Annual Meeting of the
National Association of School Psychologists in Chicago, Jesse
Jackson stated, "Parents need to do five things: (1) Take their children to school, (2) Meet their children's teachers, (3) Exchange
phone numbers, (4) Turn off the TV three hours each day, and (5)
Pick up report cards every nine weeks." These recommendations
not only reflect the credence given to parental responsibility for
children's learning but also are databased findings with respect to
successful students. For example, three factors over which parents
exercise authority—attendance, variety of reading materials in
the home, and amount of television watching—explain nearly 90%
of the difference in mean achievement of students in 37 states and
the District of Columbia on the National Assessment of Educational Progress (Barton & Coley, 1992). Over 120 studies have described the relationship between family influences and student
learning (i.e., a systems approach) by reporting significant, positive correlations, generally in the low moderate–moderate range.
It is important to note that the identification of correlates of students' school performance allows one to speak only in terms of
probabilities; that is, a correlation suggests a relationship or association (not a causal link) and allows one to think about creating
conditions that increase the likelihood of more student success in
school or reduce the likelihood of school failure. Correlates can be
viewed as ways to enhance student performance; however, they do
not determine student outcomes. For example, Table 2.2 provides
a list of empirically supported ways that families encourage, not
determine, their children's school success.

   Parent involvement in schooling is positively associated with
many benefits for students and the kind of benefits desired by educators. When parents are involved, students show improvement in
grades (Fehrmann, Keith, & Reimers, 1987); test scores, including
reading (Clark, 1988; Comer, 1988; Epstein, 1991; Stevenson &
Baker, 1987) and math achievement (Epstein, 1986); attitude toward schoolwork (Kellaghan et al., 1993); behavior (Comer &
Haynes, 1991; Steinberg, Mounts, Lamborn, & Dornbusch, 1991);
self-esteem (Collins, Moles, & Cross, 1982; Sattes, 1985); completion of homework (Clark, 1993; Epstein & Becker, 1982); academic
perseverance (Estrada, Arsenio, Hess, & Holloway, 1987); and participation in classroom learning activities (Collins et al., 1982;
Sattes, 1985). Additionally, benefits for students include fewer
placements in special education (Lazar & Darlington, 1978),
greater enrollment in postsecondary education (Baker & Steven-

TABLE 2.2. Examples of Families as Facilitators of Student Learning

Families do not determine, but rather foster students' school success by
- Encouraging and discussing leisure reading.
- Monitoring and joint analysis of television viewing.
- Showing interest in children's academic and personal growth.
- Engaging in frequent dialogue with children.
- Encouraging children's academic pursuits.
- Setting clear and consistent limits.
- Monitoring consistently how time is spent.
- Communicating regularly with school personnel.
- Attending and participating in school functions.
- Displaying parental warmth and nurturance toward the child.
- Providing quality reading materials and math experiences.
- Modeling learning by reading and using math in daily life.
- Reading with children.
- Believing children's effort, not luck, will result in learning.
- Orienting a child's attention to learning opportunities.

son, 1986; Eagle, 1989; Marjoribanks, 1988), higher attendance rates (Collins et al., 1982), lower dropout rates (Rumberger, 1995), fewer suspensions (Comer & Haynes, 1991), and realization of exceptional talents (Bloom, 1985). Furthermore, the home environment has been shown to make a difference in the health of American youth. Findings from the National Longitudinal Study on Adolescent Health revealed that adolescents have a higher probability of avoiding high-risk behavior (e.g., substance abuse, violence) when they feel connected to their families and their parents are involved in their lives (Resnick et al., 1997). The importance of "parental connectedness" is reflected in coordinated school health programs (Carlyon, Carlyon, & McCarthy, 1998). Health education programs that include family involvement have been shown to effect positive changes in children's diets, smoking behavior among parents, parental eating and exercise habits, and child–parent discussion about health topics (Birch, 1994).

Benefits of parent participation in education are evident for key stakeholders, suggesting they help create conditions that facilitate home–school connections. For example, benefits for teachers include recognition from parents for better interpersonal and teaching skills, higher ratings of teaching performance by principals, and greater satisfaction with their jobs, resulting in fewer requests for transfers (Christenson, 1995). Parent benefits include an increased sense of self-efficacy (Davies, 1993; Kagan & Schraft, 1982), increased understanding of the school program (Epstein,

1986), greater appreciation for the role they play in their children's education (Davies, 1993), improved communication with their children in general and about schoolwork in particular (Becher, 1984), and greater involvement in home learning activities (Epstein, 1995).

The benefits for key stakeholders vary as a function of the type of family involvement activity. The differential effects of varied forms of family involvement raise the question: Family involvement for what purpose? Epstein (1995) has demonstrated that expected results for parents, teachers, and students differ as a function of her six types of involvement activities, and that student achievement is not influenced directly by all types of family involvement. For example, parenting activities (i.e., helping families establish home environments to support children as students) have been associated with improved student attendance, enhanced teacher awareness of parenting challenges, and more parental respect for teachers' efforts. Home learning activities (i.e., providing families with information about how to help students with homework and other curriculum-related activities, decisions, and planning) have been associated with greater homework completion or gains in skills for students, increased parental knowledge of how to support and help students at home, and better design of homework assignments and respect of family time by teachers. Finally, decision-making activities (i.e., developing parent leaders and including parents in school decisions) have been related to increases in student awareness of family representation in school decisions, parental ownership of school, and teachers' awareness of parental perspectives for policy development and decisions.

3. *The distinction between family status and process variables is critical.* We know family process variables (what parents do to support learning) predict scholastic ability better than do family status variables (who families are). Social class or family configuration predicts up to 25% of variance in achievement, whereas family support for learning or interaction style predicts up to 60% of variance in achievement (Walberg, 1984). There is a moderate to strong correlation between income level and student achievement when data are aggregated; however, this correlation is substantially reduced when family processes are also considered. White (1982) analyzed 101 studies and concluded that the following aspects of the home environment had a greater impact than socioeconomic status (SES) on students' school performance: parents' attitudes, guidance, and expectations for their children's education; quality of verbal interaction; participation in cultural

and learning-related activities; and overall stability in the home. There are high-achieving students who live in low-income families (Bempechat, 1998). Also, the considerable variation in family environments within a social class supports the conclusion that what parents do vis-à-vis their children's education is more important than who they are. Milne (1989) stated, "Family structures are not inherently good or evil per se; what is important is the ability of the parent to provide proeducational resources for children—be they financial, material, or experiential" (p. 58). In addition, Bempechat's (1998) research underscores the critical nature of parents' motivational support for children's learning, particularly the subtle messages parents (and teachers) convey about children's abilities to learn and master new skills. In a study of parents' roles for low-income and ethnically diverse fifth and sixth graders' attributions for success and failure in math, Bempechat (1998) found that (a) poor and minority parents are involved in their children's education, and (b) high achievers, regardless of ethnic background, credited success to their innate ability and effort, and tended not to blame failure on lack of ability. In particular, she noted the critical parental role in socializing children for the schooling process. Her data suggest the need to encourage children's persistence and performance in the face of difficulty and challenge.

On the other hand, educators' use of students' background characteristics (e.g., parent educational level, family social class) as an explanation of students' school performance has been found to influence which families become involved in education (Epstein, 1991). There is no question that social background is moderately correlated with school achievement (e.g., White, 1982). However, the effect of family process was cogently stated by Clark (1990): "Of the many studies that have shown a statistical correlation between background, life chances, and life achievements, few seem to explain adequately the fact that many youngsters with disadvantaged backgrounds perform very well in school and in later life" (p. 18). Background or contextual factors may be useful in identifying target students, those who are most likely to be "at risk" for not succeeding in school. Under no conditions, however, should it be inferred that background characteristics are the reason why students do not succeed. Similarly, it may be more important to understand the number of adults available to support children's learning (what Coleman referred to as "social capital") and the nature of the family–school connection for learning than to discuss or explain achievement differences as a function of the intactness of the family (i.e., married, divorced).

    4. *The specific actions families take to facilitate their children's educational success, referred to as the "curriculum of the home" by Walberg, chart a course for intervention.* According to Walberg (1984), the curriculum of the home includes informed parent–child conversations about everyday events, encouragement and discussion of leisure reading, monitoring and joint analysis of television viewing, expression of affection, interest in children's academic and personal growth, and delay of immediate gratification to accomplish long-term goals. In his intensive observational study of the home environment of 10 high-achieving and 10 low-achieving secondary-level students, all of whom were low income and African American, Clark (1983) identified home variables that differentiated high and low achievers. Family life of high-achieving, low-income students was characterized by frequent dialogues between parents and children, strong parental encouragement of academic pursuits, warm and nurturing interactions, clear and consistent limits, and consistent monitoring of how time was spent. Parents of high achievers felt personally responsible to help their children gain knowledge and basic literacy skills, communicated regularly with school personnel, and were involved in school functions and activities. Both parents' attitudes (i.e., "I expect you to do well in school") and behavior (i.e., "I will communicate and support your learning") toward schooling for their children were evident. These findings have been replicated in numerous other studies with children and families across income levels and from different ethnic backgrounds (Kellaghan et al., 1993).

    There is, however, no consensus about a prescription for the precise ways families help to facilitate student learning. In fact, few studies have been conducted on which family process variables are most influential for student learning. One exception is an investigation by Peng and Lee (1992), who identified parental educational expectations, talking with students about school, providing learning materials, and providing learning opportunities outside of school as family process variables that showed the strongest relationship with student achievement for students in grades K–8. Rather than an exact prescription, collective research findings support several ways for families to implement important family process variables. Various indicators of the presence of four family correlates of positive school performance—structure, support, expectations, and enriching environment—appear in Table 2.3. These indicators, which are drawn from descriptive studies across student grade and income levels, represent the idea that families can and do play different roles in supporting their children's learn-

TABLE 2.3. Varied Indicators of Family Correlates of Student Performance

Correlate	Indicators
Structure	◆ Priority given to schoolwork, reading, and learning. ◆ Consistent monitoring of how time is spent. ◆ Authoritative parenting style. ◆ Development of a reflective problem-solving style. ◆ Availability of learning materials and a place for study. ◆ Delay of immediate gratification to accomplish long-term goals. ◆ Routine for completing home tasks. ◆ Regular communication with school personnel. ◆ Attendance at school functions. ◆ Parental knowledge of child's current schoolwork and strengths and weaknesses in learning.
Support	◆ Parental responsibility to assist children as learners. ◆ Encouragement and discussion of leisure reading. ◆ Modeling learning by reading and using math. ◆ Positive emotional interactions. ◆ Responsiveness to child's developmental needs/skills. ◆ Expression of affection.
Expectations	◆ Expectations for child's success. ◆ Use of effort and ability attributions. ◆ Interest in and establishment of standards for children's schoolwork.
Enriching environment	◆ Frequent dialogue. ◆ Informed conversations about everyday events. ◆ Opportunities for good language habits. ◆ Orienting children's attention to learning opportunities. ◆ Reading with children. ◆ Monitoring and joint analysis of television. ◆ Enriching learning experiences.

ing. School personnel increase the probability of family involvement when they value each role and help parents see the importance or benefits of different roles for their children. Obtaining a match between parents' availability and what they can and are likely to do is critical. Parents do not necessarily have a stated preference for a specific role; however, they seek guidance from educators as to what will help their children on school-related tasks.

They want to help, and they also need educators to understand their personal constraints for home support for learning.

The degree to which these correlates have been present over time for students is important to consider. Every child has a home environment; however, not all home environments are learning environments. This led Kellaghan and colleagues (1993) to propose the direct teaching of home conditions and activities that relate to learning as necessary for parent involvement in education. Defined as the "home process approach," they recommend sharing information about the significance of the family for children's learning and providing ongoing support in the following areas: work habits of the home, academic guidance and support, stimulation to explore and discuss ideas and events, language environment, and academic aspirations and expectations.

5. *The power of out-of-school time, which includes community and peer influences for school learning, is also important.* The use of out-of-school time—or how and with whom students spend time—helps to explain school performance differences (Christenson & Buerkle, 1999). Clark (1990) reported that students' involvement in constructive learning activities outside of school was strongly associated with higher academic achievement. Low-income, high-achieving students in grades K–12 in large, urban school districts were involved 25–30 hours per week in learning activities that involved thinking while completing the task and receiving supportive input and guidance from an adult or peer. Supportive guidance from adults, not just families, was a determining factor for the availability of these activities. Clark stated, "The attitudes and relationships between youngsters and their parents, relatives, teachers, ministers, coaches, instructors, and tutors can be among the most important factors in creating an environment that will maximize the chances for success during their school years and throughout their lives" (p. 23). Additionally, in an examination of data in the Baltimore Public Schools, Entwisle, Alexander, and Olson (1997) found that home resources (e.g., books, computers, learning opportunities) had the greatest impact on children's academic progress during the summer. Furthermore, low-income families were less likely to secure the resources needed for the ongoing cognitive growth of their children. What is key is that both low- and high-income children made comparable gains in reading and math when schools were open; however, low-income children lost ground and high-income children continued to improve their academic performance during the summer.

6. *Programs that improve student performance are compre-*

hensive, well planned, and provide options for family involvement that allow schools to be responsive to family diversity. Many studies have demonstrated a ceiling effect with respect to achievement gains for low-income students, particularly in urban education settings; that is, students' achievement scores have been raised; however, their overall performance is still below the national average. Studies that correlate levels of parent involvement with gains in student achievement invariably find that the more extensive the involvement, the higher the student achievement. In programs that are designed to be full partnerships, where the programs are comprehensive and address attitudes, philosophy, structure, and day-to-day practices, student achievement not only improves but it also reaches levels that are standard for middle-class children (Comer, 1995; Comer & Haynes, 1991). Children who are the farthest behind make the greatest gains (Henderson & Berla, 1994). Programs and practices are stronger in schools where teachers perceive that they, their colleagues, and parents all feel strongly about the importance of parent involvement (Dauber & Epstein, 1993). In comprehensive programs, family involvement is an integral part of what the school does to enhance learning opportunities and educational progress for students.

7. *The degree of match between home and school contexts is a contributing factor for students' school success.* Hansen (1986) demonstrated achievement gains from third to fifth grade for those students who experienced congruence in rules and interaction styles across home and school environments. He also found that the greater the discontinuity between home and school, the more students' academic grades declined. Finally, he concluded that there was no preferred classroom (e.g., open, traditional) or home (permissive, restrictive) type; rather, the similarity in the message received by students between home and school contexts was the critical factor for children's academic success.

Research on conjoint behavioral consultation has found that interactions involving parents, teachers, and school psychologists in joint problem solving are effective with academic, social, and behavioral concerns (Sheridan, 1997). Sheridan et al. (1990) found that when parents were involved actively in consultation-based problem solving, students' demonstration of important social skills was greater and longer-term than when consultative problem solving occurred in the school setting only. Likewise, Galloway and Sheridan (1994) reported a study wherein students with inconsistent academic performance responded more favorably and more consistently when conjoint (i.e., parent and teacher) problem solving occurred, as compared to conditions when parents were only peripherally involved (i.e., told what to do by school personnel).

With respect to mesosystemic interventions, Bronfenbrenner (1974), over 25 years ago, noted: "To use a chemical analogy, parent intervention functions as a kind of fixative, which stabilizes effects produced by other processes" (p. 34). There appears to be little or no contention over the notion that the informal education provided in homes positively impacts the formal education provided at school.

The following quote by Sloane (1991) sums up the influence of families on children's learning well: "It is now well accepted that the home plays an important role in children's learning and achievement. Some children learn values, attitudes, skills, and behaviors in the home that prepare them well for the tasks of school" (p. 161). The literature paints a picture supporting our contention that families are essential, not merely desirable, vis-à-vis their children's school performance. We know that (1) families are facilitators of student's enthusiasm for learning and level of achievement; (2) continuity between home and school affects student achievement and engagement with learning; (3) how students spend their time in- and out-of-school influences their educational productivity; and (4) there is inequity for students. School personnel—administrators, school psychologists, and teachers—hold the promise to alter influences in home inputs for students' learning.

Given the database, several questions are raised. Why is there so little constructive family involvement across grades K–12? How long will individuals refer to the rhetoric rut when discussing family and school as partners? Our response is that policies relevant to family involvement are often lacking, and family involvement programs are often viewed as an appendage rather than an integral part of school practices. We know that comprehensive programs to date hold promise for closing the achievement gap between students engaged and disengaged with learning. With respect to policy, we suggest that school personnel must deliver an essential message: Student performance depends on the curriculum of the school, the curriculum of the home, and two-way communication between school and home to enhance consistency of influence and to handle conflict across home and school. Consistent with systems theory, we suggest that this message is the umbrella under which to implement family involvement activities. Empirical support for creating consistent messages for learners is strong.

Creating Consistent Messages for Learners

What helps students learn? What helps students develop positive habits for learning? What helps students do their best in school? What conditions enhance the probability that students will be optimally successful in school and/or engaged as learners? The All Parents Are Teachers Project (formerly the Live and Learn Project), funded by the Minnesota Extension Service at the University of Minnesota, sought to answer these questions. A primary goal of the project was to disseminate evidence based on information about conditions that foster learning success and engagement for school-age children. Because of the strong outreach efforts in early childhood education in the state, parents of preschoolers noted the lack of support for families of school-age children. The project was funded, in part, to address this statewide need.

It is important to note that this project has been guided by a medical analogy, namely, the field of medicine that routinely suggests to individuals what to eat to reduce the probability of having colon cancer, or conversely, what foods to avoid because they have been shown to increase the probability of coronary heart disease. In education, we have less often adopted this strategy. To use such a strategy, it was necessary to identify alterable family, school, and community influences on children's learning in grades K–12. Across the over 200 studies reviewed, indicators of positive school performance were varied: standardized tests, grades, teacher ratings of academic performance, and measures of school adjustment, including improved attendance, fewer suspensions, increased classroom participation, and improved self-esteem and motivation to learn (Christenson & Christenson, 1998). A major conclusion of this review was that there is evidence for a common set of contextual influences important for learning regardless of the child's immediate microsystem (i.e., home or school setting). Remarkable similarity in the contextual influences that enhance student learning emerged as a result of simultaneously examining studies from family, school, and community literature. Correlations between family, school, or community influences and indicators of positive school performance were significant and fell within the low (.10) to strong (.80) range; however, most were in the low-moderate to moderate range. Actually, the size of the correlation has been argued to be less important than the fact that findings are consistent and point in a similar direction, suggesting convergence in the factors critical for students' school success (Brophy & Good, 1986; Christenson, Rounds, & Gorney, 1992).

Specifically, project personnel concluded that students perform most optimally when they experience the following six factors in school—from teachers, and outside of school—from parents and their community:

◆ *Standards and expectations*—the level of expected performance held by key adults for youth. Student success in school is facilitated when parents and teachers clearly state expectations for student performance, set specific goals and standards for desired behavior and performance, discuss expectations with youth, emphasize children's effort when completing tasks, and ensure that youth understand the consequences for not meeting expectations.

◆ *Structure*—the overall routine and monitoring provided by key adults for youth. Students' success in school is facilitated when families and schools provide a consistent pattern of events and age-appropriate monitoring and supervision. Students perform better in school when they understand their schedule of daily activities, directions for schoolwork, rules for behavior, and so forth.

◆ *Opportunity to learn*—the variety of learning options available to youth in the home, at school, and within the community. Students' success in school is facilitated when youth are provided with various tools for learning, such as reading materials, access to clubs and organizations, varied teaching strategies, and time to practice/master new skills. Also, success is enhanced when the key adults in the youth's life communicate with each other.

◆ *Support*—the guidance, communication, and interest shown by adults to facilitate students' progress in school. Student progress is facilitated when adults give frequent verbal support and praise; provide the youth with regular, explicit feedback; talk directly to youth about schoolwork and activities; and teach problem solving and negotiation skills. It is *what* adults do on an ongoing basis to help youth learn and achieve.

◆ *Climate/relationships*—the amount of warmth and friendliness; praise and recognition; and the degree to which the adult–youth relationship is positive and respectful. Student success at school is enhanced when students experience cooperative, accepting environments; a nonblaming relationship between home and school; and encouragement, praise, and involvement from key adults. Continuity in relationships and interactions between adults at home and at school will greatly influence the degree of academic achievement of youth. Climate/relationships is *how* adults in the home, in the school, and in the community work together to help youth learn.

 ◆ *Modeling*—how adults demonstrate desired behaviors and commitment/values toward learning and working hard in their daily lives. Students' success at school is enhanced when teachers establish an academically demanding classroom that has clearly defined objectives, explicit instructions, and an orderly and efficient environment, and when the parent(s) or other adults read, ask questions, discuss the importance/value of education, set long-term goals, and are able to intervene and be involved with the youth's school.

Several points are noteworthy about organizing research findings related to family, school, and community conditions that enhance students' success in school. First, this organization is guided by systems theory. Project personnel assumed that student characteristics—how time is spent both in school and outside of school—mutually influence student success in school. Also, this coordinated conceptualization of the research provides parents and teachers with a common language for discussing students' learning progress and performance, yet there is a differentiation of roles and responsibilities. Both parents and teachers have an important role to play; their roles do not replace but rather reinforce the other's role, thus providing the student with a consistent message about learning. In Table 2.4, examples of ways parents, educators and community members help to facilitate optimal student success are provided. Because we need to move from merely identifying contextual influences on children's learning (whether family, school, or peer influences) to understanding the reciprocal interaction of multiple influences for children's school success, it is recommended that parents and school personnel communicate about ways to enhance student learning by discussing the six factors and sharing ideas with each other. Finally, there are many ways for these factors to be reinforced at home, in school, and within the community. Thus, there is not one prescription for helping children, such as "Read with your child 10 minutes daily." Rather, the critical variables are the degree to which children's family and school contexts are learning environments, and complementary, not symmetrical roles are created between families and schools.

We know that students who are high achievers and/or engage in learning activities at school have experienced these six influences from family *and* school on a consistent basis and over time (i.e., across grade levels). Christenson and Christenson (1998) in-

TABLE 2.4. Creating Conditions for Student Success
_____

Standards and expectations
At home . . .
  ◆ Parents communicate that effort and a positive attitude in school are ex-
    pected.
  ◆ Parents support children and encourage them to strive for good grades
    (e.g., children teach parents one thing they learned in school each day).
  ◆ Parents discuss the importance and value of education (e.g., set clear
    academic goals with their children, encourage their children to enroll in
    challenging courses).

In school . . .
  ◆ Expectations are based on the level of student performance and are mea-
    surable and attainable (e.g., write specific behavioral objectives).
  ◆ Students understand that assignments are to be neat and turned in on
    time.
  ◆ Students are expected to respond when called on.

Within the community . . .
  ◆ Members of the community share common values.
  ◆ The community sets high standards for public behavior.
  ◆ The community values and places priority on learning and education.

Structure
At home . . .
  ◆ Routine daily events such as eating dinner together, completing home-
    work, and bedtimes are reinforced.
  ◆ Children are held accountable for their actions.
  ◆ Children's behavior is monitored, and age-appropriate supervision is pro-
    vided.

In school . . .
  ◆ A clear instructional sequence is used.
  ◆ Teachers remind students of behavioral expectations and standards prior
    to unique or novel activities (e.g., fields trips, assemblies, guest speakers,
    etc.).
  ◆ Teachers monitor student engagement and attention to determine level
    of student understanding.

Within the community . . .
  ◆ Youth in the community are involved in interesting, challenging pro-
    grams that allow and promote productive use of time.
  ◆ The community has a feeling of cohesiveness and a collective sense of
    well-being and physical security.
  ◆ The community monitors and supervises the behavior of youth.

Opportunity to learn
At home . . .
  ◆ Children are involved in extracurricular activities (e.g., youth groups,
    sports, or music lessons).
  ◆ Parents spend time discussing current events and issues with their chil-
    dren.
  ◆ Parents use everyday tasks to provide learning opportunities.

TABLE 2.4 (continued)

In school . . .
- Students are provided with prompts and cues to help them answer a question.
- Students are provided sufficient time to practice a new skill, and their success rate on independent tasks is 90–100%.
- A variety of task-relevant assignments are used when teaching a new skill.

Within the community . . .
- Community institutions collaborate for the benefit of youth programs.
- Youth have opportunities to have conversations and interactions with adults other than their parents in the community.
- A wide variety of high-quality, extra activities are available to youth in the community.

Support
At home . . .
- Parents are involved in the children's school by participating in school events and/or spending time working with their children on school-related topics.
- Parents recognize children's effort and progress (e.g., give a high five for a 10-point improvement on a math test).
- Parents talk with their children about what they are learning/studying in school.

In school . . .
- Teachers contact parents at first sign of a problem.
- Students are provided specific, immediate, and frequent feedback about their behavior and progress (e.g., recognize improvements, not just perfection).
- Teachers use student errors as an opportunity to reteach skills or concepts (e.g., appropriate instructional modifications are provided).

Within the community . . .
- Adults in the community are available to help youth reach personal and group goals.
- Youth receive guidance and recognition from a variety of community organizations (e.g., churches, families, youth organizations).
- The community is responsive to the diverse needs of its members.

Climate / relationships
At home . . .
- The parent–child relationship is generally positive and not strained (e.g., hugs, smiles, "I am proud of you").
- Parents talk to and listen to their children to understand better their opinions and needs (e.g., listen to children's questions and concerns, ask for their opinions or ideas).
- Parents advocate for their children when concerns arise.

(continued)

TABLE 2.4 (*continued*)

In school . . .
- ◆ Classrooms are warm and friendly, and students obviously feel comfortable and accepted in the environment (e.g., use praise when students enter or leave the classroom, smile, the teacher greets the students).
- ◆ Teachers listen to students' opinions and ideas (e.g., demonstrate interest by nodding, eye contact, open arms, etc.).
- ◆ The classroom promotes cooperation rather than competition.

Within the community . . .
- ◆ The community provides an environment that recognizes individual and group accomplishments.
- ◆ Youth in the community have access to competent and caring adults who provide them with additional counsel and guidance during crisis.
- ◆ There is an available social support network to address concerns for individuals.

Modeling
At home . . .
- ◆ Parents model the importance and value of education by using reading and math in the home (e.g., balance a checkbook, read a book).
- ◆ Parents talk positively with their children about school projects and activities.
- ◆ Parents set long-term personal goals and use their progress as an example of persistence and hard work for their children.

In school . . .
- ◆ Teachers perform the desired classroom behavior (e.g., talking softly vs. talking loudly; problem solving).
- ◆ Teachers model classroom guidelines and rules (e.g., listen to students, do not chew gum, drink pop, etc.).
- ◆ Teachers demonstrate important steps students must follow to complete assignments.

Within the community . . .
- ◆ The community has adult mentoring programs to teach appropriate behaviors and decision-making skills to youth involved in high-risk behaviors.
- ◆ Youth can turn to adults in the community, other than parents, for advice and support.
- ◆ The youth's peers model responsible behavior.

Note. Abstracted from Christenson and Christenson (1998).

terviewed students from grades 4–12 who were nominated as consistent and inconsistent learners by their teachers. The consistent learners were students who worked hard in school, took school and learning seriously, and performed at their "level best." Although they were viewed as responsible, productive, and competent learners, they were not necessarily the valedictorians of their class. In contrast, inconsistent learners performed inconsistently in class, did not take school and assigned activities seriously, and lacked an overall connection with school. They often displayed behaviors inconsistent with being a responsible, productive learner, such as tardiness, absenteeism, not completing assignments, and disruptiveness. Based on this pilot study, both consistent and inconsistent learners in elementary and secondary schools reported experiencing each factor. However, the consistent learners' descriptions of these influences in their lives suggested that these factors were more frequent, systematic, and noticeably evident over time.

Although not the focus of this review, the six factors are readily applied to the development of children from birth to school entrance, which is the objective of the National Education Goal 1: School Readiness. Based on a review of the literature for preschoolers, it appears that home and school influences that help to facilitate the development of preschool children, particularly for school-related tasks, are an *enriching environment* (e.g., material and personal resources, interaction with others, play, reading), *management/disciplinary practices* (e.g., understanding family rules, guidance in teaching, such as reasoning and explanation, affirmations), *responsivity/support* (e.g., warm, nurturing relationship, positive adult–child relationship when teaching), and *language* (e.g., exposure, interaction with others, use of language facilitators). We know that preschoolers benefit (or are being prepared for school-related tasks) from specific interactions with caregivers. We know caregivers who (1) model reading and writing to children frequently; (2) talk to children frequently, provide positive feedback, and foster vocabulary development by explaining the meaning of words and describing objects in the environment; (3) incorporate language, reading, and writing into play themes with children, such as singing silly songs that substitute sounds and playing rhyming games; and (4) develop environments that are "literacy rich" with available print materials and learning resources to help to foster children's identity as learners and prepare them for the tasks of school (see Ramey & Ramey, 1998).

In conclusion, schools and teachers alone seldom help students achieve their full academic potential. This is not an indictment of schools or teachers. Rather, this is a fact of child development (Comer et al., 1996). Students' personal investment in and interest for learning are influenced in particular by the degree to which home and school environments—in concert—create optimal conditions for learning. An implication of this conceptualization of family–school relationships is the presence of two curricula—the curriculum of the school, and the curriculum of the home—as well as the significance of communication between families and schools to maintain a consistency of influence and handle conflict. Because children traverse family and school contexts, the degree to which their primary socializing agents—parents and teachers—have developed a sense of shared meaning (Pianta & Walsh, 1996) or a common language about conditions that enhance children's learning may be integral to the success of ongoing collaborative relationships.

A NEW APPROACH

Garbarino (1982), an advocate of systems theory and systems intervention for children and youth, aptly notes that support for children's development is represented by "connections that occur whenever individuals (e.g., parents, teachers) or systems (schools, churches, families) have ongoing contact with each other that is organized around concern for the welfare of the child" (p. 125). It appears the paradigm shift called for relates to the manner in which we conceptualize the relationship between families and schools. We recommend an approach in which the significance of families is clear, and shared, meaningful roles are established for families and educators. In other words, the intersection of family and school is considered vital for student performance and learning, and *the emphasis* is placed on the quality of the relationship rather than roles (i.e., activities) to be executed by home or school.

In the contextual-systems model for the socialization of youth, Pianta and Walsh (1996) described a necessary belief system for educators. Specifically, they advocate one in which educators understand that children develop and learn in the context of the family, and *that* system (i.e., child/family) must interface in a positive way with the school system and schooling issues for children's educational performance to be optimal. Not all educators recognize families and schools as contexts for children's learning or believe interventions should encompass the family. We contend this difference is looking at families as "essential partners" and at families as "desirable extras."

Equally important for student outcomes is the development of a collaborative family–school relationship over time across grades K–12. Rimm-Kaufmann and Pianta (1999) have argued that the development of supportive family–school relationships should not be considered a correlate or antecedent, but rather an outcome of the successful transition of children to school. They contend that the quality of the parent's relationship with the teacher and school personnel is as valid an indicator of a successful transition to schooling as the child's competence in kindergarten. Furthermore, they suggest that the quality of this relationship may forecast later school success, particularly for situations in which discontinuity between the systems is present. Thus, greater consideration should be given to the development of family–school relationships early and over time, because parents may be more helpful in the educational process than in the educational outcome. Seeley (1985) called for individuals to move from the concept of relationships in terms of service delivery—of "provider" and "client," of "professionals" and "target" populations—to one of complementary efforts toward common goals. He argued:

> Partners may help one another in general or specific ways, but none is ever a client, because the relationship is mutual. Providers and clients can deal with one another at arm's length; partners share an enterprise, though their mutuality does not imply or require equality or similarity. Participants in effective partnerships may be strikingly different, each contributing to the common enterprise, particular talents, experiences, and perspectives and sometimes having different status within the relationship and control over aspects of the work to be done. (p. 65)

Family–school collaboration is an attitude, not merely an activity. The goal of constructive family–school relationships is to change the interface between home and school to support students as learners, not merely to arrive at a solution for the immediate school-based concern (Weiss & Edwards, 1992). The view that parents are essential for children's learning and school progress is certainly an implicit assumption of collaborative family–school relationships. A missing piece is the explicit acknowledgment, particularly in school attitudes, related to the interdependent nature of the relationship; that is, parents are essential partners. Adopting an approach that recognizes the *significance of families* and the *contributions of schools* for children's engagement with school and learning provides a necessary framework for constructive family–school connections.

SUMMARY

The approach we believe is necessary for interacting with families is characterized by (1) focusing on the relationship; (2) recognizing that collaboration is an attitude and not just an activity; (3) creating a vehicle to co-construct the bigger picture about children's school performance and development; (4) sharing information and resources; and (5) establishing meaningful co-roles for the partners. We speculate that family and school as partners can be accomplished with any specific model provided it fits the needs of teachers, parents, and students, thereby resulting in a "goodness of fit" for the specific family–school context. Therefore, the approach for interaction is not based on use of a specific model, but rather specific characteristics. Working as partners is a way of thinking about how to create constructive connections between the critical socializing agents for children and youth. It requires delivery of the right message: "that mutual respect and interdependence of home, school, and community are essential to children's development" (McAfee, 1993, p. 21). In Chapter 3, we explore the role of attitudes in productive family–school connections.

QUESTIONS TO CONSIDER

1. Define the distinction between systems approach and systems theory.

   ◆ How does this distinction influence conclusions drawn from research?
   ◆ How does this distinction influence school-based practices, including the model of family involvement selected and characteristics of the family–school relationship?

2. How would you explain the notion of informal and formal education for children's school experiences and learning?

3. What are the benefits of establishing co-roles for parents and teachers, or families and schools, with respect to educational outcomes for students?

CHAPTER 3

♦♦♦

Attitudes: Values and Perceptions about Family Involvement

♦

As already emphasized, working constructively with families requires more than activities—it requires positive and open attitudes. An important way that a school's approach toward families
is communicated is through the attitudes conveyed by school personnel. Similarly, family members often hold attitudes about
schools and education that contribute to the establishment of relationships. The development of positive and constructive attitudes
between families and schools is an important component of collaborative activities and the responsibility of both parents and educators.

In this chapter, we define "attitudes" as perceptions that families and schools hold about one another and, consequently, the
relevance of the family–school relationship for children's learning.
They serve as a manifestation of the way school personnel think
about families, and the way that family members think about
schools. Furthermore, attitudes convey essential beliefs and principles that school personnel and families have about one another
and take into account all that we consider within the purview of
appropriate and effective roles, rights, and responsibilities for
families and schools. We consider attitudes to be variables that
schools and family members can alter or modify. Attitudes can be
positive and promote effective relationships, or they can be negative and preclude constructive relationships between schools and
families.

As you read this chapter, consider the extent to which the following conditions are apparent in your school community:

- ✦ Attempts to understand the needs, ideas, opinions, and perspectives of families and educators.
- ✦ A nonblaming, no-fault problem-solving stance in interactions with families.
- ✦ Willingness to share perspectives across home and school.
- ✦ Perception of family involvement as essential (i.e., bringing a critical element to the team that is otherwise unavailable) rather than simply desirable.
- ✦ A positive attitude that focuses on school, family, and child strengths, rather than only on problems or deficits.
- ✦ Willingness to co-construct the whole picture about children by discussing, exploring, and understanding different perspectives.
- ✦ Willingness to listen to and respond to concerns across home and school—viewing different perspectives as a way to better understand students' needs, and viewing parents' and educators' concerns as a way to offer mutual support.
- ✦ Mutual respect across home and school (i.e., respect for family members by school personnel, and respect for school personnel by family members).
- ✦ Understanding that barriers for positive family–school relationships (i.e., constraints of each system) exist for parents and educators.

ATTITUDES AS PRINCIPLES

Attitudes about home–school relations are often manifested in the way parents and teachers act toward, speak to, and think about one another. Through their communications and actions, school personnel can convey family-oriented attitudes (e.g., concern for and attention to family needs and perspectives, and understanding of family constraints). Alternatively, they can suggest attitudes that limit family outreach and concern. The former attitudes are consistent with a term coined by McWilliam and his colleagues—"family-centered services."

McWilliam and his colleagues (McWilliam, Harbin, et al., 1995; McWilliam, Lang, et al., 1995; McWilliam, Tocci, & Harbin, 1998) explored various dimensions of family-centered services, and found in their research that parents who express positive experiences report that their service providers are "responsive, supportive, caring, competent, and encouraging of parents' participation as team members. . . . The professionals' interpersonal characteristics were judged to be supremely important ... [and] friendly to families, oriented to the whole family, encouraging, and flexible" (1998, p. 207). Interestingly, when family-centered service providers were interviewed, almost identical characteristics were identified. Specifically, five underlying components of family-centered services were noted: positiveness, responsiveness, orientation to the whole family, friendliness, and sensitivity. Additionally, a sixth characteristic, skills with children and the community, was identified as important. Table 3.1 provides descriptions of these underlying components that characterize effective family-centered services (McWilliam et al., 1998).

Beliefs or attitudes that families and schools hold about each other are essential in the formation of relationships. Attitudes that are conducive to establishing constructive, collaborative relationships are presented in Table 3.2. Additionally, Liontos (1992) summarized the following new beliefs and principles about families that can foster healthier relationships between homes and schools:

- All families have strengths, and their assets and strengths rather than their deficits are emphasized.
- Parents can learn ways to help their children if they are provided with the opportunity and necessary support.
- Parents have important information and perspectives about their children.
- Schools and families influence each other.
- A no-fault model is necessary—blame is not attributed to the family or the school, because there is no single cause for any presenting concerns.

Implicit in these new beliefs and principles is the notion of empowerment, which implies that many competencies are already present or at least possible within families. From an empowerment perspective, a failure to display competence is not due to the deficiencies of families and/or children but rather to the failure of social systems, including schools, to create opportunities for competencies to be displayed. Rappaport (1981) argued that "in those cases where new competencies need to be learned, they are best learned in the context of living life rather than in artificial programs where ... it is really the expert who is in charge" (p. 16); that is, to be "empowered," parents must be actively involved in making decisions and choices related to their personal lives. It is important that parents believe that changes occur as a result of

TABLE 3.1. Underlying Components and Descriptions
of Family-Centered Services

Theme	Description
Family orientation	◆ "Opening the door" ◆ Willingness to orient services to the whole family, rather than just to the child ◆ Using sensitivity and good rapport to establish enough trust with parents to be able to ask them about their own concerns
Positiveness	◆ "Thinking the best of families" ◆ A philosophy of thinking the best about the parents without passing judgment ◆ An enthusiasm for activities for which others have reported a lack of enthusiasm
Sensitivity	◆ "In the parents' shoes" ◆ Demonstrating an understanding of families' concerns, needs, and priorities ◆ Gaining knowledge about families so service personnel can expand their own sensitivity, understanding possible cultural differences, working through interpersonal challenges with parents, and recognizing parents' aspirations for themselves ◆ Putting oneself in the parents' position to anticipate how families may feel and not prejudging them
Responsiveness	◆ "Doing whatever needs to be done" ◆ Attending to parents' concerns ◆ Paying attention and taking action when parents express a need ◆ Paying attention and taking action when parents express a complaint ◆ An individualized and flexible approach to service delivery; adapting activities to particular parents' concerns, without overregard for standard operating procedures ◆ A willingness to provide options ◆ Cooperating with parents rather than expecting them to cooperate with professionals
Friendliness	◆ "Treating parents as friends" ◆ An extension of rapport ◆ Participating in a friendship-based, rather than professional-based, relationship ◆ Developing a reciprocal relationship, building trust, taking time to talk to parents about concerns, listening to parents, encouraging them, offering practical help, and conveying care for both parents and the child

TABLE 3.1 *(continued)*

Theme	Description
Child and community skills	◆ Knowledge about child development and disabilities and methods for teaching skills and interacting with children ◆ Knowledge of the community, and a good reputation within it ◆ Eagerness to establish collaborative relationships with other community agencies

TABLE 3.2. Attitudes Necessary for Positive Home–School Relations

School attitudes	Family attitudes
◆ Families are potential facilitators, not determinants of children's educational success.	◆ Schools provide a context where support and guidance for learning are established.
◆ Families must be recognized for their essential role in influencing student success.	◆ Schools bear the essential responsibility for establishing a climate that allows families to partake in the educational development of their child.
◆ Home support for learning may help to differentiate high and low achievers.	◆ There are several ways that a home environment can support learning.
◆ Families across income levels support their children's education, although in different ways.	◆ Schools are places where individual students can grow and develop, not just groups of students.
◆ Outreach to families is essential.	◆ Interest in school activities is an important way for parents to show support for a child's education.
◆ Families need information about children, school policies and practices, and what they can do to assist their children as learners.	◆ Schools need information about how they can best support a child's unique development.
◆ Assumptions about families build walls.	◆ Assumptions about schools and teachers build walls.
◆ Open and clear communication with parents is needed.	◆ Clear communication with teachers and school personnel is needed.
◆ Judgments about families and students must be suspended.	◆ Judgments about schools and teachers must be suspended.
	◆ Parents have a responsibility to play a role in their child's development and support his or her education.

their own efforts. Therefore, strengths and competencies related to families' abilities to share in decision making and problem resolution are central. Attention is placed on the shared strengths of the home, school, and child, rather than on efforts to "fix" child- or family-centered problems.

In some problematic situations, negative attitudes between homes and schools result in unhealthy connections. Relationships become strained and unproductive, and are often fraught with barriers.

ATTITUDES LEADING TO "BARRIERS"

Along with attitudes that foster the formation of healthy home–school relations, a number of attitudes may produce barriers to effective relationships. Several of these are listed in Table 3.3. It is noteworthy that many educators consider barriers as obstacles to overcome, or as challenges to tackle. This attitude focuses on problems and will influence subsequent interactions with families by increasing the potential for conflict. We believe that barriers can

TABLE 3.3. Attitudinal Factors That Produce Barriers to the Establishment of Effective Relationships

1. Partial resistance toward increasing home–school cooperation.
2. Assumptions about others that are based on specific labels or structural characteristics.
3. Stereotypical views of people, events, conditions, or actions that are not descriptive of behavior, but portray a causal orientation.
4. Assumption that parents and teachers must hold identical values and expectations.
5. Failure to view differences as strengths.
6. Limiting impressions of the child to observations in only one environment.
7. Lack of belief in a partnership orientation to enhance student learning/development influences interactions.
8. A blaming and labeling attitude that permeates the home–school atmosphere.
9. A win–lose rather than a win–win attitude in the presence of conflict.
10. Tendencies to personalize anger-provoking behaviors of the other individual.
11. Lack of perspective taking or empathizing with the other person.
12. Failure to recognize the importance of preserving the family–school relationship.

also provide opportunities to increase perspective taking and understanding among individuals. The presence of such opportunities will strengthen relationships and promote the identification and development of actions that are uniquely meaningful and worthwhile to specific families.

When working with parents and families, the emergence of challenging situations is inevitable. Many times, school personnel are heard describing families as "hard to reach" or as "problem parents." Characterizing families in this way places blame on individuals rather than emphasis on solutions toward goals. It is necessary to recognize the difficulties inherent in *situations* by focusing on contextual circumstances that can be altered (e.g., "This is a challenging situation"), and not on individuals with unalterable characteristics (e.g., "This is a resistant parent"). A constructive tactic may be to frame challenges in terms of an unsatisfactory, unproductive interface between the home and school systems. As such, this presents a problematic situation that requires the collective attention and efforts of families and school personnel to correct.

Effective family–school relationships work systematically to remove barriers between families and educators. There is an ongoing process to identify and recommend constructive suggestions for improvement in the family–school interface rather than assigning blame. The categorization of typical barriers by Liontos (1992)—barriers for educators, barriers for parents, and barriers for family–school relationships—is particularly helpful, because it suggests that barriers are expected for all and the emphasis must be on understanding and removing them. Barriers for educators include ambiguous commitment to parent involvement; negative communication about students' school performance and productivity; stereotypes about families, such as dwelling on family problems as an explanation for students' performance; doubts about the abilities of families to address schooling concerns; lack of time and funding for family outreach programs; and fear of conflict with families. For parents, barriers include feelings of inadequacy; adoption of a passive role by leaving education to schools; linguistic and cultural differences; lack of role models, information, and knowledge about resources; suspicion about treatment from educators; and economic, emotional, and time constraints. Finally, barriers for the partnership include limited time for communication and meaningful interaction; communication primarily during crises; differences in parent–educator perspectives about child performance and behavior; and limited contact for building trust within the family–school relationship. Conceptualizing barriers for each system, as well as the relationship, may serve to promote perspective taking and enhance the understanding of constraints involved for all individuals.

With respect to major barriers for effective family–school connections for children's learning across the nation, Moles (1992) focused on attitudinal barriers, such as psychological and cultural differences, and interactional barriers, such as the low rate of contact, limited skills and knowledge on which to build collaboration, and restricted opportunities for meaningful dialogue. Similarly, Weiss and Edwards (1992) identified three comprehensive, key barriers: school personnel's limited conception of the roles families can play; psychological and cultural differences that lead to assumptions that build walls between families and educators; and the lack of a routine communication system, particularly to prevent misunderstandings between families and educators. To these we would add the educators' failure to examine systematically school practices that "fail" families. For example, responding only in a crisis, defining (and labeling) the family solely by structure (e.g., single parent), and viewing the family as deficient are far too common examples of school practices that result in an uncomfortable atmosphere for discussion and interaction between families and school personnel. As a result, there is too little outreach to families and children about whom school personnel are most concerned. Of these barriers, none is as severe as our infrequent use of practices that focus on family *and* schools as contexts for children's development and learning. Integral to advancing outcomes for children and youth are school-based actions that include families and account for how the family–school interface socializes students as learners.

Attitudes that characterize differences as deficits are often conveyed in schools. Schools in America today typify a culture characteristic of a middle-class, educationally oriented, Euro-American lifestyle. Furthermore, schools tend to perpetuate the values, norms, and practices of individuals who "fit into" this culture. Families who differ are often seen as "deficient" (Davies, 1993). In many cases, there is an overemphasis on labels. Common labels often surround "what" parents and families are (such as uneducated or poor) or what they are failing to do (how they are failing their children) as defined by the school's agenda. Concomitantly, there is a lack of attention to personal characteristics of a parent or family ("who" they are) and what they do to support their children. In fact, parents who experience diverse ethnic, cultural, socioeconomic, linguistic, and educational backgrounds *are* involved in the lives of their children, regardless of whether they are formally involved in their school life (Bempechat, 1998; Edwards, Fear, & Gallego, 1995). Furthermore, many families are involved in the education of their child, albeit in ways that school personnel may not consider because they see no concrete outcome or product (Wright & Smith, 1998). In reality, it does little good to concentrate on status variables that are not amenable to intervention. Attitudes and actions that focus on competencies and identify strategies to promote success in the face of challenges are more constructive.

A focus on status variables rather than individuals and actions often leads quickly to stereotypes and preconceived judgments. We fail as educators when we form conclusions based on what we believe families need. This is heightened when we fail to consider how families may be supporting their children's education already. For example, an educator might believe that families need help supporting their children's homework, when they may not need that form of assistance at all. Rather, other forms of assistance, such as how best to communicate with teachers or understand school policies or practices, may be necessary. In such scenarios, it is the schools, not the families, who fail students.

THE IMPORTANCE OF PERSPECTIVE TAKING

It seems necessary that schools and parents begin thinking differently about their respective roles and responsibilities. In particular, both schools and parents must begin to recognize the relationship they enter with each other when children enter schools. The attitudes of and about *all* families, including those who differ from the majority culture, are important. Each family is unique in terms of its ethnic heritage, level of acculturation, SES, language practices, belief systems, religious and lifestyle orientation, and involvement with extended family members, to name a few examples. Collectively, these characteristics provide families with an inherent uniqueness that defines who they are and must be recognized as special to them. It is likely impossible for individuals who fit more comfortably into the predominant culture to understand all families whose cultural makeup differs from their own. Nevertheless, it is essential that sincere efforts be made to understand all families for *who* they are rather than *what* they are or are not. The only way to accomplish this is to acknowledge and embrace differences among families and be open to the practice of taking multiple perspectives.

How does one take multiple perspectives? This often difficult process requires that each individual take a "personal inventory" and engage in self-assessment and reflection. To truly connect with parents, educators and other professionals must get in touch with their own values, priorities, perspectives, and assumptions (Lynch & Hanson, 1998). Similarly, parents must be willing to explore their role in relation to their child's educators. It is only when these sometimes difficult tasks are initiated that educators are able to begin working toward establishing personal relationships with families and valuing them for who they are, and vice versa. A "personal inventory" for school personnel and parents is presented in Table 3.4. This inventory (or checklist), developed by Vosler-Hunter (1989), prompts school professionals and parents to consider actively their respective roles and interactions with each other around a child's education by engaging in important, albeit difficult, self-reflection.

Beyond self-reflection, school personnel must be willing to learn not only *about* a family's uniqueness but also to learn *with* and *from* them. It is essential that families' differences be recognized and accepted, and that these differences be appreciated and embraced. This level of acceptability must be bidirectional; that is, to be in relationship with each other, families must also value the different cultural and interpersonal norms of school personnel. For example, learning "from" each other allows parents opportunities to ask questions about the school and their child's education that can promote an understanding of school policies and practices. When learning "with" one another, school personnel begin to discard judgments and understand a family's reality from a different perspective, and vice versa. Together with families, educators can then learn ways to form meaningful relationships to achieve educational goals for students.

Parents generally want educators to take a personal interest in their children and in them. They want to be included in the dialogue about their children's education and to share important perceptions they have about their children. For example, consider a mother who requests feedback about how her daughter, Anna, is progressing in kindergarten. This mother (like most) is concerned with her own child's progress and what she is learning. She may feel disenfranchised by a teacher who responds with a statement

TABLE 3.4. Personal Inventories for Educators and Parents

For educators

♦ Have I put myself in the parent's place and mentally reversed roles to consider how I would feel as the parent of the child about whom there are concerns?

♦ Do I see the child/adolescent in more than one dimension, looking beyond the concern?

♦ Am I able to keep in mind that the child/adolescent is a person whom the parent loves?

♦ Do I really believe that parents are equal to me as a professional and, in fact, are experts on their child?

♦ Do I consistently value the comments and insights of parents and make use of their reservoir of knowledge about the child's total needs and activities?

♦ Do I judge the child/adolescent in terms of his or her progress and communicate hope to the parents by doing so?

♦ Do I listen to parents, communicating with words, eye contact and posture that I respect and value their insights?

♦ Do I ask questions of parents, listen to their answers and respond to them?

♦ Do I work to create an environment in which parents are comfortable enough to speak and interact?

♦ Am I informed about the individual child's case before the appointment or group session, placing equal value on the parents' time with my own time?

♦ Do I treat each parent I come in contact with as an adult who can understand a subject of vital concern?

♦ Do I speak plainly, avoiding the jargon of medicine, sociology, psychology or social work?

♦ Do I make a consistent effort to consider the child as part of a family, consulting parents about the important people in the child's life and how their attitudes and reactions affect the child?

♦ Do I distinguish between fact and opinion when I discuss a child's problems and potential with a parent?

♦ Do I make every effort to steer parents toward solutions and resources, providing both written and oral evaluations and explanations as well as brochures about potential services, other supportive arrangements, and financial aid?

♦ Do I tell each family about other families in similar situations, recognizing parents as a major source of support and information and, at the same time, respecting their right to confidentiality?

♦ At the request of parents, am I an active part of their information and referral network, expending time and energy to provide functional contacts to points in the service system and to parent support networks?

♦ Do I express hope to parents through my attitude and my words, avoiding absolutes like "always" and "never"?

♦ Do I see as my goal for interactions with parents the mutual understanding of a problem so that we can take action as a team to alleviate the problem?

♦ Do I actively involve the parents of each child in the establishment of a plan of action or treatment and continually review, evaluate and revise the plan with the parents?

♦ Do I make appointments at times and in places that are convenient for the family?

(continued)

TABLE 3.4 (continued)

- ◆ When I make a commitment of action to the family, do I follow through and complete that commitment?
- ◆ Do I obtain and share information from other appropriate professionals to insure that services are not duplicated and that families do not expend unnecessary energy searching for providers and services?

For parents
- ◆ Do I believe that I am an equal partner with professionals, accepting my share of the responsibility for solving problems and making plans on behalf of my child?
- ◆ Am I able to see the professional as a person who is working with me for the well-being of my child?
- ◆ Do I see as my goal for interactions with professionals the mutual understanding of a problem so that we can take action as a team to alleviate the problem?
- ◆ Do I maintain a file of important documents and correspondence so that I have a complete history of services provided to my child and family?
- ◆ Do I clearly express my own needs and the needs of my family to professionals in an assertive manner?
- ◆ Do I state my desire to be an active participant in the decision-making process concerning my child, and do I seek mutual agreement on the means to insure my involvement?
- ◆ Do I take an active, assertive role in planning and implementing intervention plans or special services for my child?
- ◆ Do I come to appointments having thought through the information I want to give and the questions I want answered?
- ◆ Do I accept the fact that a professional often has responsibility for service coordination and communication with many families, including my own?
- ◆ Do I treat each professional as an individual and avoid letting past negative experiences or negative attitudes get in the way of establishing a good working relationship?
- ◆ Do I communicate quickly with professionals who are serving the needs of my child when there are significant changes or when notable situations occur?
- ◆ Do I communicate with other parents, thereby reducing my isolation and theirs, and sharing my expertise?
- ◆ Do I encourage the professionals involved with my child to communicate with each other and to keep me informed as well?
- ◆ When I have a positive relationship with a professional or an agency, do I express support for that professional or agency in the community?
- ◆ When I make a commitment to a professional for a plan of action, do I follow through and complete that commitment?
- ◆ Do I maintain realistic expectations of professionals, myself and my child, knowing that complete and definitive answers are unlikely when there are concerns about children?

---

such as "Children this age are learning primarily how to get along with others." This mother requested information about *her* child, Anna, and not "children this age." The parent's perspective concerns primarily her daughter, who happens to be part of a larger group. The teacher's perspective, on the other hand, often relates to a classroom of students, of which Anna is a part. Clearly, both are important and valuable perspectives that highlight the different responsibilities held by parents and educators in relation to the education of children. The key to establishing constructive relationships is identifying ways that these perspectives can be communicated and valued by both parents and teachers.

Several dimensions on which parents and educators may hold slightly different perspectives are outlined in Table 3.5 (Mendoza & Cegelka, 1986; cited in Chrispeels, 1987). Note that these differing perspectives have a high probability for resulting in communication difficulties and misunderstandings. Although they may not cause serious conflict, they can increase social and physical distance between family members and educators, which can lead to negative attitudes about uninvolved families. Unless there is an understanding and acceptance of the logical differences between home and school responsibilities, differing perspectives can create inherent communication difficulties; that is, a lack of perspective taking results in a potential for labeling families (e.g., uninvolved, hard to reach). Similarly, lack of perspective taking on the part of parents can result in labeling of teachers (e.g., difficult to talk to, unconcerned).

TABLE 3.5. Differing Perspectives of Parents and Educators

Parents	Educators
◆ Are concerned with their child's individual progress and needs.	◆ Must focus on whole class or group.
◆ Are concerned with what their child is learning.	◆ Have knowledge of what the child has mastered.
◆ Have a perspective of how far the child has come.	◆ Are concerned with present development of the child.
◆ Have an emotional involvement with their child.	◆ Are able to distance themselves from the child; more rational–cognitive approach.
◆ Want to have their child approached and taught as an *individual*.	◆ Look for one best method or way to work with all children.

The potential for labeling parents was illustrated in a study by Davies (1993) that spanned three countries. In this study, Davies discovered very divergent perspectives about contacts and roles among parents and teachers. Specifically, teachers and school officials believed that some parents (i.e., those living in low-income conditions) were "hard to reach," and cited character-istics of the parents as the primary causes (i.e., their socio-economic conditions, lack of time or competence, or little inter-est). However, contrary to school officials' perspectives, parents did *not* consider themselves difficult to reach. They indicated that they were willing to come to school when asked and ex-pressed strong interest in their child's education. Nonetheless, they did not understand school policies and practices, nor did they realize that their involvement was actually *desired* by school per-sonnel.

Perspective taking is an important activity when working with all families, and not simply those who represent diversity in various sociodemographic variables (e.g., ethnicity, socioeconomic class, primary language, marital arrangement, household compo-sition). Differences in the manner in which some families are able to participate in their child's education also must be considered. Educators must be sensitive to all family members with whom they interact and attempt to put themselves into their place. For example, some parents are limited in their ability to engage open-ly and regularly in their child's education because they lack custo-dial rights, travel frequently, or work long hours. When consider-ing perspectives, it is important to recall that both parents and school personnel are interested in the welfare of the student. Fur-thermore, perspectives are always couched in a particular context; that is, each perspective has a distinct reality to the individual holding it, formed in relation to the context and lenses through which it is viewed.

Perspective taking is also important from the vantage point of dialogues about what families and educators need from each other in order to help children become successful learners. This high-lights the notion that individuals within the home and those in schools are always in relationship with each other, sharing com-mon goals. It also emphasizes that neither parents nor teachers can fully support learning alone. However, clear communication about what parents need from teachers, and what teachers need from parents, is essential and possible if both are able to accept the perspective of the other.

ATTITUDES AND REALITIES OF FAMILIES

Taking the perspective of families requires that school personnel and parents engage in meaningful dialogue with each other. Finders and Lewis (1994) interviewed parents who were considered "hard to reach" to understand how the diverse realities of their lives affected home–school relationships. These parents reported that their own school experiences, economic and time constraints, and differences in linguistic and cultural practices presented important roadblocks.

Diverse School Experiences among Parents

Personal experiences with educational institutions can contribute to parents' attitudes regarding their child's school and schooling. For some parents, an adverse history with schools can create negative attitudes, such as mistrust, and prevent parents from fully participating in their child's education. At times, parents also may lack confidence in the manner and effectiveness with which they can be helpful in their child's education. For some, family and work responsibilities, coupled with limited or difficult schooling, may make it difficult to help at home. Taking this perspective, including understanding and empathizing with the constraints of the other system, requires school personnel to rethink expectations and assumptions about parents. As children advance through the educational system, increasing academic demands may begin to exceed the skills level of some parents. If "helping with homework" is the only manner in which parental involvement is presented to parents, their ability to interact with their child around schoolwork is truncated. Alternatively, if *processes* are reinforced (such as encouraging effective organizational skills and discussing events at school), parents have ongoing mechanisms by which to engage with their child.

Attention to process (and not simply content) is important regardless of the level of the activity engaged in by parents (Epstein, 1995), or whether traditional or partnership models are espoused (Swap, 1993). The primary issue concerns whether parents have enough information (and how to deliver that information), so that the necessary supports are provided or constructed to match parents' skill or availability. For example, parents can value homework and demonstrate this by talking to their child about class assignments—this represents Epstein's Level 1. Or, parents can value homework and demonstrate this by tutoring their child in fractions or word attack skills—this represents a different level of parent assistance. Both are necessary and important, and appropriate within given familial situations.

Economic and Time Constraints

Many parents have practical and logistical realities, such as difficult work schedules, child care needs, and transportation issues, that limit their involvement at school (Finders & Lewis, 1994; Leitch & Tangri, 1988; Norman & Smith, 1997). For parents who work outside of the home, time constraints present a primary obstacle to becoming involved in the school. Schedule conflicts and work demands are apparent for families whether events occur in daytime or evening hours. For example, parents who work evening shifts may need daytime hours to attend to family care and obligations, or to sleep. A mother who works during the day often has immediate responsibilities to her family upon returning home and may lack the energy to attend meetings in the evening. And efforts to resolve family needs on a regular basis take parental time—time that might otherwise have been available for helping with homework or engaging in discussions about school and the importance of education. Schools that are sensitive to families' practical realities and support them by scheduling events at multiple times, so that parents may attend, making arrangements for child care, or providing free or inexpensive meals for hurried families are more successful in implementing parent involvement programs with all families (Norman & Smith, 1997; Smith et al., 1997; Williams & Chavkin, 1989).

For example, school psychologists in Minneapolis, Minnesota, held workshops for parents of students with emotional and behavioral disorders. To maximize parental attendance, several anticipated barriers were addressed (e.g., transportation to the workshops was provided, food was served, and day care for young children was included). On one occasion, when arriving at a home to drive a family to the school, the parents informed the project staff that a ride to the grocery store had become available, so they would not be attending the workshop. Although the staff were disappointed that the parents would miss the workshop that day, they did not allow their personal feelings to become known to the parents—this could have been perceived as judgmental. Rather, they expressed happiness that the parents secured a ride to the grocery store and visited the home the following day to provide them with information from the workshop. This kept the parents interested, involved, and current in terms of their child's education. Because the school staff appreciated and respected the divergent realities, priorities, and perspectives of the family, the parents felt supported and tended to miss meetings only when other family priorities took precedence.

Family economic hardship may also affect the monetary resources available for children's school activities. For example, a field trip that costs $5 for children to attend may be an impossibility for some families who must struggle to pay household bills, or who live on a stringent budget. Educators must be careful not to interpret lack of financial contributions as signs of uncaring. More realistically, these families must often make the difficult decision to prioritize family needs (e.g., meals, household bills) over their child's participation in extracurricular (or sometimes costly curricular) activities. To the extent that these realities cause families to feel misunderstood or out of place in schools, they can present important and powerful barriers and represent another example of how we fail rather than support families.

As yet another example, in a group meeting for parents that focused on dropout prevention, a parent posed a poignant question. Parents and teachers attended the meeting to jointly develop a course of action to address common concerns. The school had a high percentage of students living in disadvantaged conditions (e.g., 93% on free and reduced lunch). Although the educators knew this, one teacher commented on the difficulty of teaching children who came to school unbathed. Imagine the teacher's surprise when a parent raised her hand and asked, "Have you ever had to choose between buying a loaf of bread and a bar of soap?" This example also illustrates how easy it is to project stereotypes and fail to engage in perspective taking. When educators stress the importance of parents giving more of themselves and their resources to their children, the needs of families and children must be conceptualized broadly. It is not safe to assume that all children "need" the same things to develop fully.

Taking this perspective, school personnel must recognize that children live in families that exist in neighborhoods, communities, and other systems. As Jane Conoley aptly put it, "To understand children is to understand families" (1987, p. 193). Thinking of children separate from the family system perpetuates a disjointed, narrow conception of what may be most beneficial to the child. To be concerned with children from this perspective means being concerned with *family* needs, resources, successes, and challenges—adopting a family-centered attitude (McWilliam et al., 1999).

Diverse Linguistic and Cultural Practices

Language can often present a challenge to school staff when interacting with families. Not only can differences in language and dialect cause concrete difficulties in communicating, they can also cause family members to feel uncomfortable and out of place in a setting where they are not easily understood. When problems communicating pervade home and school relationships, the frequency and quality of interactions may be affected in a negative way. Differences in language may make standard communication channels between school and home ineffective.

Taking the perspective of parents in situations with communication barriers requires professionals to reconsider common efforts to communicate. For example, single attempts to share information or "reach out" to parents may be replaced with ongoing efforts, using diverse methods. Homework sent home should be understandable to parents if they are expected to offer different types of assistance, such as monitoring or helping (Scott-Jones, 1995b). Common language, directions for completion, and expectations for performance are essential features of homework that contribute to its clarity and allow for more active parental participation.

Different Values

Just as linguistic problems can cause barriers, differences in values held by schools and families may be common. Cultural mismatches occur when values held sacred in one culture are misunderstood or invalidated in another. Various norms and principles common to schools are the need for structured, organized approaches to problem solving that require specificity and directness. In the Euro-American tradition, this may be seen as important and logical. However, this orientation may be counterproductive when interacting with participants from diverse backgrounds, who hold different orientations toward values such as social relationships, achievement, activity, and time (Brown, 1997). Tolerance for certain behaviors or levels of performance may differ within and across groups, and result in very diverse conceptions of performance. Likewise, the temporal nature of much of educational problem solving and educational goal setting (e.g., "John will complete 85% of his work by the end of the school day") may be inconsistent with the cultural values of groups that perceive dimensions of time differently than the Eurocentric tradition (Brown, 1997; Lynch & Hanson, 1998). On a concrete level, the use of positive reinforcement programs—a widespread practice in American schools, and a common element of behavioral interventions—may be seen as inappropriate to some family members, who do not believe in providing concrete reinforcers to manage their child's behavior.

At times, parents and teachers may disagree about the methods that are most effective in addressing concerns about a child's learning or behavior. For example, some parents may accurately believe that teachers and school staff do not understand their preferences, and an educational professional may believe that parents are not cooperating ("resisting") when he or she suggests strategies with which parents disagree. What is missing in situations such as these is open and effective dialogue to understand the other's behaviors or perspectives. The ambiguity of the situation for both parties clearly creates the potential for misunderstandings.

Taking different perspectives, it is important for parents and school personnel to entertain the premise that multiple, effective child management strategies exist (Delpit, 1995). Customs and values that are important in some cultures must be respected among school personnel. Likewise, parents must be open to different customs and cultures of which they are now a part. For example, individuals from some racial–ethnic groups believe in the importance of community over independence. For these parents, extended family involvement and group membership are important. Involvement efforts may include in the definition of family not only parents and siblings but also extended members (e.g., grandparents, aunts, uncles). Likewise, respect for the uniqueness of a culture and community is important to groups whose cultural background emphasizes the tenets of connectedness and collectivity (Nobles, 1985). Families who maintain a connection to their cultural origins through rituals and other practices can provide opportunities for those from other cultures to learn about and from the rich traditions being demonstrated.

School Policies and Procedures as Sources of Barriers

Too often, educators espouse the belief that family structures, values, or practices are the culprit for a lack of meaningful parental involvement. Less frequently do school personnel recognize various school policies and procedures that actually limit opportunities for involvement. In other words, too often the responsibility (or blame) for lack of participation is placed on the family, without giving due consideration to school factors. Davies (1993) found that educators across three countries identified parents as "hard to reach" and named parental characteristics as the source of the problem. School practices were rarely raised as a contributor to poor parent–school relations. However, Dauber and Epstein (1993) found that teachers' practices were a better indicator than family characteristics at predicting which parents were involved in their child's education.

In a well-conceptualized and well-conducted path analytic study, Grolnick and Slowiaczek (1994) found that parents display their involvement in their child's school life in multiple ways, and that the manner in which parents are involved in their children's school experiences may vary according to background characteristics. They found that background variables, such as educational level of the parents, may distinguish among some, but not all, measures of parent involvement. Thus, according to these researchers, "The stereotype of the low involved, less educated parent may not hold true for all types of involvement. . . . Attitudes teachers hold about parents can have important ramifications for how they treat them, and, in particular for whether or not they try to involve them . . . [however,] involving parents is not a strategy restricted to highly educated families" (pp. 248–249).

Examination of school practices and their effect on a family's level of and opportunity for involvement is essential. For example, institutional policies and procedures often fail to consider differences in family structures, demands, and resources. Frequently, all families are approached in an identical fashion, representing an institutional approach and not a family–centered approach. Furthermore, schools often focus on a child's and family's weaknesses and deficits, rather than on assets that can be important in the resolution of concerns. A unidirectional interactional style with parents results in educators explaining deficits and making recommendations to families, without asking them to help understand the child's behavior and codesign a solution. This "expert" approach fails to recognize that it is actually the *family* that knows the child best (Malatchi, 1997).

One salient, although possibly unidentified, barrier to involvement of families is the "menu-driven approach" (Turnbull & Turnbull, 1997) to family involvement, which assumes that all families need or prefer the same general types of plans. Family-involvement efforts are more meaningful when they are tailored to meet the unique and specific needs of a situation, and when family members play a role in their development rather than being perceived as simply recipients of services (Thorp, 1997). When activities are perceived as important and purposeful to families, they will be more likely to identify them as priorities. Alternatively, if services are delegated to families (Seeley, 1989), there can be a mismatch between the school's need for information giving and the family's need for participation in services.

Another common school procedure utilizes problem resolution strategies that do not adequately involve family members. Oftentimes, positive relationships with families are not established before problems arise. Or problems are allowed to escalate before school staff call parents in to "help." Educators typically identify which individuals will attend the meetings, without asking parents whom they would like to have present, and the number of school personnel often far outweighs the number of family members present. If parents were asked who should be present to help in the resolution of concerns, the group composition might differ and the issue of unequal numbers might be resolved. It should be noted that a significant modification in special education law occurred in IDEA 97 (U.S. Congress, 1999), when schools (i.e., special education departments) were required to recognize the definition of "parent" to include extended family members or identified guardians. By extension, inviting parents or guardians to identify the individuals they deem important to attend the meeting represents best practice.

In the face of problems, systematic problem-solving strategies are not always used to resolve conflicts or design coordinated intervention plans. When handled insensitively, interactions that involve planning or decision making may increase parents' feelings of intimidation (Fine, 1990). Likewise, school personnel may be quick to offer interpretations, without considering input or perspectives from parents. They might refrain from sharing information openly, jump to conclusions, and move quickly to provide solutions, without adequately exploring the concerns.

When employing perspective taking, it may be useful for school personnel to explore the impact of school policies on families. Common procedures in schools are sometimes implemented because of their historical relevance ("It's always been done that way"), not because they have a logical rationale. Many schools are beginning to develop action teams or leadership councils that actively include parents in policy development. This establishes a common ground, allowing an open discussion of issues or concerns between parents and educators. It also provides a formal mechanism in which parents may have a voice and present perspectives that might make a meaningful difference in fostering effective relationships.

In summary, when handled constructively, "barriers" can create colearning opportunities (Harry, 1992). They allow educators to learn about families (e.g., their social realities, their cultural beliefs and practices), and they allow families to learn about schools (e.g., their social realities, beliefs and policies, and important procedures). With increased understanding, school and community professionals will be in an ideal position to support families' efforts to engage meaningfully in their children's education and development and at a systems level.

HOW ATTITUDES ARE CONVEYED THROUGH ASSUMPTIONS AND PRACTICES

Assumptions that educators make regarding families (and vice versa) often contribute to attitudes that are conveyed through words and actions. A prerequisite to healthy and effective relationships is a set of assumptions about families that allows openness, fosters respect, and invites meaningful participation. Mostert (1998) delineated 10 assumptions, presented in Table 3.6, that can enhance or damage educators' relationships with parents and families.

Attitudes espoused by educators (e.g., teachers, school psychologists, principals) often translate into the manner in which relationships with families are developed. Several models for interacting with families are prominent in the literature, each conveying a consistent pattern of attitudes, assumptions, and goals that structure parent–educator relationships. When these patterns occur over time, they begin to take on a history of their own (Power & Bartholomew, 1987). Norms that are prevalent in school systems and home–school mesosystems can become organized in such a way that they govern the nature of home–school relationships, shape the multitude of interactions between families and educators, and become a systematic model for interaction. The protective, school-to-home transmission, curriculum enrichment, and partnership models (Swap, 1993) serve as a heuristic framework for understanding different models, each serving a different purpose with inherent advantages and disadvantages.

The *protective model* has as its goals the protection of the

TABLE 3.6. Assumptions Made about or between Educators and Families

1. It is important that you work under the assumption that parents generally wish to cooperate with you and your colleagues in the best interests of their child. Beginning with such an assumption invites parents and families to collaborate, communicates that you are willing to consider their point of view, and conveys the expectations that they are valued collaborators in solving their child's problem.

2. Begin your work with the family with the assumption that the parents and other family members know a great deal about the student that you might not know. Parents and caregivers usually possess a great deal of important information that can expedite treatment interventions.

3. It is crucial to understand the distinction between what you know about each student and what the parents know about their child. These perspectives are likely to be different but overlapping sets of information.

4. Students only spend minimal amounts of time under direct supervision of any professional and a much greater proportion of their time in other situations where family members are in much closer contact. Professionals rely heavily on the support of families to carry through with interventions outside school and when direct professional supervision is impossible.

5. The nature of each educational intervention is often modified or changed according to the unique needs and configurations of each individual family.

6. You have a professional obligation to include families wherever possible in the entire decision-making process that leads to effective intervention with their child. Family members, especially parents, have a legal and ethical right to be fully aware of the potential implications of any intervention and their responsibilities before, during, and after any intervention.

7. Guard against stereotyping parents for any reasons whatsoever. Remember, there is much you don't know about families' lives, and to be helpful you need to view each family as a separate entity with its own unique set of strengths, weaknesses, and life history.

8. While it is essential that you accord families and parents appropriate respect, it is equally important not to be overwhelmed or intimidated by parents who might be aggressive, overly passive, or in some way socially inappropriate.

9. In all of your interactions with parents, be forthright about your limitations as a professional. Parents must sometimes be reminded that there are practical, legal, and ethical parameters within which you must operate. This can help to communicate your role in assisting them and their child.

10. Be aware that in any collaborative venture with parents and families, there is a continuum of involvement that overlays any action you, the parents, or your colleagues may take. The continuum of parent involvement can stretch from absolute noninvolvement on the one hand to excessive overinvolvement on the other. Wherever parents fall on the continuum of involvement, it is important to remember that there are many reasons, often unknown to school personnel, for any level of involvement or disengagement.

Note. From Mostert (1998). Copyright 1998 by Allyn & Bacon. Reprinted by permission.

school from parental interference, based on the assumptions that parents delegate to schools the responsibility of, and hold schools responsible for, educating their children and that educators accept this responsibility. The primary, prevalent attitude in this model holds that schools should work independent of families to educate children—parental involvement in decision making or collaborative endeavors are inappropriate or unnecessary. Thus, the potential for home–school collaboration is restricted in this model, and opportunities for sharing resources and responsibilities are extinguished.

The *school-to-home transmission model* attempts to enlist parents to support the school's mission as its primary goal. This model assumes that children's achievement is fostered by continuity of expectations and values across home and school. Attitudes conveyed suggest that school personnel should identify appropriate values and practices that contribute to success, and parents should reinforce the school's values and expectations. Although this model endorses the importance of continuous interactions between home and school, it continues to be unidirectional in its influence.

The *curriculum enrichment model* recognizes the expertise that families possess and is based on the assumption that interactions between families and school personnel can enhance curricular and educational objectives. One main attitude of this model asserts that parents and educators each hold unique expertise related to curriculum and instruction, and an essential element of its success appears to be the degree to which educators can draw on parents' knowledge and experiences to inform instruction rather than simply to transfer school practices into home contexts. Potential problems arise when teachers who see the curriculum as the centerpiece of their professional expertise (an attitude related to differences in roles) perhaps are not willing to invite parents to help in curricular decisions or to think broadly about how school and home resources can be bridged in efforts to enhance curricular objectives.

The *partnership model* for working with families endorses as its goal the desire for families and schools "to work together to accomplish a common mission . . . for all children in school to achieve success" (Swap, 1993, pp. 48–49). Success at accomplishing this mission requires an attitude that collaboration among parents, educators, and community members is essential. Two-way communication, parental strengths, and mutual problem solving with parents are important aspects of this model. Furthermore, given the challenge associated with its broad and comprehensive mission, school environments must undergo a "re-visioning" that explores new policies, practices, relationships, and attitudes.

Development and implementation of a partnership model for home–school relationships requires the presence of four essential elements. First, it is essential that *two-way communication* processes be established. According to the PTA's *National Standards for Parent/Family Involvement Programs* (1998), regular and meaningful communication is the foundation upon which other standards develop. Educators may share with family members information about school programs, curriculum, and student progress. Parents can convey to school personnel information about their child's background, strengths, and characteristics. To the greatest extent possible, both parties share their thoughts and ideas about expectations, goals, and responsibilities.

Second, the partnership model recognizes that *learning is enhanced at home and at school*. Development occurs across settings, and various opportunities and practices pertinent to each setting are seen as integral to supporting the child in relevant ways. For example, parents can provide structure, guidance, discipline, and assistance to prepare their children to take advantage of learning opportunities (Scott-Jones, 1995b). Likewise, teachers develop curricula, activities, and relationships with children that create optimal conditions for learning. Across home and school settings, unique, respective, complementary roles and practices inherent in a partnership model maximize learning and development.

Third, *mutual support* across home and school is an important element of partnerships. Parents can support educators in many ways, including activities such as fund-raising, volunteering, reading to their child, monitoring homework, or talking with their child about the school day. Teachers can support family members by keeping parents apprised of activities, functions, student responsibilities, and school progress. Such supportive gestures from parents and teachers can be instrumental in the establishment of trust.

Mutual support also suggests the ability of parents and school personnel to identify common ground on which they share priorities and concerns, and together design a plan to begin addressing these. This is related to the fourth element of partnership models, in which parents and educators make *joint decisions* at various levels. For example, decisions about an individual child's educational program may be shared, or schoolwide decisions concerning scheduling or other systemic issues may be the focus of partnership activities.

These elements of partnerships reinforce the notion of "co-roles" (Moles, 1993) adopted by parents and school personnel introduced in Chapter 2. In this context, cooperation entails striving to attain a common goal (i.e., student development and engagement with learning) while coordinating one's own feelings and perspectives with a consciousness of another's feelings and perspectives. Clearly, mutual and bidirectional perspective taking is essential when engaging as partners.

Positive, constructive, effective relations between homes and schools are possible in all forms of models, including those that convey protective to partnership attitudes. Furthermore, attitudes influence the activity selected to involve families in schools. For example, a school operating from a school-to-home transmission model may establish a newsletter that provides information about ways parents can help prepare their child for learning or volunteer in their child's classroom. Similarly, columns in the newsletter might be devoted to parents' ideas, responses, and agendas to promote the attitude of joint roles regarding decisions and priorities at the school. This illustrates how one activity could be altered to promote different attitudes.

School psychologists and other mental health service providers have much to offer in the development of positive relationships and partnerships in schools. They are in a unique position to work within and across systems to establish relationships at several levels. As systems consultants, they can assess situational needs, explore conditions across systems that affect the establishment of relationships, coordinate teams of individuals to establish goals and objectives, assist in the development of meaningful actions, and evaluate progress toward desired outcomes. These points are explored more fully in Chapter 5.

A key point in this discussion centers around the need for individual schools to adopt approaches and actions that are relevant and important within their unique context, and responsive to the individual relationships within and across their systems. In other words, effective practices for one school are not necessarily efficacious for another. Within a particular school setting, what is appropriate and beneficial for one school and family is not necessarily helpful for another. Developing an understanding of alternative models is useful for understanding parent–educator relationships at a school. Swap states, "Realizing that there are different approaches to parent involvement can stimulate debate among the faculty about the most appropriate goals and assumptions for a parent involvement program and help avoid the random, scattershot programming for parents that is so characteristic of many schools" (1993, p. 28). Although we agree with her statement, we would note the absence of input from families. From our point of view, the degree to which a productive family–school relationship underlies each model is contingent upon whether there is adequate "fit" between the model and the particular family–school context. Similarly, Epstein (1995) speaks about the need for the family–school–community action team to tailor its menu of practices to the needs of families, educators, and students.

To be true partners, school and family interactions must embrace collaboration as a central mode of operating. We contend that the common denominator across all models and actions of effective home–school partnerships is the establishment of a "collaborative ethic" as an attitudinal framework for home–school relationships.

"Home–school collaboration" is defined as *a student-centered, dynamic framework that endorses collegial, interdependent, and coequal styles of interaction between families and educators, who work together jointly to achieve common goals* (adapted from Welch & Sheridan, 1995). It is considered an evolving process that enables parents and educators to have access to, and develop, new creative alternatives. The "collaborative ethic" (Phillips & McCullough, 1990) is a guiding belief, philosophy, or set of values about the importance and essential nature of family participation in educational efforts. It is a framework for the overall operation of a school and not a concrete activity or event. The emphasis is on relationships between family members and educational personnel rather than distinct roles that each may play. As such, the responsibility for educating and socializing children is within the shared domains of home and school in relationship with each other. Both families and schools are essential for the growth and success of children.

Effective collaboration is dependent on the belief that the home–school relationship is a priority. A willingness to make the relationship a priority (as reflected in such actions as creating two-way communication, increasing learning opportunities for children, providing mutual support, and engaging in joint decision making) is a prerequisite for collaboration to occur. For successful negotiation across systems, participants must act in ways that preserve the relationship (Christenson & Hirsch, 1998). These various characteristics of collaboration are summarized in Table 3.7. Benefits of a collaborative approach to home–school relations are listed in Table 3.8.

TABLE 3.7. Characteristics of Collaborative Home–School Relationships

Maintenance of a positive home–school relationship is a priority:
- ◆ Personal needs and goals are put aside to allow the needs and goals of the group to take precedence.
- ◆ All parties believe that the expenditure of time and energy necessary to maintain the relationship is worthy.

Relationships are balanced:
- ◆ Each member has generally equal opportunity in decision making, but decisions are based on more than what is most "acceptable."
- ◆ The status of parents and teachers is complementary, recognizing the benefits of unique contributions of parents and educators that are not necessarily identical or "equal."

Relationships are cooperative and interdependent:
- ◆ Families and schools share in the ownership for identifying, addressing, and solving problems.
- ◆ Goals are determined in a mutually beneficial way.
- ◆ There is joint responsibility for the child's success, and for the establishment and maintenance of a trusting relationship.

The relationship occurs in a context with the student at center:
- ◆ Main attention is afforded to the benefits and outcomes for students.
- ◆ Approaches are developed, based on the specific needs and contexts within which relationships are formed.
- ◆ Family-based services and programs are useful only to the extent to which they are responsive to needs within a particular context (i.e., they are contextualized).

Actions between homes and schools are flexible, responsive, and proactive:
- ◆ The manner in which home–school relationships are defined and actions developed vary depending on the unique context and situation.
- ◆ Family members and educators will be involved in very different ways depending on the nature of the contact, the needs presented, the goals for the student and family, the resources available, and a host of other relevant factors.

Differences in viewpoints and perspectives are seen as a strength, not a hindrance:
- ◆ The respective vantage points of family members and educators enhance the understanding of a child and his of her situation.
- ◆ The unique knowledge, resources, talents, and expertise that parents and educators bring to a situation enhance the potential outcomes for students.

There is a commitment to cultural diversity:
- ◆ Services are delivered in a way that is respectful of the cultural values and traditions that families and educators bring with them.
- ◆ Services that are sensitive to important cultures and traditions of families and schools are most likely to be effective.

There is an emphasis on outcomes and goal attainment:
- ◆ Goals are clearly specified, and progress toward goals is closely monitored through databased decision-making processes.
- ◆ Goals and objectives are outcome-based and include problem resolution or management, prevention, and development of skills and competencies.

TABLE 3.8. Benefits of Collaborative Home–School Relationships

---

- Enhanced communication and coordination among family members and educational personnel.
- Continuity in programs and approaches across home and school contexts.
- Shared ownership and commitment to educational goals.
- Increased understanding and conceptualization of the complexities of a child and his or her situation.
- Pooling of resources across home and school increases the range and quality of solutions; diversity in expertise and resources; and integrity of educational programs.

In collaborative relationships, there is shared ownership for identifying and working toward solutions and goals. Likewise, there is recognition of and respect for individual and cultural differences in developing and adapting to changes that come out of mutual and shared decision making. Collaboration involves both *equality*—the willingness to listen to, respect, and learn from one another, and *parity*—the blending of knowledge, skills, and ideas to enhance both the relationship and outcomes for children. Thus, parents and teachers "share joint responsibilities and rights, are seen as equals, and can jointly contribute to the process" (Vosler-Hunter, 1989, p. 15). There is a commitment to *interdependence*; that is, parents and educators in collaborative relationships depend on one another equally and reciprocally (Welch & Sheridan, 1995). One person cannot achieve to the best of his or her ability and contribute fully without the other; that is, teachers cannot bear the sole responsibility for educating children to their greatest capacity without the active involvement of families, and vice versa.

In collaborative patterns of interaction, there are clear and flexible boundaries. Individuals (parents, teachers, school psychologists) defer to the others in their respective domain, work together in a reciprocal and complementary fashion, and complement each other's efforts (Power & Bartholomew, 1987). Three important characteristics of collaboration identified by Power and Bartholomew include (1) understanding inherent constraints of systems; (2) lack of rigid roles and responsibilities, but clearly defined boundaries; and (3) the opportunity to voice concerns without being perceived as a "problem" by the other parties.

Collaboration portends a constructive attitude when working together across systems. It includes mutual respect for skills and knowledge, honest and clear communication, open and two-way

sharing of information, mutually agreed-upon goals, and shared
planning and decision making. In practice, collaboration is
demonstrated and modeled by parents and educators by the following:

- Listening to one another's perspective.
- Viewing differences as strengths.
- Focusing on mutual interests.
- Sharing information to co-construct understanding and in-
  terventions.
- Respecting each other's skills and knowledge by asking for
  ideas and opinions.
- Planning together and making decisions that address par-
  ents', teachers', and students' needs.
- Sharing in decision making about a child's educational pro-
  gram.
- Sharing resources to work toward goal attainment.
- Providing a common message about schoolwork and behav-
  ior.
- Demonstrating a willingness to address conflict.
- Refraining from finding fault.
- Committing to sharing successes.

SUMMARY

Working together in collaborative relationships with families is
crucial to a child's learning and academic success. When put into
practice, the constructive attitudes identified in this chapter allow
us to ask: How can we work together to address a concern or
shared goal? We believe that attitudes are among the most salient
and powerful precursors to healthy partnerships with families.
Constructive attitudes allow for the development of effective listening, nonblaming messages, and trust. Positive attitudes allow
parents and educators together to identify concerns, analyze situations, develop and implement plans, and evaluate goal attainment. Problem solving, information gathering, and resource sharing are all heightened. The attitudes parents and educators hold
about each other set the stage for an atmosphere conducive to the
formation of effective relationships. School personnel who attempt
to put programs into place in the absence of constructive attitudes
and a healthy atmosphere will likely experience limited success.
The importance of atmosphere is explored more fully in Chapter 4.

Specific actions that are possible and desirable at the systemic and individual-child levels are explored fully in Chapter 5.

QUESTIONS TO CONSIDER

1. Read the following case study twice. The first time, consider the perspective of Mr. Moore, Servio's 10th-grade math teacher. The second time, take the perspective of Ms. Gonzalez, his single mother.

   Servio is a 10th-grade high school student who is failing math. According to his teacher, Mr. Moore, Servio daydreams and fails to complete any math worksheet problems during independent seatwork. When his teacher tells him to get to work, he argues that he is working. Although he sometimes writes down random answers, he does know how to complete the problems and does fine on weekly quizzes. Servio is required to bring uncompleted or incorrect work home. He often doesn't turn in his worksheet the next morning, and gets a "0" in the gradebook.

   Ms. Gonzalez, Servio's single mother, doesn't understand why he is failing. According to her, Servio has always been good with numbers and has never received failing grades in any subject area. Besides, he knows how to do the math problems, so why should he fail? She works nights and leaves the house at 6:30 P.M. to be on time for her 7:00 P.M. shift. This leaves just enough time to get her two children fed and the chores done. She reminds Servio to do his homework before leaving, but she presumes that he probably spends his time watching TV and arguing with his younger brother. Servio leaves to catch the bus at 7:15 A.M., before his mother gets home from work.

   After reading the scenario twice, answer the following questions:

   ◆ What is most important to the Servio's teacher (Mr. Moore) in this case? What is most important to Servio's mother (Ms. Gonzalez)?
   ◆ What are some issues on which Mr. Moore and Ms. Gonzalez may disagree? What are some things that they likely agree on?
   ◆ Given some differences and agreements between Mr. Moore and Ms. Gonzalez. What might they do to work together to maximize Servio's academic success?

2. McWilliam, Tocci, and Harbin (1998) discuss family-centered service providers as persons who demonstrate a "friend-like" attitude toward parents and listen to the problems and personal concerns that parents experience apart from those related to their child. This approach

demonstrates sincere care for parents as individuals and as partners. In school-based services, what are the appropriate boundaries between a school's need for information and a family's problems? Where is the line between establishing and maintaining positive rapport within a healthy relationship, and blurring the boundaries between home and school?

3. What is the role of the school psychologist or other mental health worker when a school system and a family system have conflicting expectations, beliefs, and practices regarding a child's education? If the school's views and practices would benefit the child, to what extent should these ideas be imposed on the family? What effect can this have on the home–school relationship?

4. How can school and community personnel assist in overcoming negative connotations that parents associate with schools? For example, the manner in which a school handles a child's difficulties may contribute to problems in the home–school relationship. How can parental attitudes that may have built up over a long history of negative interactions with school personnel be addressed?

5. If school personnel speak about "dysfunctional" families, is it possible for them to create constructive relationships with the families to whom they refer?

♦♦♦

Atmosphere: The Climate in Schools for Families and Educators

♦

As indicated in Chapters 1 and 2, the empirical bases and conceptual frameworks for home–school partnerships are clearly established. In Chapter 3, the importance of constructive and positive attitudes between parents and educators was also stressed. However, research, theory, and attitudes provide only a foundation; they do not ensure that positive home–school relations will occur as a result. In addition, the *atmosphere* (or climate) in and around schools must be conducive to establishing healthy relationships for families and educators. In other words, an atmosphere that is open, trusting, and inviting provides an important, supportive infrastructure within which attitudes can be shared and actions implemented. Two particularly notable characteristics about a school's atmosphere that serve as essential prerequisites are the frequency and quality of interactions among its participants (i.e., communication) and feelings of trust and respect existing within the school community (Haynes et al., 1996). These will be explored more fully in this chapter.

When reading this chapter, consider the extent to which the following conditions are apparent within your school community:

- ♦ Recognition of the value, and active solicitation, of family input regarding important decisions about their child.
- ♦ Use of family and school input to promote positive outcomes for students.
- ♦ A welcoming, respectful, inclusive, positive, supportive climate and atmosphere for *all* children and families.
- ♦ A variety of communication strategies to reach all parents

in a manner that is sensitive or responsive to family background (e.g., language, skills, knowledge level), easy to understand, and "jargon-free."
+ A variety of communication strategies to share information
  and/or monitor children's performance.
+ Parental and school trust in each other (including motives,
  objectives, and communications).
+ Mechanisms for listening to and responding to concerns
  across home and school.
+ Meaningful ways and flexible options for parents and students to be involved.
+ Opportunities for parents and school personnel to learn
  from one another (e.g., cross-cultural communication opportunities).

SCHOOL CLIMATE

School climate has been defined in many ways. According to Tagiuri (1968, p. 27), climate is "a relatively enduring quality of the
internal environment of an organization that (a) is experienced by
its members, (b) influences their behavior, and (c) can be described
in terms of the values of a particular set of characteristics (or attributes) of the organization." It includes both tangible and intangible qualities of the school and its personnel. Bell (1985) described it as "a school's personality, ranging from schools that are
"open" and respect individuality to those that are "closed" and emphasize "toeing the line" (p. 27).
    In a healthful climate for family participation (Comer et al.,
1996), collaboration is the norm (Swap, 1993) and a no-fault orientation is adopted. Collaboration was explored fully in Chapter 3. A
"no-fault" orientation to identifying and addressing concerns allows for the establishment of a safe environment in which
thoughts and feelings are shared directly with those who have a
concern. Also, decisions by consensus allow for "brainstorming, in-
depth discussion, cross-fertilization of ideas, and a plan for trying
different solutions in some sequence" (Comer et al., 1996, p. 9).
The behavior of individuals (students, educators, parents) is understood to be adaptive rather than sick or well; that is, the context in which individuals function influences their behavior. Thus,
it is understood that some children behave in ways that are appropriate on the playground, at home, or at other places outside of
school, but inappropriate to the culture of school. In this case, the

collaborative relationship between parents and school personnel is integral for providing supportive resources to foster children's adaptation to the demands of the school environment.

There appears to be a reciprocal relationship between a school's climate and parental involvement; that is, schools with a positive, open climate enjoy greater levels of parental participation, and schools with a high degree of parental participation tend to be characterized as having a positive climate. Research reviews summarizing the characteristics of effective schools have consistently included parent involvement as an important element (Bickel, 1999; Edmonds, 1979). Furthermore, the more comprehensive the school programs (e.g., those that are schoolwide, varied, and long term), the greater the level of parental involvement (Henderson & Berla, 1994). Schools that welcome parents in their physical (i.e., displaying indicators of openness around the school building) and psychological environment (i.e., friendly and warm staff interactions) begin to address inhibition and distrust that might impede involvement (Finders & Lewis, 1994; Leitch & Tangri, 1988; Norman & Smith, 1997).

Parent involvement enhances a school's climate in many ways. Likewise, school climate can facilitate or inhibit parent involvement. Bell (1985) described a study investigating the manner in which the organizational climate of a school (the degree to which internal environmental or teacher needs are met) influenced teachers' perceptions of parent involvement. According to this study, schools that are described as respectful of an individual's integrity and promote "a sense of fair play and openness" (p. 27) enjoy high levels of parent involvement. Those described as closed, with little opportunity for personal expression and a high degree of pressure to conform, experience low degrees of parent involvement. Similarly, Dauber and Epstein (1993) reported that parental involvement programs are strongest when there is schoolwide agreement about the importance of a positive school ecology. As summarized by Bell (1985), "Schools that are eager to secure active parent participation need to develop organizational climates that are conducive to openness, lack rigidity and show respect for . . . individuality" (p. 27); that is, a positive, open climate appears to be a prerequisite to meaningful and effective parent involvement activities and actions.

A school's climate is especially important for families from groups that have typically felt disenfranchised by institutions in the United States (Lareau, 1987). Some parents do not feel that they really have equal power to make decisions about their child

(Harry, 1992). A personal history or experience of repeated or on-going inequity and discrimination may encourage some parents (e.g., those from low socioeconomic conditions or ethnic minority groups) to refrain from participating in visible ways and question-ing or addressing school staff directly. In fact, some researchers have suggested that repeated interactions between families and schools take on their own stylistic patterns, and the climate thus developed becomes routinized over time (Doherty & Peskay, 1992; Power & Bartholomew, 1985). This is a problem when it discour-ages a constructive problem-solving dialogue, even when that is desired by both parents and teachers (Swap, 1993).

It is clear from research that most families want to be, and can be, involved in the educational experiences of their children (Davies, 1988; Epstein, 1990). It is also clear that educators must engage in certain practices to ensure that all families feel welcome in schools. A family's ethnicity, language, religious beliefs, and SES are among the variables that help a family as a unit form an identity. These unique qualities can be highlighted as strengths rather than partialed out as barriers to forming relationships. Furthermore, differences among parents' backgrounds, experi-ences, and beliefs contribute to their uniqueness. For example, a parent's own educational experiences (be they positive or negative) and previous interactions with teachers, administrators, or other school representatives add to their current perspective on partner-ing options. Beliefs of parents and educators, and the degree to which they match with each other, are also important to parents' potential role in educational programs. This was discussed more fully in Chapter 3.

Schools are among the first places where children learn about race and culture. Representations and discussions of race and cul-ture (or their omission) in literature, history, and social studies communicate a very potent message. Likewise, treating all chil-dren and parents in an identical manner despite differences in home backgrounds, differences in approaches to parenting, and potential differences in language and dialect communicates the message that "different is not welcome here" (Delpit, 1995; Heath, 1983). Oftentimes, a failure to recognize individual differences openly leads to psychological barriers among "mainstream" schools, children, and families. Assumptions are often made be-cause families and school personnel do not know each other as in-dividuals, and the lack of a relationship precludes their abilities to learn about or from each other. These psychological barriers tend to be more difficult to address than physical barriers due to their intangible nature.

SCHOOLS AS WELCOMING COMMUNITIES

To begin to ameliorate psychological barriers, schools must become welcoming, "family-friendly" communities. Table 4.1 outlines some possible practices that educators may consider in efforts to enhance the atmosphere in their school.

Although parent involvement does not necessarily mean involvement at the school building, there are several benefits to this form of involvement. According to Wright and Smith, "Involvement at school may be a proxy for other types of partnering activities including the nurturance of social networks, facilitating cohesion, and establishing common goals and objectives. . . . Well-placed efforts to promote involvement at school may pay off in ways that have not often been recognized in the literature" (1998, p. 156). When parents come to school, they develop a better understanding of the educational context (i.e., the needs, constraints, and issues faced by educators in their school building). For similar reasons, some researchers have recommended that educators make visits to the homes of their students. Possible misperceptions and assumptions of educators regarding a child's family life can be modified through social visits to their homes.

When family members feel welcome and wanted at school, and know what their role is or can be, they will generally be better able to participate meaningfully and actively in the education of their child. Likewise, parents may be more willing to share their ideas if they feel that school personnel will listen to them and value such input. Feeling welcome can also increase parents' participation in available activities that enhance their own and their child's experiences. Similarly, they may be more open to support the ideas of educators and provide assistance in programs related to educational missions. Importantly, when family members recognize the school as a place (and schooling as a process) in which they belong, and the meaningful role they play, their beliefs that their efforts make a difference for their child may increase. Unless parents feel connected, they may question their ability to recognize the essential nature of their role.

Parents also must see how their efforts are related directly to improvement, or the possibility of improvement, in their children's

TABLE 4.1. Possible Practices that Promote Schools
as Welcoming Communities

At-school efforts
* Develop a clear, welcoming parent involvement policy, publish it for all to see, and post it in an obvious location in the school.
* Display welcome signs in various languages.
* Ensure that the school office is friendly and open.
* Organize the school so each child is known well by at least one person.
* Provide a full-time parent contact person responsible for connecting parents and educators.
* Post a school map to help visitors find their way around the school building.
* Arrange flowers, murals, children's pictures, and photographs in the main hallways.
* Consider a "family center" or parent room to allow family members to meet formally or informally with each other.
* Have available toys for young children to encourage parents with toddlers and infants to attend school functions.
* Post a welcome sign at the front door or in the school's entrance corridor.
* Arrange for translators for family members who do not speak English.

Family outreach efforts
* Make at least one complimentary phone call to a parent each day.
* Sponsor a regular (e.g., monthly) parents' luncheon for informal social interactions.
* Consider special events for fathers, such as "Significant Male Day" or "Doughnuts for Dad."
* Ask a parent or grandparent to greet other parents at drop-off and pick-up times.
* Develop a friendly and inviting greeting for secretaries.
* Smile.
* Invite parents to visit the school or classrooms.
* Use an "open school" policy or designate times when staff are available to talk.
* Host social events and multicultural celebrations.
* Make a home visit to welcome parents, invite them to visit the school, or provide a book as a friendly gesture.
* Ask parents about their needs and provide necessary services.
* Sponsor parent-to-parent communications and events.

---

education. Comer (1995) identified this as the "linchpin" for parents to sustain their involvement. Parents' sense of efficacy, or the belief that they can help their child succeed in school, enables them to assume that their involvement activities may influence their child's learning and performance in a positive way (Hoover-Dempsey & Sandler, 1997). When parents judge their success in involvement practices to be unlikely, their feelings of low efficacy might keep them from becoming involved (Lareau, 1989). Indeed, some parents place their trust completely in the schools and do not expect to play an influential role in their child's learning (Harry, 1992). Parents' perceptions of their abilities to assist in their child's development, and in the attainment of important educational goals, may be partly a function of the degree to which they identify the school as open and approachable.

In order to establish an atmosphere that is comfortable, friendly, and approachable for *all* families, it is crucial that educators consider the predominant *culture of the school* (i.e., the belief systems and values that are promulgated in the school context). This culture can be imposed on family members inadvertently and communicate a lack of openness to different cultural beliefs. The attitudes this encompasses (e.g., a willingness to learn about and from each other, a recognition of individual differences not only between but also within groups) are explored in Chapter 3. If a school perpetuates beliefs about how children learn or about appropriate discipline strategies, there may be little openness to differing viewpoints that are characteristic of some cultural groups. Consider a situation in which a school emphasizes independent work and personal accountability for student performance. A family who embraces a culture that values community efforts and maximizes group accomplishments over personal achievement may encounter roadblocks when trying to work within this school's culture.

The *ecology of the school,* or its physical and structural aspects, is also important (Weiss & Edwards, 1992). Schools and classrooms that are welcoming and inviting to all families reflect the various and diverse communities from which children and parents come. Pictures, bulletin boards, books, visual images, and curricular materials should reflect the children and families of the school. Importantly, respect for families and their cultures is shown by recognizing their role in contemporary society, and not simply in traditional dress or historical renditions (Thorp, 1997).

CORRELATES OF PARENT INVOLVEMENT

What types of influences at the school and family levels are related to parental involvement in their child's education? From an ecological perspective, variables can be identified within and across systems (i.e., school, home). Teacher practices, school and neighborhood climate, and parental background and attitudes have all

been identified as contributors to involving parents as collaborators in their child's education, both at home and at school. Clearly,
this suggests the importance of examining school practices when
families are uninvolved.

School Correlates

Smith et al. (1997) reported an ecological study that investigated a
model incorporating parent, teacher, school, and community factors that were hypothesized to influence school- and home-based
parental involvement. They found that factors at each of these levels contributed to involvement at home and at school. Family
background variables (including education, income, and two-
parent family structure) were related to living in a neighborhood
whose climate supported the school's endeavors. Parent education
was related to being comfortable and familiar with involvement
practices, especially when these practices occurred at school
rather than at home. This highlights the point that efforts to help
parents feel comfortable at school are integral to their presence
and that climate-enhancing and trust-building activities are important for all.

Another finding of the Smith et al. study was that highly educated parents were more likely to express dissatisfaction with the
efforts of teachers in engaging them in school. It is possible that
roles that these parents believe to be truly meaningful have not
been identified or articulated. Family variables were related to
higher levels of involvement, especially in the school setting.
Home factors were not the only, or even the strongest, influences.
Positive school climate was related to proactive teacher strategies
and to the removal of practical barriers to involvement. Schools
with positive climates were found to have parents less likely to report that scheduling, lack of child care, and transportation inhibit-
ed their ability to be involved at school. This implies that school
policies can impact home involvement through flexible scheduling
and the provision of tangible resources.

At the school level, it appears that strong leadership and administrative support are essential to increasing meaningful family
involvement. Schools that are responsive to the needs of parents,
such as providing transportation and child care, report higher levels of parental involvement. Likewise, those that are friendly and
welcoming to parents report greater success (Berninger & Rodriguez, 1989; Haynes, Comer, & Hamilton-Lee, 1989). Schools
can function as an important liaison by linking families with other

resources and providing parents with support that allows them to focus more of their energy to their child's education (Smith et al., 1997).

In that school policies communicate expectations, guidelines, and incentives, they can serve as macrosystemic influences on the type and frequency of parental involvement. For example, school policies may provide guidelines for the frequency and type of home–school communication, process of parent–teacher conferences, and expectations regarding other ways of involving parents. Consider, for example, a policy stating that parents are not allowed to observe at their child's school or help in their child's classroom, a situation experienced by one of the authors (SMS). Although we hope such policies are rare, some schools or teachers may not allow observation during specific times or under specific conditions, or without implementing onerous procedures. Whereas such policies may be necessary in some circumstances, when reasonable rationales are not provided to families, the strong message to parents is a desire to keep them out of the school environment. Limited opportunities to visit the school building circumvent parents' abilities to learn firsthand about realities of their child's school day.

Teachers' practices have been the focus of some research investigating family involvement levels. Epstein and Dauber (1991) concluded that "when teachers make parent involvement part of their regular teaching practice, parents increase their interactions with their children at home" (p. 289). Teacher self-efficacy and training in parental involvement practices are also important (Hoover-Dempsey, Bassler, & Brissie, 1992; Swick & McKnight, 1989). Grolnick, Benjet, Kurowski, and Apostoleris (1997) found teacher practices to have their strongest impact when other factors (e.g., context, parent attitudes) were optimal. Parents who saw themselves as teachers and felt efficacious, as well as those in more optimal contexts, became more involved when teachers actively involved them. Parents who did not see themselves in this manner or those in difficult contexts were less affected by teachers' attitudes and behaviors. It is important to note, however, that school and teacher practices are a more important predictor of parent involvement than family status variables (Dauber & Epstein, 1993).

It is possible that parents who are extremely stressed, or whose values and attitudes clash with those of educators, may not receive a teacher's message, even if the teacher is attempting to involve them. If this is the case, educators must go further than making singular efforts to involve families. Relationships are not formed when one party attempts to connect with others without monitoring its effects. If outreach efforts are initially unsuccessful (or only marginally successful), more and perhaps different efforts must follow. For example, one of us (SLC) has witnessed directly that persistence in connecting with families for enhancing children's performance at school can pay off. In working with disengaged youth at risk for dropping out, a monitor on the Check and Connect project made five home visits and even had the door slammed in her face once. On the sixth visit, the parent commented that the monitor really cared about her child. They talked. Although time consuming (and these efforts would not be necessary to build connections with all families), these persistent outreach efforts are needed to create connections with students and families who feel very alienated from the schooling process. In this case, the monitor was successful because her focus was on the adolescent and was nonjudgmental. Her efforts were to build a relationship with the family, not to fix the family, and her persistent efforts were to help engage the student at school and with learning.

Home Correlates

Research has been conducted to identify parental factors related to involvement in education. Home and family factors include those that are structural or status-oriented (e.g., SES, parental education, number of adults in the home; Grolnick et al., 1997; Lareau, 1987; Stevenson & Baker, 1987), and psychological or process oriented (including parents' role conceptions, sense of self-efficacy related to involvement, attitudes toward education, expectations for their child's performance, and what they say and do to communicate these to the child; Hoover-Dempsey & Sandler, 1997).

Before discussing status variables and correlates to involvement, a cautionary note is in order. Research on the relationship between family factors and parental involvement should not be interpreted to mean that all families sharing certain demographic features are identical on any dimension. In other words, there is likely as much variability within demographic groups as between them. Results of research must be interpreted with the understanding that all individuals within a group are not equal or identical in terms of what they do or believe vis-à-vis children's learning (Phinney, 1996). Furthermore, process variables have been demonstrated to be relatively more powerful than status variables in predicting school outcome (Delgado-Gaitan, 1991; Scott-Jones, 1987). Based on a review of 66 studies, Henderson and Berla (1994) concluded, as have others, that the most accurate predictors of student success in school are the ability of the family, with the help and support of school personnel, to create a positive home learning environment, communicate high and realistic expectations for children's school performance and future careers, and to become involved in children's schooling. All emphasize the value of education. And lower-income parents are involved when the school has an inclusive policy that values and supports families (Lewis & Henderson, 1997).

Family status variables, such as SES and parents' education level, have been investigated in relation to involvement activities. Research has yielded mixed results regarding the relationship between SES and parental involvement. Most research has concluded that SES is not related to overall family involvement; however, the type of involvement varies as a function of SES. In general, it is believed that school-based family involvement is significantly related to SES, whereas home-based involvement is not (Grolnick et al., 1997; Hoover-Dempsey et al., 1992). For example, some parents may be unable to come to programs or conferences at school but still able to engage in interventions related to reading with their child at home. According to the Metropolitan Life Survey (Binns et al., 1997), students report that their parents are available to help regardless of ethnicity, although parents in urban areas tend to be less involved at the school building. This may be related to logistical or psychological variables, such as work or transportation conflicts, comfort level coming to school, perceptions that parents have about their roles and efficacy in relation to their child's education, and school practices to invite and involve parents (Hoover-Dempsey & Sandler, 1997).

The nature, but not the level, of involvement seems to vary according to SES. Supportive and "learner" roles (e.g., teaching their child new skills) appear less typical for parents in low-SES conditions compared to those in higher socioeconomic classes; however, overall levels of involvement did not differ among these groups (Grolnick et al., 1997; Hickman, Greenwood, & Miller, 1995). Parents in low SES conditions tend to be less involved in cognitive–intellectual activities (e.g., providing help studying for exams) than parents in higher SES groups. However, personal–affective types of involvement (e.g., discussing a child's school day) may occur equally at all parental occupational and educational levels (Grolnick et al., 1997).

Parental marital status and family stress are additional demographic variables that have received some attention in the literature. Mothers from single-parent households were less involved than those in dual-parent families across all variables (school, cognitive, affective). However, when SES was held constant, only school involvement was lower compared to other family configurations. In other words, no difference may be expected for forms of involvement other than school-based ones. A difficult family context (economic hardship, family stress) and lack of social support have been found to be negatively related to parental involvement in the school building for boys (Grolnick et al., 1997). There was also a direct negative relationship between the difficult context and personal involvement, suggesting that a difficult context may make it hard for parents to attend to the subtleties of what is going on at school.

What does this mean for professionals working in schools? It is critical that we look beyond how a family "appears" and consider the family's assets as a starting point. That it is not appropriate to interpret familial structural variables as predictive of the meaning families place on their child's education is an important lesson. Likewise, it is inexcusable to judge parents because they experience life priorities ahead of their child's schooling. When one considers a family's hierarchy of needs, there are several (e.g., nutrition, safety, housing) that may take precedence over activities such as parent–teacher conferences or homework monitoring. In some circumstances, educators want certain types of involvement and judge parents' commitment or skills on the basis of how well they fulfill predetermined (i.e., school-defined) roles. This not only extinguishes opportunities for collaboration but also precludes the possibility for communicating openly and empowering parents to participate in shared decision making.

Psychological variables are also related to involvement. Parents' construction (or beliefs) of their role vis-à-vis their child's education seems to contribute to what they do (Hoover-Dempsey & Sandler, 1997). It appears that the manner in which parents perceive their own role in their child's education establishes a range of activities that they consider appropriate, necessary, and important. These role conceptions are based partly on the groups to which parents belong and the expectations that these groups hold for parental involvement, including the school community and school groups. This points to the importance of considering schools' expectations for parents to be involved and setting the stage for, and conveying, a positive atmosphere for their meaningful participation.

Several researchers have found that parents who have well-developed, positive perceptions of their own efficacy tend to demonstrate higher levels of involvement (Grolnick et al., 1997; Hoover-Dempsey et al., 1992; Swick, 1988); that is, parents who believe that they are important and efficacious with regard to their children's learning tend to demonstrate higher levels of involvement (Ames, 1993). School personnel who can communicate directly the importance of parental activity help parents recognize the usefulness of several practices, and believe in their ability to help in various ways (i.e., not only in "traditional" ways) may be more successful in achieving relevant levels of participation.

Perceptions that parents hold of teachers and schools are related to parental involvement. The extent to which parents believe that they are wanted and invited to participate may be relevant here. Specifically, parents in classrooms where teachers engage in many high-parent-involvement activities, and work to involve all parents, are generally more positive about school and more aware of teachers' interest in their involvement (Epstein, 1986). In a related way, parents with positive perceptions of schools and education are more likely to be involved (Lindle, 1989).

Invitations for parents to be involved may come also from students. According to Hoover-Dempsey and Sandler (1997), children may influence their parents' participation due to their "emotional influence over parental decisions because of the personal relationship involved" (pp. 27–28). Specific invitations from children for parents to attend meetings, review homework, or participate in special events provide an "overt affirmation of the importance of parental approval and participation" (p. 28) that can facilitate action on the part of parents. There may even exist a reciprocal relationship: If parents are involved proactively (e.g., participate as a result of child or school invitations) rather than reactively (e.g., hear from school only when problems persist), children may value and accept family involvement more when support is needed.

THE IMPORTANCE OF TRUST

A prerequisite to any effort to involve parents in educational partnerships is an atmosphere characterized by *trust* (Haynes et al., 1996). "Trust" is defined as "confidence that another person will act in a way to benefit or sustain the relationship, or the implicit or explicit goals of the relationship, to achieve positive outcomes for students" (Adams & Christenson, 1998, p. 6).

Many parents may avoid interfacing with school personnel due to their own feelings of insecurity or uncertainty about what the school promotes or believes. They may view the school as an institution that is static, unwelcoming, distant, and inflexible. This is particularly likely for parents whose previous experiences with schools and other agencies have been adversarial, intimidating, or otherwise uncomfortable.

Trust is an intangible characteristic that develops *over time*. An educator's ability to develop and foster an ongoing personal relationship with family members does much toward establishing trust and sending a message that the school is a friendly, warm, and open environment (Finders & Lewis, 1994). The need to allow trusting relationships to develop often runs counter to practices in schools wherein quick and efficient solutions are sought. In many such circumstances, efficiency is valued over the interaction process that requires time to build trusting relationships and get to know one other. It is important that interactions with family members be considered in the context of whether they facilitate the development of trust or inhibit the formation of relationships.

It is a reality that some families may be willing to trust school personnel more readily than others, particularly if they are accustomed to the traditional practices and norms established in schools. Family members who vary in terms of culture, values, or language may appear more hesitant to interact freely and openly. "One-shot" events or interactions with family members do not allow educators to learn about family beliefs, practices, values, or preferences. They do not allow families to explore their feelings about the school microsystem or their comfort level with adults in that environment with whom they may differ in a number of important dimensions. And, they do not provide ongoing opportunities to allow parents and educators to learn from and about each other, increase acceptance, and build trust.

Ideally, the outcome of a positive, open, supportive school atmosphere facilitates the establishment of trust among parents and educators. Likewise, bidirectional trust between families and schools is vital to a healthy atmosphere and an essential feature of productive home–school relationships. However, the atmosphere itself does not secure trusting relationships—these are established over time, with repeated contact and exposure. Too often parental involvement is initiated in the midst of a crisis situation, such as when a child's behavior at school becomes uncontrollable. Trust between parents and teachers in such situations is vital to yield a positive outcome for the student (e.g., the development and implementation of an intervention plan to address the behavioral concerns). If trust between home and school has not already been established, intentions, communications, and, subsequently, outcomes for the student will be less than optimal.

In a study that explored trust between homes and schools, Adams and Christenson (1998) surveyed 123 parents of regular and special education students, and 152 teachers in three urban middle schools in the Midwest. Slightly over half of the parent sample reported their ethnicity as European American; the majority of nonwhite participants self-identified as African American. Approximately half of the sample was eligible for free or reduced lunch (an indicator of income), and 45% of the sample represented parents of students receiving some special educational services. Consistent with their hypotheses, the authors found that parent trust of teachers was significantly higher than teacher trust of parents. Furthermore, parents who were characterized as "high trust" reported significantly more behavioral indicators of parental involvement than parents characterized as either moderate and low in trust. Parents of students who received more intensive special education services reported higher levels of trust than parents of students receiving less intensive special education services. Contrary to predictions, however, there were no significant differences between groups who differed on the variables of income, ethnicity, or type of educational service (special education vs. regular education). Similar results were found in a subsequent study in which 1,234 parents and 209 teachers from one school district were surveyed. Adams and Christenson (2000) found that parent trust was higher than teacher trust at elementary, middle, and high school grade levels; however, significant differences between parents and teachers emerged only at elementary and high school levels. They also found that parent trust for teachers was significantly higher at the elementary than the middle or high school levels, and teacher trust for parents was significantly higher for elementary than for high school teachers. Regardless of school level, parents and teachers identified communication and parental dedication to education as important means to increase mutual trust between families and schools, and satisfaction with the parent–teacher relationship was predictor of trust for both parents and teachers. Finally, parent trust for teachers was significantly correlated with credits earned per year, grade point average (GPA), and attendance for students in grades 9–12.

How does trust between homes and schools develop? Certainly, it does not occur accidentally or coincidentally; rather, it develops as educators engage in certain actions that promote trust. According to Margolis and Brannigan (1990), such behaviors include (1) accepting parents as they are; (2) sharing information and resources; (3) focusing on parents' aspirations, concerns, and needs; (4) keeping your word; (5) discussing objectives openly; and (6) preparing for meetings. Also important are focusing on the interactive process with parents, using structured problem-solving approaches, and listening empathically. Findings from Adams and Christenson (1998) suggested that we also (1) create opportunities to build personal relationships with families; (2) create opportunities to be co-learners with parents; (3) engage in shared governance with parents; (4) develop effective conflict management strategies; and (5) maintain a focus on student outcomes.

If heeded, suggestions by these researchers can guide school personnel to send strong messages and engage in outreach activities geared toward building trusting relations with families. First, however, some personal reflection is necessary. Questions that professionals can ask themselves include the following: (1) Do I accept parents as they are, or try to change them to "fit" a predetermined parent role? (2) Do I try to build relationships or stay aloof in my interactions with family members? (3) When I tell parents that I will do something, do I follow through? and (4) Am I always trying to teach, inform, or instruct parents about something, or do I also try to learn from and about them?

Second, preparing for meetings or interactions with families is helpful to build positive and constructive relations. This sends the message that parents are important and valued. Interactions that convey appreciation for parents' ideas and input (e.g., using open ended questions, validating their statements) are also important. Clear, open communication is necessary to connect with families in meaningful ways.

THE IMPORTANCE OF COMMUNICATION

Open, two-way communication is another important element of an atmosphere that is conducive for effective home–school partnerships. In an interesting study, Ames (1993) investigated the manner in which communication between school and home influenced parents' beliefs and practices across a number of dimensions (including their awareness of communication efforts, children's motivation to learn, self-reported involvement, and comfort with the school). Teacher self-reports on the use of communication strategies and feelings of self-efficacy were also assessed. Compared to parents who did not experience high levels of communication, parents of children whose teachers communicated at a high level found these teachers to be more effective. Teachers who self-reported being "high users of school-to-home communications" (p. 46) reported higher levels of their own teaching efficacy. Furthermore, compared to parents who received little communication from teachers, parents whose children were in "high users" classrooms reported greater belief in their own ability to influence their children, viewed their children as more motivated, and reported higher levels of involvement in their children's learning. Interestingly and importantly, children's self-ratings of academic competence and interest were strongly related to each other and to their parents' involvement. Ames hypothesized that teachers' communications may have influenced "how parents talked to their children about school, whether they monitored their schoolwork, and how much time they spent helping their children learn; in other words, their involvement in their children's learning" (p. 47). Ames' study highlighted the importance of sending an optimistic and hopeful message to parents about their child's education and what they can do to help.

We believe that effective communication is the foundation of all family involvement in education. According to Weiss and Edwards (1992), an underlying goal of communication is "to provide consistent messages to families that the school will work with them in a collaborative way to promote the educational success of the student" (p. 235). Accordingly, all communications should strive to convey at least three consistent themes to families: the desire to develop a working partnership with families; the crucial nature of family input for children's educational progress; and the importance of working together to identify a mutually advantageous solution in light of problems (Weiss & Edwards, 1992).

Frequent, effective communication is necessary for a number of reasons. It is required for parents and teachers to share information about children's progress, needs, and interests. Through two-way communication, parents and teachers can be informed of what is expected relative to student behavior, achievement, and discipline. This can in turn set the stage for establishing shared goals and mutual decision making, avoiding misunderstandings, and helping parents understand how to reinforce learning and school instruction in the home.

Sources of Miscommunication

The probability for miscommunication between parents and school personnel is high for a number of reasons (Christenson & Hirsch, 1998), including infrequent contact, emotionally charged situations, and ineffective communication.

In many situations, parents and educators maintain infrequent contact. When they do interact, "teacher talk" dominates the interaction (Christenson & Hirsch, 1998, p. 315); that is, information shared by educators tends to take precedence over that provided by parents, both in terms of amount and importance.

Another important source of miscommunication occurs in emotionally charged situations. Parents are always emotionally attached to their child. Emotionally charged situations between home and school occur when there are fundamental differences in opinion about learning, goals, objectives, or interventions for a student. When these differences in perspective form the context for interactions, there is typically no explicit step to co-construct the bigger picture about a child's performance. When neither party is willing or able to adjust its perspective or stance, problems, rather than solutions, are focal.

Many times, contacts between school personnel and parents are not made at the first sign of a concern, but rather after problems have exacerbated. In such exchanges, the first message conveyed to families concerns issues that have an established pattern and need remediation. In such encounters, parents or school personnel may inadvertently attribute responsibility for the child's academic or behavior problems to the other system or an individual within that system. A blaming orientation interferes with communication because the focus is set on another person rather than a situation wherein solutions are stressed. Oftentimes, communications that occur during such situations are ineffective and nonconstructive.

A final reason that miscommunication occurs between parents and educators is that the parties are not always careful in using effective communication strategies. Inadequate communication between families and educators can lead to misunderstandings that may turn into conflict. As in all relationships, parents and educators do not always exhibit empathetic understanding and listening when concerns are raised. Rather than using constructive and empathetic strategies, defensiveness often prevails. For example, when first hearing that their child has been "causing problems on the playground for several weeks," a parent may raise systemic issues such as lack of adult supervision or the presence of unruly groups of children. At the same time, school personnel may argue vehemently about the adequacy of supervision and appropriateness of others' behaviors, tcuting the parent's responses as resistant or irresponsible. Effective communication skills, including objectivity, clarity, and constructive problem solving, are conducive to depersonalizing anger-provoking behaviors and decreasing conflict.

What Do Parents Prefer?

Parents have specific desires about the nature and tone of communication with school personnel. They appear to value sincere interaction with school personnel over structured programming. Less professional, more personal interactions with schools that promote communication and parents' abilities are preferred over interactions that suggest that the parents have deficits to overcome. According to one parent, quoted in Finders and Lewis (1994, p. 53): "Whenever I go to school, they want to tell me what to do at home. They want to tell me how to raise my kid. They never ask me what I think. They never ask me anything."

Understanding parents' perspectives and preferences is important in fostering positive relationships. In a study of 69 parents and 102 early intervention professionals, Dunst, Johanson, Rounds, Trivette, and Hamby (1992) uncovered various elements of effective parent–professional partnerships. Both parents and professionals ranked the same five elements most highly, and each of these is directly related to a context for healthy interpersonal communication. Parents ratings were, in rank order, trust, open communication, mutual respect, active listening, and honesty. Early interventionists' rank orderings were slightly different; they ranked mutual respect highest, followed by trust, open communication, honesty, and active listening. In a similar vein, Lindle (1989) identified three areas of school communication viewed by parents as pivotal: congeniality, patronage, and partnership. Sincerity and a desire to be helpful were more important to them than a desire for a standard or set approach to interactions between parents and teachers.

GUIDELINES FOR EFFECTIVE COMMUNICATION

Personnel in schools and communities have many opportunities to communicate with families. It is essential that verbal and written communications be delivered with care. Guidelines and practices that may be followed to achieve effective communication are summarized in Table 4.2 (Christenson & Hirsch, 1998).

Although the guidelines in Table 4.2 are not "surefire" ways to guarantee clarity of communication, they can minimize the chances that miscommunication will occur. And as suggested guidelines, it is important to reiterate that implementation in the absence of a constructive attitude and welcoming climate will not result in the intended goal. Parental involvement practices, or activities, are nested within the larger framework of the attitudes and atmosphere present in the school; that is, the attitudes and atmosphere drive the activities, and not vice versa.

• *Strive for a positive orientation rather than a deficit-based or crisis orientation*. Ames (1993) suggested that parents may be more willing to participate in their child's education when they have a sense of optimism or hopefulness. Findings of a study on communication practices and perceptions of parents, teachers, and students led her to hypothesize that when parents believe that they can make a difference, and that their child has an ability and desire to learn, they may be more involved.

Results of Ames's study are important given the typical types of communication that parents receive from educators. Generally speaking, school-to-home communications are often sent to report some form of inappropriate behavior or inadequacies that the child is demonstrating. From a parent's perspective, then, calls from school connote something "bad." To the greatest extent possible, communications that focus on the positive (and realistic) aspects of the child and family, and the constructive and helpful ways that families and educators can work together, may be more facilitative. Alternatively, receiving "good news" phone calls about a child's positive behaviors or accomplishments a student earned would be highly welcomed by most parents.

A common contributor to communication breakdown is messages to the home that convey an authoritarian tone (Weiss & Edwards, 1992). Many individuals do not respond positively when they feel that they are being ordered to take some form of action. For example, a letter may be sent home indicating that a meeting will be held on a certain day at a certain time to discuss options for

TABLE 4.2. Guidelines and Practices for Effective Communication

Guideline	Possible practices
◆ Strive for a positive orientation rather than a deficit-based or crisis orientation.	◆ Good-news phone calls ◆ Invite and incorporate parent reactions to policies and practices. ◆ Contact parents at the first sign of a concern. ◆ Communicate an "optimistic" message about the child.
◆ Consider tone as well as content of your communications.	◆ Reframe language from problems to goals for student. ◆ Focus on a parent's ability to help.
◆ Develop and publicize regular, reliable, varied two-way communication systems.	◆ Systemwide family–school communication/assignment notebooks ◆ Shared parent–educator responsibility for contacts ◆ Handbooks ◆ Newsletters ◆ "Thursday folders," including relevant home and school information ◆ Telephone tree ◆ Electronic communication technology
◆ Emphasize a "win–win" orientation rather than placing blame.	◆ Discuss and focus on mutual goals and interests. ◆ Use words such as "we," "us," and "our," versus "you," "I," "yours," and "mine."
◆ Keep the focus of communication on the child's performance.	◆ Bidirectional communications regarding classroom activities, progress, suggested activities for parents ◆ Home–school notebooks/notes ◆ Family–school meetings with students present ◆ Shared parent–educator monitoring system (e.g., educational file, contract)
◆ Ensure that parents have needed information to support children's educational progress.	◆ Several orientation nights, with follow-up contact for nonattendees ◆ Parent support groups to disseminate information on school performance ◆ Home visits ◆ Home–school contracts with follow-up ◆ Curriculum nights ◆ Monthly meetings on topics of mutual interest

(continued)

TABLE 4.2 (continued)

Guideline	Possible practices
◆ Create formal and informal opportunities to communicate and build trust between home and school.	◆ Multicultural potlucks ◆ Grade-level bagel breakfasts ◆ Family fun nights ◆ Committees designed to address home–school issues ◆ Workshops where parents and school personnel learn together ◆ Principal's hour
◆ Underscore all communication with a shared responsibility between families and schools.	◆ Communicating the essential nature of family involvement ◆ Sharing information about the curriculum of the home ◆ Discussing co-roles (e.g., co-communicators) and implementing shared practices (e.g., contracts, common language about conditions for children's success) ◆ Back to School night

addressing a child's behavioral problems. Although the parent may be requested to attend, what does the tone of this communication convey? To many parents, it may be interpreted as the school ordering them to show up to a meeting to hear about problems and issues. Oftentimes, their input is not invited in scheduling the meeting. The parent may not know of the issues in advance, and he or she may not know who will be present. Taking the parents' perspective, educators may begin to understand the difficulty for parents inherent in this common practice. Alternatively, respect for families is conveyed by determining a mutually agreed-upon time for the meeting, sharing concerns in advance, emphasizing the desire to work together to discuss and address the concerns, and clarifying the specific goals, objectives, and participants in the meeting.

Oftentimes, educators try several strategies to help a child who is demonstrating some type of difficulty in the school environment. For example, they may try several behavioral interventions to help a distractible child stay focused on academic tasks. They sometimes attempt different strategies to help a young reader increase his or her comprehension skills. Although these are typically worthwhile efforts on the part of educators, they may still be unsuccessful after several trials. Parents may understandably respond with surprise and dismay when, months later, a teacher wants to refer their child to specialists for testing. Contacting a parent early on to share concerns and invite input in a caring and positive manner, rather than waiting until several school interventions have been tried, may help build trust and convey the message that there is much a parent can do to help. Furthermore, a proactive stance by parents may enhance the effect of their academic and motivational support for the child's learning (Bempechat, 1998). This reinforces the importance of an ecological systems approach to working with families.

♦ *Consider tone as well as content.* Up to this point, we have focused on the content of communication with parents, or *what* is said or conveyed. Also important is *how* messages are conveyed (the tone). A communication style that connotes a desire to relate positively and constructively with parents is important to enhance an atmosphere wherein collaborative partnerships can occur. "What" is said and "how" it is delivered can either invite parental participation or close off good communication.

Tone within a conversation with parents is generally conveyed in the manner in which concerns about a child are raised. Concerns can be framed in a manner that expresses investment in and commitment to a child's progress, with an invitation and expectation of parental assistance. Or concerns can be presented in a way that provides an evaluation of the student's problems and shifts responsibility onto the parent. Rather than inviting parental input, the latter overture communicates the fact that the teacher's concern is now the parents' problem and displaces the opportunity to engage in joint, shared problem solving.

Consider the following interaction, wherein an educator "tells" the parent the problem.

> "Joey is really different from the other kids. I think he must have some kind of a learning disability. I can't hold everyone back just because Joey is behind. There is nothing that I can do for him—I'm going to have to refer him to a specialist."

Consider for a moment how the parent felt in this interaction, and what a likely response might be. It is possible that this teacher's statements might have produced feelings of inferiority in the parent. Such potentially degrading statements could be restated in more supportive terms. For example, consider a slightly different approach:

> "Joey is certainly a unique child! Let's talk about his specific strengths and challenges. I'd really like your input on what

we might do to make sure that he understands what is going on in the classroom."

A simple reframing of the child's situation in a positive, constructive tone can foster the development of a more trusting and encouraging interaction that invites the parent's ideas and involvement.

Reframing is the act of providing an alternate point of view about a set of facts to relay a more positive, productive meaning. The practice of reframing encourages participants to take a different perspective by interpreting a problem or concern in a proactive way (Thorp, 1997). It can be used by educators to increase understanding and decrease stereotyping of families. For example, if families do not attend school-sponsored activities such as "Back to School" nights, educators might reframe the facts of the situation by considering all the possible reasons for parents' absence, exploring how the school may have contributed, and assume that the parents were interested but the structure of the meeting was not conducive to their participation at that time.

An important aspect of reframing is the expression of sincere and shared concern for a child. Oftentimes, professionals focus on "problems" or "issues." A simple reframing reorients participants to consider concerns, hopes, and desires held for children. When the focus is on a "problem," the discussion is directed toward its extinction or removal, but when it is on shared concerns and goals for a child, dialogues can be directed toward helping him or her develop competencies.

A related communication tactic was offered by Canter and Canter (1991), who stressed the importance of the manner in which concerns are presented to parents. When educators have a concern to present to parents, it is essential to do so in a way that is not interpreted as an evaluation of the parents. The language used by educators must invite parents' contributions and input for a solution. This can be accomplished by using statements that express concern for the student and state the problem. For example, a statement such as "I'm concerned about how Brian gets along with the other students" is more positive, inviting, and constructive than "Brian's behavior with other students is getting worse and worse." Similarly, "I'm concerned about how little work Tess is doing" invites more parental input than "I'm not at all pleased with Tess's progress."

 ◆ *Use effective conflict management strategies.* When interactions between parents and teachers include constructive attitudes and mutual respect, open communication is the result. However, differences in opinions and viewpoints are inevitable in encounters between parents and school personnel. At times, these differences may lead to conflict. Differences are not necessarily detrimental to the relationship; in fact, we argue that different perspectives are healthy in collaborative relationships. Rather, it is the way conflict is managed that can challenge or strengthen the development of constructive partnerships.

When conflicts occur, strategies that focus on both resolving the specific concern and maintaining the home–school relationship take priority. Negotiations that emphasize efforts toward mutual benefit (a "win–win" orientation), rather than those that place one party against the other (a "win–lose" approach) are essential. A helpful framework is offered by Fisher and Ury (1981), who suggest four important elements of negotiation: separate the person from the issue, focus on mutual interests, generate options prior to making a decision, and base final decisions on objective criteria.

First, it is important to separate the person from the issue. Approaching a conflict from a competitive ("me" vs. "you") rather than cooperative ("we" vs. the problem) perspective breaks down opportunities for open communication and objective, collaborative problem solving. In this regard, a simple technique that professionals can use when discussing concerns with parents is to use terms that connote shared responsibility, such as "we," "us," and "our."

Second, participants are advised to focus on mutual interests. Parent and teacher agreement on what is at the center of their concerns relates to positive educational outcomes for children. Keeping that at the forefront of communications helps retain a constructive focus. Third, it is useful to explore several options prior to making decisions. In this way, decisions can be made with a reasonable amount of information. Finally, ultimate decisions should be based on objective criteria to minimize the potential of emotionally laden and often ineffective strategies. Note that these latter two suggestions of Fisher and Ury (1981) are highly congruent with the problem-solving orientation that we stress throughout this book, and especially in Chapter 5.

The "me" versus "you" conflict paradigm (vs. one that emphasizes "us vs. the problem") sets up a pattern wherein parents and schools are likely to begin placing blame on each other for a child's difficulties. This not only leads to ineffective communications but it also potentially destroys the home–school relationship. A number of techniques may be used to "block" blame in parent–educator interactions (Weiss & Edwards, 1992). These are illustrated in Table 4.3. Importantly, educators must enter their relationship with families proactively and with an orientation toward solutions, rather than blame. This will allow for the consistent and effective use of communication strategies with parents that facilitate the development of plans that are appropriate and effective across systems, rather than the identification of obstacles to such programs.

◆ *Develop and publicize regular, reliable, varied, two-way communication systems.* There is no one surefire communication technique that will work well for all families, schools, or situations. Consistency in communication includes regular procedures on which families and educators can rely (Swap, 1993). For example, a systemwide home–school communication notebook that is sent home the same day each week provides a common mechanism by which important messages can be communicated. A method by which parents can return the notebook with questions, responses, or issues can promote two-way communication and shared responsibility for assuring open communication among teachers and parents. The establishment of telephone trees among classrooms may be helpful to convey urgent messages, with a backup plan (e.g., brief home visits shared among a group of parents) for families who do not have telephones. Other forms of electronic technology, such as electronic mail and a school homepage on the worldwide web, present numerous additional opportunities to explore ways to communicate with families.

The development of a system designed to establish two-way communication is an important first step in promoting openness in information sharing. It is also the school's responsibility to ensure that all parents know about the system and how it operates, and that it is effectively reaching all families. It is not sufficient to produce a communication mechanism without attention to its outcome; it is also essential that the messages are being received appropriately by a school's constituencies. Since parents are in the best position to know what communication mechanisms work best for them, a system developed by both parents and educators for use by both would seem to hold the most promise.

◆ *Keep the focus of communication on the child's performance.* Importantly, the overall purpose for partnering with families—to enhance the educational experiences and successes for all students—must be kept clear in home–school communications. Delving into a family's personal background or experiences, when there is no clear educational need for such information, is inappropriate.

TABLE 4.3. Techniques for Blocking Blame

Direct blocking: Signaling that the purpose of the interaction is not to blame but to solve a problem. Example:

♦ Student: *Johnny always starts the fights—it's not my fault.*
♦ Teacher: *We're not here to find out who's to blame but to figure out how you and Johnny can get your work done instead of fighting.*

Reframing: Providing an alternate point of view about a set of facts which gives the facts a more positive, productive meaning. Example:

♦ Teacher: *These parents drive me nuts—all they're concerned about is whether their child is going to get into the top class. It starts in prekindergarten.*
♦ Teacher: *It sounds as if they're trying to be an advocate for their child's education and get them started off on the right track.*

Probing: Eliciting additional information to clarify the context leading to the blaming. Example:

♦ Student: *The teacher always picks on me.*
♦ Teacher: *I certainly don't intend to pick on you, David. What do you see me doing that makes you think I'm picking on you? Give me some examples.*

Refocusing: A statement that redirects the discussion from a nonproductive or nonessential area to an area relevant to helping the student. Example:

♦ Parent: *José did great last year with Ms. Johnson. We think that Ms. Williams is just not as good a teacher.*
♦ Guidance Counselor: *I can see that you're very concerned that José has a good year this year, too.*

Illustrating: Giving concrete examples of areas of concern. Example:

♦ Parent: *He doesn't act that way at home. You just don't know how to deal with him.*
♦ Teacher: *What I've observed is that Johnny acts that way when he is with his friends. They enjoy talking with each other so much that they don't seem to be able to stop when it's time to get down to work.*

Validating: Recognizing the validity of another's perception or efforts. Example:

♦ Parent: *I know Jane needs me to spend more time with her—maybe I should quit going to school.*
♦ Principal: *I can understand your concern about spending time with Jane, but your going to school is also a positive role model for her. Let's see if there are other ways you could be helpful to her.*

Agreeing: Confirming someone's perception of a situation. Example:

♦ Teacher: *It really drives me nuts when people come in and think they can just take over the classroom.*
♦ Parent: *It would drive me nuts, too, if I thought someone was trying to take over something that I was responsible for.*

Note. Training handout reprinted with permission from Howard M. Weiss, Center for Family–School Collaboration, Ackerman Institute for the Family, New York, NY.

A good place to start may be to ask the question: "What do I need to know, or what information is essential for me to work effectively with this child?" Communications that attempt to obtain information in unrelated areas can then be considered "off limits."

Many procedures for communicating with parents about a child's academic performance are available. For example, classroom assignment notebooks can include a "parent column" to invite parents to note questions or comments about their child's work. Alphabetized lists of activities can be provided to parents, with ideas for how they can support and enhance what is occurring in their child's educational program. Information about events and lessons in the classroom can be conveyed through students' journal writings. Furthermore, family–school meetings with students convey a partnering or collaborative orientation wherein all individuals (family members, teachers, students) share in the establishment of educational goals, objectives, and solutions.

An interesting example of constructive communication focused on students' educational programs is being promoted in many states through comprehensive guidance initiatives. For example, in the state of Utah, student educational and occupational plans (SEOPs) are developed conjointly among teachers, parents, and students, and evaluated regularly. Similar procedures are used in Minnesota, through the development of individualized learning plans (ILPs). By design, SEOPs and ILPs bring parents, teachers, and students together to identify important learning objectives in order to attain mutually determined goals. Examples of learning objectives may include successfully completing an individually tailored spelling curriculum or engaging in 10 minutes of reading to a parent daily. At other grade levels, vocational goals such as learning to use a word processor efficiently or developing skills in graphic design may be appropriate.

♦ *Ensure that parents have needed information to support children's educational progress.* It seems clear that all parents want what is best and desire their children to succeed in school. However, not all parents have the needed informational tools to support their children in these endeavors. It is difficult, if not impossible, for parents to participate actively in their child's educational program if they do not know the goals and activities used to meet their child's needs. Beyond simply knowing the school's agenda for a student's education, parents may be in a better position to assist if they (1) understand the rationale for certain academic goals and activities, and (2) assist in formulating an agenda based on adequate information.

Well-meaning professionals often identify practices or activities that they believe will be helpful (e.g., sending notes home with prescriptions for what parents should be doing with their child). However, such activities are often completed without soliciting parents' opinions or giving them options as to the ways they can be involved. This school-initiated approach (or agenda) precludes two-way communication and fails to ask parents what information they need, or what would be helpful, so that they can help to foster their child's enthusiasm for learning, school performance, and success in school.

Another area in which parents desire information about their child's schooling concerns school policy (Christenson, Hurley, Sheridan, & Fenstermacher, 1997). School policies about discipline, homework, and other important procedures are often considered elusive by family members. Likewise, although they affect family life in a significant way, they are often established and implemented without parental input. Demonstrating respect and openness in relationships with family members would suggest inviting parents to respond to a school's policies and procedures as a normal course of planning and evaluation. This also increases the diversity of ideas, perspectives, and expertise from individuals who share a vested interest in a child's education and development.

One-shot "Back to School" nights or orientations are no longer sufficient vehicles to reach all parents and provide necessary information. The reality is that many families are unavailable when educators schedule such events, or they experience other constraints that preclude taking advantage of this mode of outreach. Several orientation nights may be necessary, with follow-up contacts conducted for nonattendees via alternative mechanisms (e.g., phone calls, home visits, newsletters, or letters in the mail). Parent support groups are also often useful to disseminate information about children's school programs and performance. Some schools are also experimenting with home–school contracts that outline the unique and shared responsibilities of educators, parents, and students. As with any event, it is important that such outreach does not occur as a "one-shot" activity. Follow-up contacts should be scheduled and supported by both educators and families.

♦ *Create formal and informal opportunities to communicate and build trust between home and school.* Formal events that occur in schools and invite parental participation (e.g., parent–teacher conferences) provide a consistent mechanism for interaction. However, they are not sufficient to ensure regular, open communication. Other vehicles for initiating and maintaining positive relationships with family members are necessary, such as informal social gatherings that allow parents and educators to form relationships (Swap, 1993). Although such events may seem a trivial form of parent involvement, their importance in setting the stage for further participation and establishing a climate of trust is clear (Davies, 1991). Informal activities set the context for pleasant social interactions, exchange of information, and future activities and projects among educators and family members. Furthermore, they "signal a mutual interest in establishing adult relationships on behalf of the child and in breaking down the barriers between home and school" (Swap, 1990, p. 110). Ironically, "seemingly unimportant aspects of the occasion, such as the quality of the food, the ethnic appropriateness of the food, even the smells of good cooking, can signal (perhaps more profoundly than what educators say) a welcoming attitude toward parents . . . as equals [that we welcome] as we do guests in our own home" (Swap, 1993, p. 67).

Several examples of informal events can serve the purpose of welcoming families into the school. Bagel breakfasts, family fun nights, and holiday affairs provide social opportunities that allow families to get to know one another and interact with school staff. On a more formal level, committees can be formed to address issues shared across home and school. Similarly, offering workshops, where parents and school personnel learn together, provide a task-oriented opportunity for interaction wherein both parties benefit.

Many successful events take advantage of the diverse and unique cultures that contribute to the school's makeup. Multicultural potlucks are considered enjoyable activities that serve the joint purposes of celebrating the various ethnic groups in the community and providing an important welcoming function. School assemblies that invite parents to share important traditions or practices around cultural holidays are not only interesting and informative for students, staff, and other families in the community, but they also deepen the multicultural heritage of a school.

 • *Underscore all communication with a shared responsibility between families and schools.* Our definition of family–school partnerships stresses the importance of bidirectional and joint commitments among parents and educators to attain important goals for children. Therefore, it is important that communications between schools and families occur in both directions. Furthermore, parents must internalize the responsibility and realize that their involvement is essential to maximize educational outcomes for their children. School- and community-based professionals have the responsibility to communicate this message to parents.

The importance of open communication between the home and school is evident. To be truly open and bidirectional, however, it is also incumbent upon parents to take responsibility for maintaining communication; that is, just as schools and school personnel have a responsibility to reach out to parents, parents have a responsibility communicate and participate with school personnel. With the exception of cases in which parents are unable to comprehend communications sent home (e.g., when they are sent home in a language the parent does not understand, or when phone calls are placed to a family that does not have phone service), whether parents "receive" the messages that teachers and other school personnel send is as much part of the parents' responsibility as it is the school's. That being said, school liaisons (e.g., school psychologists, social workers, counselors) are in a pivotal position to increase the expectation—in fact, "raise the bar"—for meaningful dialogue and participation among school personnel and family members. Concrete examples of what can be done include providing assistance to parents for communicating with teachers; suggesting mechanisms by which teachers can increase constructive interactions with parents; and expressing the importance, need, and expectation that parents will be involved in school decisions.

It is our belief that schools set the tone for shared responsibility through inviting involvement, using strategies that allow bidirectional communication, and structuring interactions in such a way that parental input is necessary. As an example, Weiss and Edwards (1992) describe a novel use of "Back to School" nights. They present a model in which parents and students attend the Back to School orientation together, with teachers, parents, and students all sharing their respective goals for the academic year. The stated goals are written down on a flipchart or blackboard for easy reference, and the teacher attempts to identify some consensus of opinion. The tone is very positive, with participants sharing what they want and believe is necessary for the student to learn and to have his or her best year in school. The teacher tries to identify some consensus of opinion in a very goal-oriented and positive way. The goals may be general, but the strong message of shared responsibility for achieving the goals is conveyed. Together, teachers, students, and parents can achieve many of these goals if children are reminded that their work and progress are important, and if all parties work together. Parents and teachers share information on how to contact each other and explore other mechanisms for ongoing communication.

School and community professionals can also share information with families about the "curriculum of the home," including ways that parents can make the home not only a safe and nurturing environment but also one in which learning and enrichment can occur. Although we emphasize shared responsibility, we are not suggesting that parents and teachers should engage in identical activities to demonstrate a shared commitment to learning. Rather, complementary activities that parents and educators (e.g., teachers, school psychologists) identify together to help attain mutually determined goals are important. For example, some parents may not feel comfortable tutoring their child in reading. They may, however, feel better equipped to read with the child or ask questions about stories read by the child to help foster the child's emerging literacy. Chapter 2 addresses more fully important concepts related to the "curriculum of the home."

LISTENING AS A FORM OF COMMUNICATION

Parents entrust schools to provide formal opportunities for their child's academic development. They want to talk with school personnel who are truly interested in their child and know that their concerns are heard. Effective listening skills on the part of educators are necessary to convey the message that there is a sincere desire to learn about the concerns and issues raised by parents. "Effective listening is dependent on the desire to listen; therefore, it is important for educators to create a context for conversation in which parents and educators feel relaxed, comfortable, and prepared" (Christenson & Hirsch, 1998, p. 319). A welcoming and supportive climate in the school is essential to facilitate listening and meaningful communication. Both passive and active listening skills are essential components of communication.

Passive Listening

Passive listening is a compilation of nonverbal and verbal behaviors that convey interest and involvement in what another person is communicating. It allows listeners to observe the others' behaviors and establish a foundation by which all participants can become actively involved in the communication process. Both passive (nonverbal, physical gestures) and psychological (affective) attending are important aspects of passive listening.

Physical attending refers to behaviors that allow individuals to connect with each other, and to demonstrate that connection. Nonverbal behaviors, including facing the other person, leaning slightly toward him or her, and maintaining appropriate eye contact, are examples of physical signs that send messages of interest and involvement. The importance of nonverbal cues cannot be overstated; it has been estimated that 55% of the meaning of a communication is conveyed through facial expressions and body language, and another 38% through voice tone and pitch (Friend & Cook, 1992).

Psychological attending refers to one's commitment of his or her undivided attention to a speaker and the ability to convey that attention. It also refers to the facilitative use of silence and minimal responses. Silence is important, since it provides the speaker with an opportunity to pause, gather thoughts, reflect on previous comments, and engage in self-examination. Accordingly, "listeners must learn to be comfortable with silence and squelch the urge to comment on every statement made by the speaker" (Christenson & Hirsch, 1998, p. 320).

Effective listening is enhanced by the use of responses that encourage a speaker to continue talking and relay understanding of a message. The use of minimal encouragers (e.g., head nods, "Mm-hmm") provides an indication that the listener is connecting with the speaker, without interrupting the flow of the speaker's verbal comments. Paraphrasing key aspects of the communication (i.e., repeating the essence of what is being said by the speaker) and clarifying points of uncertainty further ensure clear and accurate understanding. An example of an effective paraphrase following a parent's expressed distress about his or her child's lack of progress in reading might be "So you share our concern with Nathan's difficulties." To promote an expectation that the parents coparticipate in helping their child academically, the professional might follow with "Determining meaningful ways that we can work together to help Nathan achieve realistic goals will increase his opportunities to succeed."

Active Listening

Active listening is possible only when a listener engages in passive listening skills; however, it extends passive listening to engage in problem solving and decision making. Beyond conveying a desire to attend to and "hear" the other person, active listening communicates an acceptance of the individual, an understanding of the persons' feelings and perspectives, and an outward expression of acknowledgment.

Reflection of key comments and emotions is an important element of active listening. It extends paraphrasing by going beyond restating key things a parent or teacher says to including a comment that conveys an understanding of the parent's or teacher's affect. Reflection can be used to state an interpretation of a parent's or teacher's feelings and comments, and check the validity of this interpretation. It also has the benefit of letting the parent or teacher know that you truly understand his or her experience and perspective of a problem. For example, a parent may make a statement such as "I'm doing my best, but you school people just don't understand how hard it is for me to make sure Sam gets his homework done when I come home from work tired and still have the housework to do and the baby to care for!" A thoughtful reflection of this might be "You're frustrated because you don't think we understand how much you do in addition to being concerned with Sam's schoolwork. I can sure appreciate how important it is for us to understand that."

The effective use of questions is an important element of active listening, since questions are the primary way that information is elicited and clarified. Christenson and Hirsch (1998) provided guidelines for questions that help the parent feel comfortable and glean relevant and important information. First, they suggest that educators avoid the use of "why" questions. Such questions often have an interrogative and judgmental quality. They may result in defensiveness, which shuts off communication. Second, they suggest using open-ended questions to obtain important information and provide parents with opportunities to respond in a way that is meaningful to them. A question such as "What social goals do you have for your child this Fall?" is much more useful than "Do you want your child to interact with more children?" Third, and relatedly, it is important to limit the use of closed questions. Questions that prompt "yes," "no," or other one- or two-word answers direct the communication in a linear path and limit the amount of information provided.

A fourth guideline for obtaining information is to ask questions that view the child's behavior and the family's responses contextually, and not in a way that implies internal deficits on the part of the child or family. A statement such as "Let's talk about how homework is assigned and completed" is more helpful than "Is the work too hard for your child?" or "Does your child understand what she is supposed to do to complete her homework?"

Finally, some professionals may find it useful to phrase questions in the form of a statement. Oftentimes, this yields the benefit of minimizing a parent's feeling that he or she is being interrogated. Indirect questions that begin with a phrase (such as "I'm interested in knowing what happened . . . " or "It would be really helpful for me to understand . . . ") are often perceived as comfortable and supportive. As an example, consider the support conveyed in "I'd love you to share your observations of Kelly's work habits at home," compared to "Does Kelly have problems completing work at home?"

Although it may seem easier to establish a personal agenda for communication and ask parents very pointed or directive questions, there are many benefits that make active listening worth the effort. Through active listening, information sharing occurs on a meaningful and not just a superficial level. It allows educators and parents to gain broader insights and perspectives about situations. Recognition of different opinions and feelings, and stronger communication have been identified as additional benefits (Lombana, 1983). Margolis and Shapiro (1989) further identified that, through active listening, parental anger can be dissipated, problems can be better understood, and effective solutions can be generated.

SUMMARY

An atmosphere that facilitates collaborative home–school partnerships is characterized by trust, effective communication, and a mutual problem-solving orientation (Christenson, 1995). The physical as well as psychological messages conveyed through the school's atmosphere can serve to enhance or inhibit parental involvement. Likewise, it can contribute to or impede the productivity of family–school relationships. It is the responsibility of both educators and parents to communicate openly and honestly to build a climate that is conducive to meaningful and effective interactions on behalf of children.

In this chapter, we outlined many important elements of a supportive, inviting school climate. The tangible and interpersonal atmosphere is prerequisite to the implementation of effective strategies, or actions, that move parents and educators forward in their collaborative work. However, it is important to note that the atmosphere is a necessary but not sufficient factor in promoting successful experiences for children. In the next chapter, we explore actions that can maximize positive interactions between homes and schools, with a goal of healthy child development.

QUESTIONS TO CONSIDER

1. Consider the following interaction between a parent and a school psychologist. Try to identify elements of effective communication used by the psychologist.

   PARENT: I'm pretty upset with Samantha's teacher. She treats me like I don't care about Sam's work. She hardly ever listens to what I have to say and just doesn't understand me.

   SCHOOL PSYCHOLOGIST: What is it that you feel she doesn't understand?

   PARENT: Well, she's asked me to come in and talk to her about Sam. But I'm not able to come to school to meet with her between 8:30 and 4:00 because of my work schedule. Yet it seems as though that's the only time she's able to meet. And now she thinks I don't care, which is not at all true!

   SCHOOL PSYCHOLOGIST: Mm-hmm (*nods*). You work during the school day and can't come in at times that have been suggested by Sam's teacher.

   PARENT: Yes, and I really am concerned about her progress. I mean, I know that she's not doing well. I know that she's frustrated, and so am I, because I don't know what to do! I'd like to be able to meet with her teacher to find out what I can do to help her more. I really think something needs to be done about this situation.

   SCHOOL PSYCHOLOGIST: Mm-hmm (*nods*). So you're concerned that your daughter isn't progressing in school, and you're frustrated that you're not able to discuss the situation with her teacher. You'd like some type of arrangement whereby you can communicate directly with her teacher and discuss ways that you can help your daughter.

   PARENT: Yes, that's right!

2. In some schools, an "openness" in school climate is extended to community services or programs through full-service school options or neighborhood centers. On the positive side, a sense of community pride and increased parental involvement could be enhanced through things such as volunteer projects, provision of health care, social events, and community meals. However, many schools are becoming more "closed"

and secure due to concerns related to violence and safety in school. How can schools balance the seemingly competing priorities of providing open and inviting centers, and ensuring a safe environment?

3. What are some strategies for establishing open, two-way communication with parents and at the same time remaining aware of boundaries between home and school? Where is the line between friendly and helpful communication (e.g., rapport building/collaboration), and privacy rights of parents and schools?

4. How can organizational change occur in a school to ensure that the ecological collaborative process between family and educators continues?

♦♦♦

Actions: Strategies for Building Shared Responsibility

♦

In this chapter, we describe seven broad actions that professionals can take to work with families as partners across grades K–12: garnering administrative support, acting as a systems advocate, implementing family–school teams, increasing problem solving across home and school, identifying and managing conflict, supporting families, and helping teachers improve communication and relationships with families. Actions are purposefully distinguished from activities, because they focus on the relationship or connection between family and school relative to children's school performance, whereas activities represent a narrow focus on how to involve families in education. Thus, actions are oriented toward building shared responsibility for educational outcomes. To be successful in this goal, school personnel consider the adopted approach toward the role of families, the degree to which constructive attitudes between families and educators exist, and the present atmosphere or climate for participation and interaction between families and educators in their particular school context. Approach, attitudes, and atmosphere are the "backdrop" for the actions described.

Of utmost importance in our conceptualization of actions is the focus on schools examining their practices for partnering with families and their willingness to include parents and to be responsive to family input and desires with respect to children's learning experiences. To build a working partnership that lasts, school personnel realize that "trust-building starts with reaching out to families, a sometimes difficult task when *(some)* families are accustomed to an adversarial relationship with schools or community services" (Carter, 1994, p. 9; italics added). School personnel also recognize that parents want relevant information about their children's schooling, educators need to pay attention to parent requests and unique needs for participation, and families require varying amounts of support to actively participate in their children's education. Opportunities for meaningful dialogue provide the basis for mutual understanding across home and school about the learning experiences and performance for children and youth. Strategies for shared responsibility depend, in part, on finding ways to ensure that parents have access (i.e., parental right to inclusion in decision-making processes), voice (i.e., parents' feeling that they are heard and listened to at all points in the process), and ownership (i.e., parents agree with and contribute to any action plan affecting them) (Osher, 1997). A structured, proactive problem-solving approach with families is offered across several contexts, including those involving school teams, individual consultation, and conflict management. Such approaches provide a template for enhancing opportunities for parents to have access, voice, and ownership through meaningful dialogue and participation.

When reading this chapter, consider the extent to which the following conditions are apparent in your school community:

- Information is provided to families about school policies and practices, parents' and students' rights vis-à-vis education, and ways to foster students' engagement with learning.
- Opportunities or mechanisms are provided for the home and school to plan jointly and collaborate to resolve a shared concern or to improve learning experiences for students.
- A process exists for creating mutually supportive roles for families and educators.
- Supports and resources exist for creating and maintaining partnerships.
- Policies and practices support a coordinated, collaborative approach (i.e., shared responsibility) for home and school.
- Parents and school personnel (i.e., partners) routinely review the availability, accessibility, and flexibility of family–school roles and responsibilities for fostering children's/adolescents' learning and school engagement.

GARNERING ADMINISTRATIVE SUPPORT

Lack of administrator and teacher training for working as partners with families has been described as one of the biggest barriers for implementation of family–school partnerships for children's learning (Epstein, 1989). This statement is still highly relevant today. Although educators have always valued parent involvement and worked with parents, they have not necessarily been educated to work with parents as partners.

Working with Principals

The nature of family–school relationships in a particular school is influenced by the role, belief system, and philosophy of the principal. One characteristic of effective principals is the ability to interact positively with families (Edmonds, 1979). Principals set the expectation for involvement as well as the tone for interaction (e.g., nonblaming, inviting), encourage the development of meaningful roles for families, and provide the opportunity for initial and sustained interaction between families and educators. Effective principals take partnering with families very seriously. They ensure that parents know how and when to contact them; in a sense, they create an open-door policy with parents, and they do so with genuine friendliness. It is not uncommon to see principals have office hours such as "Carol's Corner" or grade-level breakfasts to increase interaction opportunities with parents and to provide for parent input on school practices and educational concerns. They also realize that parent input must be reflected in school policies and practices, and that good communication about how parent and educator input influences school policies and practices is necessary.

   Not all principals are comfortable working with families to alter school procedures; and often, this discomfort is due to lack of information about how to proceed. School-based professionals have been successful acting as systems consultants with respect to family–school collaboration (Weiss & Edwards, 1992). However, to garner administrative support for working with families as partners also means that consultants and educators envision their role as leaders in developing positive connections for children's learning (Epstein, 1992). We recommend discussing content related to the approach, attitudes, and atmosphere as a structure for garnering administrative support for working with families. For example, school- and community-based consultants are in an ideal position to share in the following ways their observations and evidenced-based information about methods to improve students' school experience and progress in regularly scheduled meetings with principals:

- ◆ Share information on the significance of the role played by family, home, and school influences on learning (see the six factors described in Chapter 2), or the importance of in- and out-of-school time for children's school success and, consequently, the essential nature of the home–school connection for educational outcomes.
- ◆ Discuss constructive attitudes for working with families (e.g., nonblaming, problem-solving interactions, strength-based orientation, benefits of multiple perspectives), paying particular attention to ways to foster positive interactions and to address challenges for families, schools, and the partnership.
- ◆ Discuss the effect of the school climate on family–school interaction or family participation. In particular, realistic ways to enhance bidirectional communication and a welcoming, inviting climate will be of interest to principals.

Although information provides a roadmap, the subsequent leadership role in developing a positive family–school connection, beginning with establishing policies and a family–school team, cannot and should not be minimized.

The Importance of Policy

District- or school-level policies may facilitate and/or inhibit the involvement of parents and the community in educational processes, programs, and practices. An issue is that "school level policies and expectations tend to center on what parents can provide for teachers and schools rather than what *teachers* and *schools* can provide for *parents*" (Rutherford, Billig, & Kettering, 1995, p. 15). Furthermore, policies and resource constraints in schools may inadvertently inhibit parent involvement, and working with administrators on how to develop policies that stress the bidirectional influences and responsibilities of homes and schools is possible. For example, in the absence of a homework policy, conflicting expectations for students between parents and teachers and a reduction in parent support for home learning may occur. However, clear homework policies based on empirically supported practices can go far in clarifying communications and expectations around potentially family-stressful interactions.

District-level policies often link to state and federal policies and are a component of the district's school improvement plan. Changes in family–involvement practices during transition between grades are relevant here. For example, how school personnel communicate with parents between elementary and secondary grades, and the attitudes toward students' autonomy, are seldom explicitly stated or understood by families. Without a clearly articulated policy about family involvement in education across grade levels, no one should be surprised that parent involvement is consistently reported as lower in the secondary grades (Zellman & Waterman, 1998).

Developing both district- and school-level policies for working with families as partners to achieve greater school success for students is critical. The guidelines provided by the National Coalition for Parent Involvement in Education (1990) may prove helpful when discussing the role of policy with principals. According to this coalition, policies should contain the following concepts:

- Opportunities for all parents to become informed about how the parent involvement program will be designed and carried out.
- Participation of parents who lack literacy skills or do not speak English.
- Regular information for parents about their child's participation and progress in specific educational programs whose objectives are understood.
- Opportunities for parents to assist in the instructional process at school and at home.
- Professional development for teachers and staff to enhance their effectiveness with parents.
- Linkages with social service agencies and community groups to address key family and community issues.
- Involvement of parents of children at all ages and grade levels.
- Recognition of diverse family structures, circumstances, and responsibilities, including differences that might impede parent participation. The person(s) responsible for a child may not be the child's biological parent(s), and policies and programs should include participation by all persons interested in the child's educational success.

Clearly, these concepts, which are described in detail in Chapters 3 and 4, are important to achieve the call by Rafaelle and Knoff (1999) that "we must examine the organizational climate that exists within our schools and the (often covert) messages about involvement that we send to parents from the beginning of their child's school experience" (p. 449). We concur that effective home–school collaboration must adhere to four specific beliefs and behaviors: It is proactive rather than reactive; involves sensitivity to and respect for the cultural backgrounds of students and families; recognizes and values the important contributions parents make in the educational process regardless of their formal educational experiences; and engenders parental empowerment through positive, meaningful, two-way communication between home and school, based upon mutual respect and trust. However, integral to the success of partnering with families is that these beliefs and behaviors be reflected in school- and district-level policies and become part of the school norms. Committed leadership, training for teachers and parents, clarity about home and school roles and responsibilities, and options for families are examples of necessary support to be considered by principals.

ACTING AS A SYSTEMS ADVOCATE

Researchers of family–school partnerships have consistently found that (1) parents care about their children's education and are able to provide substantial support if given specific opportunities and knowledge; (2) parents wait to be directed by school personnel about what they should do; and (3) schools must take the lead in eliminating or at least reducing traditional barriers to active parent participation. School leaders can promote change by serving as systems advocates in their efforts to promote and enhance children's learning through strengthened home–school relationships.

We recognize that the recommendations suggested in this book (e.g., establishing new strategies for home–school communication, educating school personnel about useful partnering practices) may require policy development or change. Likewise, we recognize that systems-level changes such as these are for individual practitioners challenging to implement. Innovative change is not easy and requires several important considerations. In a discussion of processes leading to educational change, Grimes and Tilly (1996) describe several principles and practices that can increase the possibility that change initiatives will become lasting components of an educational system. First, consistent with our message about the importance of local school and family needs and preferences, they suggest that change agents and system advocates consider the context and commit to "the long haul" (p. 470). Accordingly, meaningful change efforts will come about when individuals within a school community create and own them. This implies that similar strategies may look very different when implemented in unique contexts; in order to be successful, programs or activities adapt and respond to local situations.

Second, change efforts that are driven by principles are more successful than those driven by procedures. This is consistent with our concern with process-related *actions* rather than targeted *activities*. For educators to adopt new initiatives, they must recognize the need and understand why the new approach is necessary. For example, a major purpose of developing and strengthening positive and constructive connections with families is to enhance learning opportunities and experiences for children and youth. There are many avenues by which this can be accomplished in a school community. When promoting systems change, focusing on the principle of "enhancing learning opportunities and experiences" is preferable to a specific practice such as "developing a home visiting program." This "purpose focus" will help constituencies understand why change is important, allow new improvements to be integrated into its structure, and minimize the "bandwagon phenomenon" (Grimes & Tilly, 1996, p. 471).

A third consideration offered by Grimes and Tilly is that systems advocates invest in building a knowledge and skill base within the school to support the change. This includes developing and imparting information on how to implement an innovation, why it is important, and how it improves on current practices. Fourth, change agents are encouraged to "start small. . . . This translates into beginning innovation on a small scale within one's own caseload and then generalizing successes as further commitments and resources become available" (p. 472). Similarly, to start toward change, they suggest that change agents work with school leaders in planning and implementation, measure progress on an individual basis, and "communicate, communicate, communicate" (p. 473). Finally, they recommend that important changes in schools should be promoted, not sold, and that individual practitioners become strategic in their actions, which allows them to "work smarter, not harder" (p. 474).

Maher and Illback (1985) offer a pragmatic approach to facilitate implementation of new or novel services within a school. Their seven-phase approach describes actions that practitioners can take when interested in identifying important goals and actions related to home–school relations. The phases, denoted with the acronym DURABLE, are defined below:

- Discussing—occurs prior to beginning an innovation and suggests that the leader meet with relevant individuals or groups to discuss important aspects of the program.
- Understanding—reflects managerial activities designed to clarify the extent to which the school community is ready to implement the program.
- Reinforcing—includes efforts of the change agent to reinforce staff for carrying out aspects of their program roles and responsibilities.
- Acquiring—indicates the practitioner ensures that conditions necessary for program implementation are in place.
- Building—emphasizes that the change agent "builds" cooperative relationships with individuals who will be implementing the program.
- Learning—reflects activities designed to help improve the performance of individuals responsible for carrying out procedures.
- Evaluating—consists of an evaluation of the extent to which the program has been implemented and the degree to which program goals have been realized.

When trying to serve as a systems advocate and create a norm for collaboration (Swap, 1993), individual practitioners are advised to work with school personnel to develop shared responsibility for student's school engagement and performance. Admittedly, this will require educators to change the "way they do business." For example, a way to enhance shared responsibility is to identify current ways families and educators connect, and then alter the existing structure (i.e., social compact) to build-in responsibility for parents, educators, and students. Because this approach is also based in developing relationships as the basis for supporting learners, it is important to recognize that social events to get to know each other ("find friendly faces in the crowd") help to build a foundation for trust and positive communication. Such an approach is consistent with the conceptualization of co-roles for families and schools presented in Chapter 2 (Moles, 1993). It is consistent with two tenets of effective family involvement programs:

(1) Parents are their children's first teachers and have a lifelong influence on children's values, attitudes, and aspirations; and (2) children's educational success requires congruence between what is taught at school and values matched at home (e.g., Fruchter et al., 1992).

As interventionists, we must remember that families do not operate in a vacuum; they need support from institutions to fulfill their functions well (Zill & Nord, 1994). In Table 5.1, activities that represent common points of contact between families and

TABLE 5.1. Building Shared Responsibility for Educational Outcomes

Orientation / Back to School night

Traditional: Parents are welcomed by the principal and follow their child's school schedule. The degree to which parents hear about school/ teacher expectations and policies (e.g., homework, discipline) varies by school and teacher.

Partnership: Parents receive an invitation to the orientation nights, which are offered at multiple times to accommodate parents' schedules. School policies are explained and a handbook and school calendar are distributed to parents. Attendance is taken and there is follow-up (phone calls or home visit) for nonattendees. Several meetings are scheduled to receive parents' input on the policies and to discuss parents' and educators' roles and responsibilities.

Another approach is for teachers to welcome parents and students to the classroom. Teachers articulate their goals for this to be the students' best year; they request that parents and students share their goals. Teachers summarize by noting the goals for which there is consensus and reinforcing the idea that if home and school work together, students will do better. Arrangements are made for how to contact each other (Weiss & Edwards, 1992).

Workshops

Traditional: Schools offer workshops for parents to learn about school- or parent-determined topics.

Partnership: Topics for workshops that require an "institutional" and parental perspective are offered. Both parents and educators, as co-learners and co-teachers, attend. An educator and a parent organize and facilitate the workshops. Sample topics include homework, improving IEP conferences, improving parent–teacher conferences, communication (e.g., maintaining a non-adversarial approach), test standards, and so forth.

Good-news phone calls

Traditional: Teachers make positive phone calls to parents at work or at home. If secondary teachers, make two phone calls per day (40 per month), they have made 360 phone calls in one academic year.

TABLE 5.1 *(continued)*

Good-news phone calls (continued)

Partnership: Phone calls are alternated between school and family. Teachers make the first couple of positive phone calls. They request that parents call next with their good-news observations.

Newsletters

Traditional: The school sends the newsletter to parents. School personnel, whether the principal or teachers, have taken the responsibility for writing the newsletter, which contains important information about child/adolescent development, and school programs and policies.

Partnership: On the first of the month, the teacher writes the letter, and on the fifteenth of the month, the parent is given a blank newsletter to complete. Or the newsletter is written by volunteer parents, working with teachers or students. Or the newsletter reinforces a partnership orientation, such as "Our Turn" and "Your Turn" columns.

Communication system

Traditional: Most communication flows from the school to the home (principal's hour) and is in print. Home–school assignment sheets are used for individual students.

Partnership: Written communication says: We want to be partners, parent input and involvement is critical to children's educational achievement, and if there is a concern, we will work together to find a solution. Also, communication builds-in opportunities for dialogue. For example, the principal schedules "office" hours for discussion. The descriptor for this commonly used structure is changed to Principal–Parent Hour to reflect the partnership.

Home–school assignment books, diaries, and journal notebooks are used on a daily basis to set clear expectations for work to be completed. Teachers set aside time before the end of the school day to allow students to organize their responsibilities. Students write in assignments (they may copy from the overhead) and may use a buddy for checking accuracy. Parents, teachers, and students rate student behavior and academics weekly. The system is described at Back to School nights; nonattendees receive a personal contact.

Contract/partnership agreements

Traditional: Home–school contracts are used for individual students.

Partnership: Home–school–student contracts are used schoolwide. These can be linked to ILPs (individualized learning plans) and IEPs (individualized education plans), where specific responsibilities for the school, family, and student to achieve the goals are documented.

Monitoring student progress

Traditional: Schools, particularly teachers, assume the total responsibility for informing parents about student progress (e.g., report cards, personal contact–phones, notes home).

(continued)

TABLE 5.1 (*continued*)

Monitoring student progress (continued)

Partnership: Monitoring student progress is shared with parents. Parents are asked to keep educational records for their children; these can be shared with the child's teacher(s) the following year. (See K–12 examples of an educational file developed by Johnson & Johnson, 1994–1995.) Also a system can be established whereby parents request specific information about the student's progress (i.e., parent calls ninth-grade teacher to ask about child's performance in algebra class). Conferences with parents are held early (i.e., within first half of the quarter) for the purpose of developing two-way communication about student progress. Suggestions for improved class grades/learning the material are available.

Volunteers

Traditional: Schools distribute a list of volunteer activities to parents. The list specifies the needs of schools and indicates that parent involvement in this capacity is desirable.

Partnership: A list is distributed to parents. However, the wording emphasizes that parents are essential, and the list is introduced in a way to underscore the fact that involvement and participation are expected but responsive to the parents' choices. For example:

"At _____ School, we believe that teachers and parents are both needed to help students achieve their very best performance in school. This is an invitation to share your abilities and time with your child and/or other children at school. Your suggestions and expertise are needed.

"These volunteer positions include one-time commitments: _____

"These volunteer positions include ongoing, longer-term opportunities to be involved in helping students succeed/improve their school progress: _____

"In what way do you plan to be involved? (Feel free to suggest another way.)

"We know when parents are involved in their children's learning, they [list benefits for student learning]." Involvement can include activities at school and at home. Slips are obtained from all parents by making personal contact with those who do not return the slips by the designated time. A parent often coordinates this activity.

Conferencing

Traditional: One-way communication, usually focusing on teacher evaluation of child performance, results in sole responsibility being placed on teachers.

Partnership: The use of early (within first month of school) goal-setting and information-sharing conferences provides an opportunity to build the parent–teacher relationship. Parents are given sample questions to ask, and answer for, the teacher. Students are encouraged to attend the conferences so everyone is "singing from the same sheet of music." A system for ongoing communication is established. Student-led conferences pair well with this format.

schools have been altered to invite parent participation and increase parental responsibility for student learning. The contrast between the traditional and partnership approaches illustrates how school practices can be changed to expect and encourage parent participation. It also illustrates how educators' attitudes and beliefs influence the school practice in place. In schools where partnerships with families are highly valued and supported, newsletters have a column entitled, "Our Half/Your Half, school handbooks address parents and teacher questions; workshops invite parents to help resolve an educational concern, and parent–teacher conferences are co-learning opportunities. Furthermore, all activities are conceptualized as shared responsibility for student learning. Thus, a parent volunteer program is not conceptualized to assist teachers. Rather, volunteering is conceptualized as tangible evidence that parents believe education is important and learning is valued, that educators believe parents are essential, and that interaction between parents and school personnel provides positive modeling for children and youth.

Another way to enhance shared responsibility directly impacts assessment and intervention practices. Recall that Beth Harry (1992), a special education researcher, suggested that the parent–professional discourse must change to provide official channels for reciprocal rather than one-way discourse. She suggested this can be done by having parents assume active roles—specifically, parents as assessors, presenters of reports, policymakers and advocates and peer supports. When educators actively engage parents in these roles, they begin the process of developing collaborative practices, such as those presented in Table 5.2. This list is not exhaustive; school and community professionals interested in engaging in positive practices with families are encouraged to expand it. Ask yourself: How might parents be involved as active participants in assessment and intervention? The suggestions in Table 5.2 strive to create conditions whereby parents and educators understand the "bigger" picture about children's development and educational needs. Active participation of parents means they have voice, input and ownership; we do not do something "to" but rather "with" parents.

IMPLEMENTING FAMILY–SCHOOL TEAMS

Parent participation in decisions that affect their children has taken several forms in schools, including parent advisory councils

TABLE 5.2. Shared Roles and Responsibilities in Assessment
and Intervention Practices

Parents as assessors

  ◆ Parents provide questions for the assessment to address.
  ◆ Parents ask for information about assessment procedures and tools.
  ◆ Observation techniques are demonstrated to parents (e.g., ABC analysis)
    and then used to gather data to answer specific questions.
  ◆ Parents are identified as being part of the assessment team on assess-
    ment forms.
  ◆ Parents are provided with time to interview/question educators (e.g., a
    question–answer session).
  ◆ Parents monitor and record ways in which students spend their time.
  ◆ Parents describe the kinds of messages given to their child about school-
    work and effort for learning.
  ◆ Parents provide school information about what motivates the child, what
    reinforcements have worked, successes in previous years, and so forth.
  ◆ Parents explain the cultural context for child behavior to educators.
  ◆ Parents assess strengths of their child, not just deficits.
  ◆ Parents attend a pre-IEP meeting to learn about assessment results; they
    ask questions about assessment and actively participate in intervention
    planning at the IEP meeting.
  ◆ Parents validate (confirm or disconfirm) assessment findings based on
    knowledge, experience, and interaction with their child.
  ◆ Parents provide the home input, and educators the school input on the
    same, specifically defined behavior. Discussion and interpretation of the
    findings occur together.
  ◆ Parents collect data for and evaluate interventions.
  ◆ Parents offer recommendations for implementation of interventions.

Parents as presenters of reports

  ◆ Parents present observational data from home–school–community.
  ◆ Parents report on community events (gang activity, stressors) to give an
    ecological dimension to understanding child behavior.
  ◆ Parents report on child strengths in general and strengths relative to a
    specific mutually identified concern. Gather same information from school
    personnel.
  ◆ Parents use half of conference time to report about their child (send home
    sample questions for their consideration).
  ◆ Teachers take notes during conference and file in the home–school plan-
    ning/intervention or assessment-to-intervention file.
  ◆ Parents request whom they want to be present at meetings.
  ◆ Parents describe their child's specific needs related to an individual situa-
    tion.
  ◆ Parents present intervention strategies that have worked well in the past.
  ◆ Parents present information regarding child's personal or medical histo-
    ry/background.

TABLE 5.2 (continued)
_____

Parents as policymakers

* Parents are empowered/encouraged to assert their rights (refer to Parent Advocacy Coalition for Educational Rights [PACER] or other outside resources).
* Parents co-conduct forums to educate parents about policy issues.
* Parents suggest agenda items, issues for consideration for advisory meetings.
* Parents serve on policymaking committees and have voting power.
* Forums/discussion groups are created to allow parents to meet independently of teachers/administrators.
* Provide a follow-up time to share home and school perspectives.
* Provide information to parents about what issues are key for student learning and encourage them to lobby the legislature either individually or in groups.
* Parents can be part of the decision-making process by creating parent groups and learning about the school system (see Delgado-Gaitan, 1991).
* Parents from each grade level participate on shared decision-making committees. Set policies, procedures, and practices for school and on issues affecting home and school.
* Involve parents that represent the cultures of the school.
* Ask parents to draft policies/guidelines that would work for them (e.g., homework) and then seek the response of educators. Dialogue on issues raised.

Parents as advocates and peer supports

* Parents with experience with special education process, rules, and policies serve as advocates and encourage other parents to be active participants.
* Led by parents for parents, a peer support group serves as a resource and helps educate families about school–community services.
* Provide parents with opportunities to have contact with other families that share similar backgrounds and/or experiences.
* Provide opportunities to parents for advocacy training and make it a routine part of service delivery to include parent advocates/partners.
* Develop advisory groups within schools made up of school personnel, parents, and community members.
* Parents serve as advocates for each other (e.g., bring another parent to IEP meeting for support).
* Parents serve as leaders/liaisons in community.
* Parents meet/communicate with other parents regularly. Develop a system to gather accurate information from school personnel.
* Affirm parents rights. Discuss rights, responsibilities, and resources (and constraints) of home and school toward common goals.
_____

(PACs), school-based management teams, PTA/PTO, and other committees in schools. The concept of family–school teams differs from typically functioning PACs, which are often only advisory to educators and principals, suggesting that parent input is sought and helpful but may not necessarily be used in school-based decisions. In contrast, family–school teams emphasize the elements of collaboration, particularly shared decision making, which has been redefined by Epstein (1995) "to mean a process of partnership, of shared views and actions toward shared goals, not just a power struggle between conflicting ideas" (p. 705). Epstein has demonstrated multiple benefits when parents are actively involved in decision making. For example, students were aware of family representation in school decisions and, as a result, were provided with a congruent message about school behavior. Feelings of ownership of school and shared experiences and connections with other families were identified as some of the parental benefits, while benefits for teachers included awareness of parent perspectives in policy development and school practices. Furthermore, parent participation in school governance has been shown to enhance school climate and academic and behavioral outcomes for elementary students (Comer, 1995; Comer & Haynes, 1991; Eccles & Harold, 1996).

Family–school teams have been conceptualized in several ways. For example, Epstein (1995) advocated for an action team to develop a comprehensive, coordinated family–school partnership program by organizing, implementing, and evaluating options for new partnerships that represent her six types of family involvement across grades K–12. From his work on the League of Schools Reaching Out Project, Don Davies and his colleagues (cited in Palanki & Burch, 1995) have been proponents of parent–teacher action research teams whose goal is to create systemic change by (1) ensuring that parents and teachers follow a 10-step process to address a meaningful school problem, (2) creating a model for ongoing, databased problem solving in the school, and (3) creating support for creativity and innovation in the school. With an action research team approach, parents and teachers are program developers and evaluators. Together, they design, implement, and evaluate interventions. Some teams set school policies and procedures, coordinates activities, and engage in strategic planning with key stakeholders.

The School Planning and Management Team (SPMT) in the Comer School Development Program (Comer et al., 1996) is an example of a model characteristic of effective action research teams.

In the Comer model, the SPMT listens to parents and addresses their needs, and listens to educators and addresses their needs. It does not simply include parents and assume that their physical presence represents parent input. Parents and educators are valued and active participants, and consensus is obtained to address concerns expressed by both. Because of these characteristics, this team has served as a model for many successful partnership programs. A final example of a family–school team is PATHS— Parents and Teachers Heading to Success (Sinclair, Lam, Christenson, & Evelo, 1993). The purposes of PATHS are to share information and resources to address concerns of mutual interest and to find mutually supportive ways to enhance student learning and outcomes. PATHS designed changes in home–school communications, sex education curricula, and homework policies, all of which were mutually agreed upon by parents and educators.

Regardless of the purpose or format of the team, there seems to be common agreement that strong partnerships develop over time and depend on both interactions between the partners (e.g., exchanging information, clarifying responsibilities) and actions (e.g., assessing strengths and needs, setting goals, planning projects, implementing practices, evaluating results) to enhance student success in school. Many action teams are directed at developing or improving parent involvement programs. In addition to Epstein's (1995) action team, the National PTA (2000) recognizes that an action team is necessary to develop sustained parent involvement programs. Specifically, they recommend three responsibilities for the team members: to develop a formal parent involvement policy, to develop action plans to implement the policy, and to monitor and evaluate the implementation process. Other family–school teams are focused on handling issues that require family and school input, and that support decision making to change policies and practices, and to achieve desired gains for students.

Benefits of a Team Approach

The benefits of a family–school team go far beyond developing a family–school partnership program, albeit some of these are less tangible. Consider the benefit of having a mechanism for circumventing blame, providing continuity about school and family expectations, providing mutual support for the benefit of students (e.g., homework, anger management, compliance), increasing parent–educator contact and interaction over time, and engaging in collective problem solving to address concerns of parents, educators, and students. Particularly noteworthy is the opportunity for input from the many voices represented in the school community and the presence of mechanisms for observing and monitoring the dynamic quality of developing stronger partnerships between families and schools. Family–school teams provide a regular, ongoing, structured, and systematic means for family–school interaction. In addition, many interventions have been shown to be more effective when implemented across settings. Given these benefits, we strongly support the development of a well-publicized family–school team that is structured to address issues that can only be resolved well with home and school input (e.g., homework, suspension, discipline, attendance, career aspirations, dropouts, poor achievement, value of education). Memorable labels such as TGIF (Teachers Getting Involved with Families), FAST (Families and Schools Together), and BEST (Better Educational Support Team) are often used.

A primary yet often unstated benefit of the family–school team is the opportunity to use ecological systems theory in understanding student behavior, and more importantly, to develop mesosytemic interventions. The family–school team is an ideal vehicle for focusing explicitly on the connection between family and school for children's school performance. Thus, an effectively functioning team engages in much information sharing about family and school goals, expectations, policies, and practices. As a result, it may discuss the following questions: What are parents', educators', and students' rights, roles and responsibilities, and resources for enhancing student learning? What does it mean to call at the first sign of a problem or concern? What are meaningful roles for parent and teacher participation? How can parents and educators support each other in efforts for improving graduation rates, student success on high-stakes tests, development of after school programs, and so forth? The team provides a mechanism for reducing subjectivity or jumping to conclusions about the other partner and for sharing information about the resources or barriers (i.e., constraints) of each system for addressing the presenting concern. It also is an easily accessible, permanent contact point for parents and teachers when they have concerns and questions, desire clarification, or have an innovative idea for supporting and engaging students as learners. Effectively functioning teams maintain a constructive, two-way communication process about learning goals, experiences, and outcomes.

Throughout this book, we have made reference to family and school as partners for prevention. The family–school team is, from our viewpoint, a primary mechanism to alter the typical course for interacting with families. The social and physical distance between families and school personnel is great in many schools; in urban schools, the distance is compounded by significant yet rich cultural diversity. Families and educators, who often feel like strangers, far too often interact only when there is a problem, and far too often try to resolve the problem without first developing a foundational relationship. Families and schools tend to be quite autonomous. The saying "the shortest distance between two strangers is a story" is appropriate: both home and school need to share their stories about issues, concerns, observations of children/adolescents, effect of interventions, and suggestions for improving the family–school connection and children's learning.

The team provides this opportunity. It establishes the tone for the partnership that both family and school are essential, namely, that "we" (not "you" or "I") can address mutual concerns about children's learning progress and together provide improved educational experiences for students. To do so requires sharing information and resources to achieve a shared goal or mission. Table 5.3 provides a list of policies and practices that parents need to know about to monitor their children's progress in school and to feel a

TABLE 5.3. Sample Policies and Practices for Enhancing Co-Communication

- Suspension and expulsion policies
- Section 504 regulations
- Extracurricular opportunities and field trip rules
- Grading policies
- Expectations for assignment completion
- Graduating with honors
- Homework expectations and policies
- Handling conflict (student–teacher; school–family; student–student)
- Grievance procedures
- Discipline policies
- Bus/transportation policies
- Health regulations
- Special education rules and regulations
- Visitation policies (e.g., classroom observations)
- How to contact teachers/school personnel
- Ways to maintain two-way communication between home and school
- How to report good news
- Ways to communicate at the first sign of a problem
- Financing costs of K–12 education
- School schedules and events
- Policies about school safety

sense of ownership and responsibility for their children's learning. These are provided to stimulate thinking about the many possibilities for team action.

Teams convey the attitude that parents and educators have equal power in decisions that are made on behalf of students. To successfully portray that attitude, they must adopt a proactive stance. If the stimulus for parental contact and meetings is students' school-based problems, parents are placed immediately in a reactive, potentially defensive situation. Under these circumstances, they become involved with their children's learning primarily under tense and stressful conditions. Likewise, such school practices may contribute unknowingly to parent–child/adolescent communication difficulties.

Creating a Team

When creating a family–school team, an initial, important consideration is its membership (i.e., who serves on the team). There is general agreement in the literature that a team should be comprised of key stakeholders with respect to children's learning. Epstein (1995) has suggested including three teachers from different grade levels, three parents with children in different grade levels, one administrator, possibly a member from the community at large, and others central to the school's work with families. Also, based on implementation of PATHS (Christenson & Hirsch, 1998), it is important to involve parents from diverse backgrounds and with varying experiences at school. Various voices in the school need to be represented; therefore, parents from different ethnic and social-class backgrounds, parents with different educational and skills levels, parents whose children are performing with varied academic success, and parents who are more and less involved at school are examples of categories of "voices" to be considered for participation. Overrepresenting parents, particularly in urban areas, is an efficient way to maintain a "critical mass" of parents available to attend regularly scheduled team meetings. Although team membership may be based on parent and teacher interest or parent interest and teacher assignment, it is most appropriate in selecting members to attain the broadest representation of parent and educator perspectives.

Another consideration is to establish the purpose of the team. Family–school teams provide a structured way for parents and educators to study and intervene on a concern that is relevant to a specific school. Davies, Burch, and Johnson (1992) recommend that teams select a focused topic or question and use structured interviews with school personnel and parents to gather data on current practices and attitudes about the topic. Implemented in elementary and middle schools, a variety of topics have been studied and addressed using this approach. For example, the Attenville Elementary School action research team learned "that increasing parent involvement is a sum of personal connections to families, whose ties to the school are nurtured over time. To help them make the connections between individual parents' increased involvement and changes in children, the action research team designed a three-part portfolio (collection of materials compiled over time) approach" (Davies et al., 1992, p. 17). The school's parent involvement strategies are documented in a school portfolio. Families' attendance at school events, contacts with schools, and resources and skills are documented in a family portfolio. The contents of a student portfolio are jointly determined by parents and teachers, and provide a picture of student progress over time.

Procedures for operating as a cohesive team must be developed. Teams tend to select either a needs-driven or referral-oriented approach to teamwork. For the former, agenda items to be addressed can be generated by the team in concert with identified priorities. For example, one of us (SMS) worked with an elementary school whose action team identified the need to establish a family center in the school and held meetings to develop and implement an action plan around that priority. It followed a structured problem-solving approach to determine goals, objectives, and resources available to develop the family center. At their meetings, team members also brainstormed ways to attain needed resources, set up and "run" the family center, assessed possible uses of the family center based on input of the families and the school, and evaluated its effectiveness.

Alternatively, teams can adopt a referral procedure to address ongoing issues that arise. For example, at an initial PATHS meeting, team members generated a list of home–school concerns, which included home–school communication, homework, study skills for students, discipline, use of out-of-school time, ways to promote self-esteem, and ways parents and teachers contribute to students' success in school. The list, which was continuously reviewed and modified, served to maintain the focus on addressing concerns important to families and educators at an urban middle school.

Also, it is important that meetings themselves be organized and semistructured. There are advantages to employing "situa-

tional leadership," which suggests that team meetings can be facilitated by whoever is most "expert" on the issue or task at hand.
For example, if the home–school action team is working on developing a schoolwide discipline or social skills program, the school
psychologist may be the facilitator. If, however, it is working on establishing an efficient computer networking system for the school,
a parent with technology expertise may be more appropriate as facilitator or co-facilitator.

Process-related beliefs shared by team members should also
be explicated. Beliefs for working together must be shared and re-
iterated. Examples of these from PATHS were that (1) differences
of opinion are OK and helpful; (2) conflict is natural and can be
managed; (3) a good action plan satisfies parents', teachers', and
students' needs; (4) both parents and teachers are important for
student success in school; and (5) parents and teachers have inadequate information about youth because they see them in only one
context. Finally, ground rules need to be established and reviewed
at each meeting. For example, when PATHS was working on promoting home–school communication, the ground rules were as follows: (1) every participant is a consultant or coach for both
parents and teachers; (2) this is a brainstorming session—participants share what they think; (3) this is also a planning session of
action—- participants will follow up on activities; and (4) the focus
of our discussion is on solutions that benefit all students rather
than concerns about a specific student.

A final consideration concerns the language used by the team
members, and the facilitator in particular. An honest but positive
orientation during team discussions is important and should be
maintained. Words used to convey certain messages must be selected carefully. For example, in PATHS, there was no focus on
problematic individuals; rather, the focus was on problematic situations between home and school (e.g., lack of communication).
Concerns, rather than problems, were discussed because they
imply caring, whereas problems tend to increase defensiveness.
And, concerns can be reframed as goals—what families and
schools want to achieve to foster positive school experiences for
students.

In team meetings, conversations can be facilitated so that perspective taking between home and school is actively practiced. It is
important to elicit parents' and teachers' feelings and desires
about a situation. It is equally important for each party to think
about the other's feelings and desires. The facilitator can stress

that the team goal is to enhance students' academic and behavioral success in school. When the facilitator emphasizes understanding the issue, team members can be asked to consider the following: What is the issue? What do I need to say about the issue? What do I need to understand from others about the issue? How can we develop a better action plan? Important questions during evaluation include the following: What did you need? What did you get? How did it work?

Of the lessons learned over 2 years of implementing PATHS using these principles, two stand out. First, the importance of non-blaming interactions was apparent. In general, PATHS parents and teachers did not engage in "blaming the other system," perhaps because of the clearly focused purpose of the team, skill of the facilitator, or the structure provided by problem solving. However, team members were known to slip into the "world of blame." For example, even after 2 years of operation, team members found themselves engaged in finger-pointing behavior when a new issue was discussed. It is encouraging, however, that they quickly identified their unproductive behavior and focused common efforts toward a shared goal. They had learned to listen, to understand that different perspectives are acceptable, and to create a plan that addressed the needs of students, families, and schools. The second lesson, and perhaps most poignant, was that the concept of the family–school connection for student success in school had to be salient. The group facilitator was very persistent about ensuring the dominance of the goal of PATHS—partnerships for student learning.

In summary, a family–school team is a vehicle for developing constructive family–school connections, addressing a myriad of parent and teacher concerns about students, and providing a structure for routine communication on systems-level issues. Teams are flexible in that members can and should vary to address the needs of the specific school community. For example, student members may be included to address specific issues (e.g., homework completion). Successful team process is characterized by negotiation and consensus, and shifting discussion from complex rhetoric to specific and solvable problems. Teams are not, however, a panacea. The use of the team would be inappropriate if either parents or educators are too emotionally involved, upset because of previous personal experience with the topic of discussion, or have a hidden agenda to use the team to advance their own perspective to meet the needs of a specific child.

Focus on the Family–School Connection

It is clear that family–school teams stimulate a new social compact between families and schools, one in which families and educators are placed in an altered relation to one another (i.e., shared responsibility) and to the education of children and youth. We know that schools alone cannot solve the problems of today's students, and we know that shared responsibility and collaborative relationships are imperative. If we are going to improve educational outcomes in this country (what we refer to as "raising the bar"), it is equally imperative that we increase parental responsibility for educational and developmental outcomes for children and youth. Although standards for students are being set across the nation (e.g., competency tests), clearly articulated support roles for critical socializing agents—teachers and parents—to assist students in attaining the standards are less apparent.

When a goal of the family–school team is to "raise the bar" for students' educational accomplishments, the team members recognize the need for strong family–school connections with regard to children's learning. In fact, the team is an ideal mechanism to craft school- (and districtwide) messages about conditions that promote children's success, the importance of continuity and consistency across home and school about the value of learning, and ways to engage students as learners in school and at home. Examples from "Partner Up," a school newsletter from the Schools and Families Together (SAF-T) project (Christenson, 1994; see Appendix C), illustrate messages given routinely to educators and parents at an elementary school about the value and benefits of working in a collaborative fashion. From the perspective of Bronfenbrenner (1979), these messages provide the cultural blueprint for making mesosystemic intervention with individual families the norm. School personnel do not interact with a monolithic family; families bring myriad experiences and histories to school with them. For example, we know that many families do not know the best way to support or foster children's school progress; they are uncertain about their role; some families are unclear about policies and procedures in schools; other families, as result perhaps of their own schooling, believe in separate roles and responsibilities for home and school; and still others see schools as their second home. With the exception of anecdotal information, there has been little, if any, systematic study of the effect of intergenerational experiences on family participation in education. An evidence-based, regular, and systematic media campaign conducted by the family–school team holds much promise in setting the stage for positive connections and other family–school interventions (Rich, 1993).

Although it is ideal for the team to focus on preventive and proactive strategies, it also serves as a concrete forum for addressing concerns about students' learning progress, maintaining communication, and handling conflict. As the team functions, trust between home and school is built through a common knowledge base that comes from addressing mutual concerns and problem solving. Structured problem solving that purposefully includes information sharing, particularly about resources and constraints at school or at home, is essential. In structured problem solving, team participants must first be concerned with understanding, and second, with being understood.

Problem-solving models that have been used to address individual concerns are covered later in this chapter. We believe that team members' use of a structured problem-solving framework can also be appropriate to identify priorities, analyze resources and constraints, brainstorm alternatives, select specific strategies, develop an action plan, implement the chosen procedures, and evaluate the outcomes. For example, teams may find the following structured problem-solving approach helpful in addressing concerns or priorities:

- Stop. Think about the concern at home and at school.
  - Describe the concern in each setting.
  - How does the concern affect the teacher/classroom?
  - How does the concern affect the parent/home?
- What are some choices/options for changing the current practice?
- Choose one after considering consequences for each system.
  - What consequences do teachers/school personnel envision?
  - What consequences do parents envision?
- Try the option.
  - What resources or support do teachers need?
  - What resources or support do parents need?
- How did it work?
  - What were the benefits for students, teachers, and families?
  - What changes should be made?

Coequality in decision-making power among participants, including equal status of educators and parents on the team, is important. Although this is doable, it is not necessarily easily accomplished. Typical interactions between schools and families are still hierarchical, and sharing power requires a new social compact between families and school personnel. Consider the following scenario: Parents may not believe that the school has chosen the right intervention for students (e.g., requiring competency tests for high school graduation requirements). Parents also do not believe they are in a position to contradict the school, nor do they know exactly what students might need to improve academic performance. School personnel are not used to taking extra time to explain educational practices (e.g., the learning process or assessment strategies). A productive family–school connection to aid student learning necessitates that time be taken to explain the school's and parents' perspectives and to allow team members to ask and answer questions of each other. Systematic opportunities for co-communication, so that families and educators can learn from each other, are a prerequisite to the goal of being co-supporters of students' learning.

A mutual relationship between families and schools recognizes the power of co-communication to achieve cosupport. To this end, we offer an acronym, CONNECT, which was developed by the SEARCH Institute (1994). We think of this as a helpful heuristic for family–school teams to engage in dialogue about ways to support and socialize students as learners. A family–school team that places an explicit focus on the mesosytemic influence of home and school on children's learning can adopt CONNECT as its motto and begin by eliciting parent and school perspectives to the following questions:

- How can we *customize* our plan to improve student's school experiences?
- How can we *overcome* logistical barriers?
- What are *new* practices we should try?
- What *new* understanding do we need?
- How can we *expand* options for families and schools?
- How can we *create* relationships for children's learning and school experiences?
- What can our *team* do to promote student learning and development?

From our perspective, the benefit of CONNECT lies in the attitude symbolized by the name and the discussion about actions stimulated by the questions. Therefore, the necessity to obtain concrete answers to each question is very small.

INCREASING PROBLEM SOLVING ACROSS
HOME AND SCHOOL

Clearly, efforts and actions at systemic levels, such as those involving family–school teams, are necessary to achieve broad-based changes in approach, attitude, and atmosphere. Along with several approaches that support family and school systems to promote quality education for children, there is also a need for individual-level approaches that address unique needs of specific students, families, and educators. These include problem-solving meetings and communication-building strategies.

Home–school problem-solving models provide structured and supportive mechanisms by which partnerships can be operationalized. They provide the templates and tools that enable parents, teachers, and other team members to work together to achieve a positive and constructive climate aimed at addressing mutually shared concerns (Sheridan, Cowan, & Eagle, 2000). Most problem-solving models are based on at least four common principles: joint responsibility and ownership for problem solution; the child as central; open and direct conflict management; and a focus on solutions (Christenson & Hirsch, 1998). An empowerment orientation, focusing on the strengths of families as active and meaningful participants in their child's education, is typical. Similarly, most problem-solving models refrain from diagnosing problems and strive to develop cooperative relationships with parents that best meet the needs of the child.

Effective problem-solving practices empower parents to become meaningful contributors in their child's education. Empowerment implies that many competencies are already present or possible within families (Dunst & Trivette, 1987). From an empowerment perspective, a failure to display competence is not due to the deficiencies of families and their children per se, but rather to a failure of social systems, including schools, to create opportunities for families strengths to be displayed.

To be empowered, parents must believe that changes are a result of their own efforts and not due to the efforts of others in control of making decisions or sanctioning actions (e.g., educators who "tell" parents what they must do to solve a problem; administrators who limit parental input on important matters related to individual child decisions). Rappaport (1981) has argued that "in those cases where new competencies need to be learned, they are best learned in the context of living life rather than in artificial programs where . . . it is really the expert who is in charge" (p. 16). Therefore, strengths and competencies related to families' abilities to share in decision making and problem resolution are central. Attention is placed on the shared strengths of the home, school, and child, rather than on "fixing" child- or family–centered problems (Sheridan et al., 2000).

Several models for team-based problem solving are available, including conjoint behavioral consultation (CBC; Sheridan, Kratochwill, & Bergan, 1996) and solution-oriented family–school meetings (Carlson, Hickman, & Horton, 1992). Although these models are unique in their respective procedural protocols, they each include four elements that are consistent with a problem-solving approach: (1) an introductory phase between members of the school and family environments to set the stage for problem solving; (2) a collaborative brainstorming of concerns; (3) a joint selection of an immediate concern on which to focus discussions; and (4) an implementation of a solution amenable to all parties (see Table 5.4). As such, each model relies on effective communication skills and competence in problem solving, and both share a primary goal of empowering parents and creating partnerships between families and schools to promote student competence.

Conjoint Behavioral Consultation

CBC is "a structured indirect form of service-delivery, in which parents and teachers are joined together to address the academic,

TABLE 5.4. Procedural Stages of Home–School Problem-Solving Models

Solution-oriented family–school meetings (Carlson, Hickman, & Horton, 1992)	Conjoint behavioral consultation (Sheridan, Kratochwill, & Bergan, 1996)
◆ Introduction ◆ Explanation of solution-oriented approach ◆ Joining ◆ Negotiating a solvable complaint ◆ Establishing a solution goal ◆ Eliciting multiple solutions toward accomplishing smallest change ◆ Gaining agreement on the smallest change in direction of goal ◆ Clarifying individual responsibilities and task assignments ◆ Follow-up ◆ Evaluating and recycling, if necessary	◆ Preconsultation meeting ◆ Conjoint problem identification ◆ Conjoint problem analysis ◆ Treatment (plan) implementation ◆ Conjoint treatment (plan) evaluation

social, or behavioral needs of an individual for whom both parties bear some responsibility" (Sheridan & Kratochwill, 1992, p. 122). The process is guided by a consultant (e.g., school psychologist, special educator, or other team member) who uses both technical and interpersonal skill in facilitating the problem-solving process.

CBC borrows from both ecological and behavioral theories. From ecological theory, CBC addresses the mesosystem (i.e., interactions among primary systems in a child's life, such as the home, school, and other immediate settings) by bringing together important primary caregivers (i.e., parents, teachers, and other significant individuals) from the essential systems of which a child is a part (e.g., home, school). As related to behavioral theory, CBC recognizes the importance of conducting direct behavioral observations, collecting data in a continuous fashion, performing functional assessments, and employing empirically validated interventions as a critical element of educational and behavioral programs. These and other problem-solving (outcome) goals of CBC are presented in Table 5.5.

The home–school partnership in CBC is considered a process —a means to an end, and not an end in itself. The structured model allows parents to become actively involved in problem solving and decision making as behavioral, social, or academic problems are identified, defined, analyzed, and addressed across settings. Parents' unique knowledge, information, and expertise, and their active participation in decision making, place them at the center of CBC planning and problem solving. Through mutual and collaborative interactions, parents and school team members identify and explore academic and behavioral problems; analyze functional,

TABLE 5.5. Outcome Goals of Conjoint Behavioral Consultation

1. Obtain comprehensive and functional data over extended temporal and contextual bases.
2. Establish consistent treatment programs across settings.
3. Improve the skills, knowledge, or behaviors of all parties (including students, parents, family members, school personnel).
4. Monitor behavioral contrast and side effects systematically via cross-setting treatment agents.
5. Enhance generalization and maintenance of treatment effects via consistent programming across sources and settings.
6. Develop skills and competencies to promote further independent conjoint problem solving between the family and school personnel.

Note. Adapted from Sheridan and Kratochwill (1992). Copyright 1992 by Elsevier Science. Adapted by permission.

contextual/ecological, and/or curricular conditions around behaviors; develop and implement relevant interventions; and analyze the outcome of interventions (Sheridan et al., 1996).

Consistent with several premises of this book, we believe that relationships between parents and educators and success in CBC are related. Put another way, healthy and supportive relationships between teachers, family members, and consultants support conjoint problem solving. Likewise, structured problem-solving interactions implemented via CBC can assist in the development of constructive home–school partnerships. Goals related to the home–school relationship (process) within CBC, and strategies that a consultant can use to achieve these important relational goals, are listed in Table 5.6.

TABLE 5.6. Goals and Possible Strategies for Achieving Relationship Goals of Conjoint Behavioral Consultation

Goal	Strategy
◆ Increase understanding of family.	◆ Identify strengths in child and family. ◆ Support parents "where they are at." ◆ Elicit ideas, information, and perspectives using open-ended questions. ◆ Paraphrase and validate messages from parents to check for understanding.
◆ Establish home–school partnership.	◆ Establish relative goals for families based on current needs. ◆ Provide rationales and expectations for families and schools to work together (i.e., "make process overt"). ◆ Emphasize a team concept with words such as "we," "us," and "together." ◆ Highlight similarities across settings.
◆ Promote shared ownership for problem solution.	◆ Engage in shared eye contact. ◆ Verbally encourage and reinforce future, independent, conjoint problem solving among parents and teachers. ◆ Draw distinct similarities across settings. ◆ Structure interventions that require cooperation and communication, such as home–school notes.

TABLE 5.6 *(continued)*

◆ Promote greater conceptualization of problems and increase perspective taking.	◆ Increase responsibility for successful outcomes by including all participants, including the child, when appropriate. ◆ Describe rationale and expectations for joint home–school problem-solving efforts. ◆ Use nonverbal listening skills that convey understanding and acceptance of various perspectives.
◆ Strengthen relationships among participants.	◆ Verbally acknowledge different perspectives with statements such as "I see your point" or "I hadn't thought of it that way before." ◆ Reframe problems into opportunities for skills development. ◆ Emphasize positive efforts of all parties. ◆ Reframe negative comments into areas of care and concern. ◆ Point out unique strengths of parents and teachers. ◆ Use physical arrangement of meeting room to encourage eye contact and dialogue between parents and teachers (e.g., remove physical barriers such as large tables; encourage parents and teachers to sit next to each other). ◆ Use gestures to communicate joining of home and school parties (e.g., arm and hand movements that suggest coming together).
◆ Recognize the need to address concerns occurring across, rather than within, settings.	◆ Point out the importance of out-of-school opportunities for a student to experience success. ◆ Comment on the benefits of congruence and continuity of experiences for students, families, and educators.
◆ Increase parent and teacher commitments to educational goals.	◆ Ask for help. ◆ Develop plans that are consistent across settings and support achievement in and out of school.
◆ Increase the diversity of expertise and resources available.	◆ Involve students when possible. ◆ Invite family members other than parents to be involved. ◆ Allow parents to bring additional support persons to meetings. ◆ Ask parents for ideas for interventions and incorporate them into plans.

The CBC process consists of four stages, all implemented in a simultaneous, conjoint fashion (Sheridan et al., 1996). Three of the four stages are initiated via a structured behavioral interview. The stages are as follows: (1) problem identification (and the Conjoint Problem Identification Interview; CPII), (2) problem analysis (and the Conjoint Problem Analysis Interview; CPAI), (3) treatment implementation, and (4) treatment evaluation (and the Conjoint Treatment Evaluation Interview; CTEI). Interview formats are available in Sheridan et al. (1996).

Conjoint Problem Identification

The first formal stage of CBC is problem identification, initiated via a CPII. In problem identification, parents' and teachers' shared primary behavioral, academic, or social concerns are described. Clear, objective definitions of target concerns are developed to help team members focus their problem-solving efforts. Behavioral examples are explored and priorities for intervention are established. Situations where the concerns are highest (e.g., at what time, in what setting, with what subject matter) are identified and prioritized, allowing for focused observation, analysis, intervention, and evaluation during later CBC stages.

During the problem identification stage, an initial contextual/functional assessment allows the parents and teachers to explore conditions that may be supporting or maintaining the primary concern as presented across settings. An additional goal of the CPII includes delineating a valid procedure for collecting baseline data across settings. The goal in data collection is to learn more about the concerns as they present themselves across home and school, and to identify environmental conditions that may be affecting the child, and his or her behavior and achievement.

Conjoint Problem Analysis

The second stage of CBC is problem analysis, initiated in a conjoint fashion via the CPAI. There are two distinct phases of problem analysis: (1) data analysis and (2) plan development (Sheridan et al., 1996). During the *data analysis phase*, the consultant, parents, and teachers examine the baseline data and conduct a functional assessment of the target behavior across settings (i.e., discuss antecedents, consequences, and environmental conditions of the behavior). In the case of academic problems, the child's current level of performance, skills and deficits, details of the curriculum, and instructional procedures are explored. For an invaluable resource in assessing the instructional environment, the reader is referred to Ysseldyke and Christenson (1993). In the case of behavioral or social concerns, the consultation team seeks to identify setting events (Wahler & Fox, 1981), environmental stimuli, and other variables that occur across settings (e.g., home and school routines) that may affect the target behavior. For specific information on conducting functional assessments, interested readers are referred to Larson and Maag (1998), O'Neill et al. (1997), and Tilly, Knoster, and Ikeda (2000).

The second phase of problem analysis is *plan development*. Hypotheses about the function or purpose of the behavior are generated by the team prior to discussing an intervention plan. From the hypotheses generated during the instructional or functional assessment, the team collaboratively develops a program to address the target concern. Parents, teachers, and other team members develop interventions collaboratively to address the shared concerns in the natural settings of the home and classroom. Plan strategies are clearly defined, roles and responsibilities of all parties (e.g., parents, teachers, support staff) are clearly delineated, and a time line for implementing the intervention is constructed.

To facilitate the process and outcome goals of CBC, it is imperative that all team members participate in treatment plan development. Parents and teachers contribute their unique knowledge and expertise about the child and their respective contexts (e.g., home/family issues, classroom/curricular/educational considerations). Together with the consultant's intervention knowledge base, they together arrive at a reasonable plan. Data collection continues throughout the consultation process, thus promoting a goal-oriented, outcome-based, data-driven problem-solving process.

Intervention plans that are implemented across home and school need not be identical in design and structure. Home and school environments are different, and although CBC consultants strive for continuity and congruence across settings, the unique features of each system, and behaviors manifested in each system, must be recognized. It is possible (in many cases, likely) that different behaviors serve similar functions at home and school (suggesting that different behaviors need to be targeted across settings). For example, a child may cry at school to avoid exposure to challenging work, and at home to obtain attention from a parent. Similarly, different conditions may operate at home and at school (e.g., television on during homework at home; small-group work environment at school) to maintain a similar behavior (such as inattention or distractibility).

Resources across home and school settings are important to consider in the development of plans aimed at achieving consultation goals. Assuming that the goals are mutually determined and shared across settings, it is possible to focus on one setting (e.g., school) to provide the primary intervention strategy, and the additional setting (e.g., home) to engage in complementary roles. For example, when targets for intervention are academic in nature (e.g., reading skills acquisition), a structured peer tutoring program at school may be appropriate. Similarly, during the plan design phase, a discussion of the home as a learning environment is appropriate. For example, supportive practices, such as enhancement of the linguistic environment at home (Clark, 1988), an increase in the amount of reading materials via regular visits to the local library, or interactive parent–child book reading (Taverne & Sheridan, 1995) are possible, unique home interventions that support parents' roles in their child's learning and development.

There are several variables to consider when designing procedures to be implemented by parents and teachers across home and school settings. First, active participation of all team members during plan development is important (Gresham, 1989). Second, the components of the plan should be rooted in evidence-based practice. Third, the plan should be reasonable (i.e., not too complex) to allow parents and teachers to follow through easily and reliably (Yeaton & Sechrest, 1981). The parent and teacher should also agree with the plan; that is, the basic principles and strategies of the plan should match the values and perspectives of the parents and teachers who will implement it.

Treatment Implementation

The next stage of CBC is treatment implementation. During this stage, parents and teachers implement the collaboratively derived intervention procedures. This stage does not involve a structured interview; however, several practices are important to ensure effective implementation of the plan. It is essential that the consultant remain in close contact with parents and teachers throughout this stage to ensure understanding of the intervention; check for implementation fidelity (i.e., degree to which the plan is being delivered as intended); offer assistance, if necessary; provide support and reinforcement for the parents' and teachers' intervention efforts; and determine the need for immediate revisions to the plan (Sheridan & Colton, 1994).

Conjoint Treatment (Plan) Evaluation

The final stage of CBC is treatment (plan) evaluation, implemented via the CTEI. During the evaluation stage and the CTEI, the team evaluates the treatment data to determine whether the goals of consultation have been met across settings. This requires feedback from all parents, teachers, and others (including the student, when appropriate). Depending on whether the goals have been met, the team should discuss strategies and tactics related to the continuation, modification, or termination of the intervention. If the goals are not met, the team may decide to meet again for another CTEI after modifications are made and a revised plan is implemented for an agreed-upon amount of time. If the consultation goals have been met, the team should discuss strategies for the maintenance and generalization of treatment gains, and the home–school partnership.

Solution-Oriented Family–School Consultation

Solution-oriented family–school consultation (Carlson et al., 1992) is an indirect model of service delivery that draws from several conceptual frameworks, including an emphasis on ecological systems perspectives, an enabling philosophy in working across home and school settings, and solution-oriented brief therapy. Consistent with each of these orientations are the notions of the interrelatedness of home and school systems, a focus on strengths (rather than deficits) and growth-producing actions, and a shift from problem resolution to the identification of solutions.

A mental health worker, such as a school or clinical psychologist, social worker, or counselor, can serve as a solution-oriented consultant. The role of the consultant is to work with family members and school personnel to help them identify solutions through selective use of language. For example, "problems" are described as "difficulties"; "complaint" is used to denote an individual's response to unsuccessful previous attempts to alleviate difficulties. Assessment, intervention, and evaluation of concerns are mediated through verbal strategies, in the context of solution-oriented interviews.

Several potential techniques are available to move the home and school toward finding solutions rather than analyzing details of a problem. Based on the early work of de Shazer (1982, 1988) and O'Hanlon and Weiner-Davis (1989), attempts are made to change the "viewing" of the complaint by home and school participants, and/or the student's "doing" the behavior that surrounds the complaint.

Techniques for *changing the viewing* of the complaint are focused primarily on helping individuals alter their subjective reality or beliefs about why things occur as they do. According to theory, their beliefs influence their behaviors and impede their ability to consider solutions on their own. Reframing (see Chapter 4) is a common strategy used by solution-oriented brief therapists to help individuals modify their subjective beliefs. Various forms of reframing include "normalizing" or "depathologizing" the behavior or concern (i.e., suggesting that it is common or natural); "deconstruction" (i.e., acknowledging it and then breaking it down into smaller parts that are more manageable); and summarizing what has been done previously but now providing a solution-oriented framework (i.e., pointing out solutions that have worked in the past).

Other techniques are used by solution-oriented consultants to *change "the doing"* or behavior patterns surrounding the complaint. This includes focusing initial interview questions on exceptions to the complaint (i.e., asking about times when the problem does not occur); interrupting behavioral patterns (i.e., suggesting actions that change the time, frequency, or sequence of events surrounding the complaint); and attending to strengths and solutions that are evident in the participants' lives but may not have been used to deal with the complaint in the past.

The solution-oriented family–school consultation approach is structured and practiced in 10 phases, summarized here as described by Carlson et al. (1992).

Phase 1: Introduction

In this stage, the individual responsible for conducting the meeting introduces each participant and acknowledges the importance of each. The facilitator emphasizes that the unique and different perspectives each party brings to the meeting are valued, and that each participant is necessary for change. The parents are introduced as the experts in the home setting, and the teacher is introduced as the expert on the child's performance in the school setting.

Phase 2: Explanation of the Solution-Oriented Approach

During this stage, the solution-oriented approach is described. There is discussion on the notion that complaints are dissolvable, and that viable solutions are possible when all participants work together.

Phase 3: Joining

Joining involves acknowledging each person's point of view and matching the language used by that person. *Acknowledgment* requires good listening skills on the part of the facilitator. Likewise, matching involves at least three things: (1) mirroring the exact words of the speaker (e.g., "John has an attitude problem"); (2) using a speaker's metaphor later in the discussion (e.g., the speaker's comment about having a "rocky road ahead" could be referenced later by the facilitator's comment that the family now has a "four-wheel drive to handle the rocky road"; Carlson et al., 1992); and (3) matching sensory modalities (e.g., if a speaker refers to the need to "see things clearly," the facilitator may use a visual referent such as "taking a closer look").

Phase 4: Negotiating a Solvable Complaint

In this phase of the solution-oriented approach, the facilitator attempts to identify the complaint in concrete behavioral terms (e.g., by requesting that participants give a "video" description). Other techniques for negotiating a solvable complaint include searching for exceptions to the problem, identifying strengths of the child, questioning about past solutions that have worked, and/or visualizing the future without the concern.

Phase 5: Establishing a Solution Goal

Once the solvable complaint is established, the facilitator helps participants determine a mutually agreed-upon goal for positive change. Stating the goal in positive terms (stating what will happen, or behavioral change that will occur in the positive direction) is encouraged, rather than in negative terms (stating what will not happen, or behaviors that will decrease).

Phase 6: Gaining Agreement on the Smallest Change in the Direction of the Goal

During this phase, the facilitator works at gaining agreement on the smallest amount of change possible in the desired direction. This helps participants focus on noticing positive change and noting when it is observed.

Phase 7: Eliciting Meaningful Solutions toward Accomplishing the Smallest Change

When eliciting possible solutions, the facilitator assists participants in brainstorming possible strategies for initiating the change. Resources and strengths of the participants are identified to increase the probability that a viable solution will be found. Likewise, comments made in relation to exceptions to the behavior are revisited in an attempt to increase acceptability of possible solutions.

Phase 8: Clarifying Individual Responsibilities or Task Assignments

During this phase of solution oriented consultation, participants' understanding of their respective roles is clarified. Furthermore, the facilitator offers to consult with participants as they implement the agreed-upon solutions.

Phase 9: Follow-Up

In the follow-up phase, the consultant assesses the implementation of the solutions and progress toward the goal. The focus is on what is different, what has already changed, and what participants want continued. The main emphasis is on substantiating the fact that the participants did implement some small change. If no change occurred, the process can be recycled. Emphasis is initially focused on the goal of a small change, and not complete alleviation of the problem.

Phase 10: Evaluating and Recycling If Necessary

In the final phase, evaluation, the solutions are evaluated relative to the participants, their goals, and their respective systems. Advantages and disadvantages of the solution plan are noted, and additional planning occurs if no change has been noted.

In summary, "the hallmark of the solution-oriented approach is the consultant's shift from a detailed analysis of the problem to an active search for solutions . . . [using] techniques that introduce doubt into the existing perceptions of clients, reduce the uncontrollability of the behavior surrounding the complaint, and provide multiple solutions to the complaint, thus allowing the complainants to construct their own workable solutions" (Carlson et al., 1992; p. 200). The multiple values of the solution-oriented approaches convey an optimistic framework and attitude for resolving concerns of families and schools about students. They encourage open and constructive dialogue, consensus building, and attainment of achievable goals. Finally, they can be incorporated into several interactions among families and schools, including conferences, phone calls, and virtually all communication opportunities.

IDENTIFYING AND MANAGING CONFLICT

We have emphasized the importance of increasing frequency and quality of interactions between family members and school personnel to address concerns or to enhance learning experiences for students. One of the benefits of increased interactions is that greater opportunities for different ideas, perspectives, and resources can unfold. Parents and educators do have different vantage points; clear differences exist between homes and schools. Thus, we can expect differences to be revealed in parent–educator interactions. As interactions among family members and school personnel increase, and as differences become visible, the likelihood of some conflict is inevitable.

"Conflict" has been defined in many ways. Webster (1981) defined it as "competitive or opposing action . . . antagonistic state or action (as of divergent ideas, interests or persons)" (p. 235). In the educational literature, Friend and Cook (1992) defined conflict as "any situation in which one person (or group) perceives that another person (or group) is interfering with his or her goal attainment" (p. 118). Some may view conflict as negative and undesirable, and necessary to extinguish or avoid. However, we believe that conflictual situations can be considered *opportunities* for families and educators to explore objectives, priorities, ideas, feelings, and strategies. When addressed constructively, conflicts can actually strengthen the home–school relationship and lead to better outcomes than might have been achieved otherwise. The manner in which conflict is managed by individuals, and by the group, will determine its effect on the home–school relationship.

Conflict Management Styles

Individuals who participate in home–school interactions will likely vary in the manner in which they approach conflicts. There are generally five conflict management styles that vary along the dimensions of cooperativeness and assertiveness (Friend & Cook, 1992; Thomas & Kilmann, 1974), or importance of interpersonal goals and relationships. The five styles can be characterized as competitive, avoidant, accommodating, compromising, and collaborative:

1. Persons who use a *competitive style* of conflict management perceive their own goals as highly important and relationships as low in importance. These people tend to be highly assertive but low in cooperativeness. Called "sharks" by Johnson and Johnson (1991), such individuals try to overpower others by forcing them to accept the solution that they favor. A "win–lose" attitude is prevalent; sharks believe winning is of the greatest importance, even at the expense of the home–school relationship.

2. Some individuals try to avoid conflicts at all costs. *Avoidant styles* of conflict management are characterized as uncooperative and unassertive. These individuals tend to withdraw when faced with conflict, perceiving their own goals and those of the home–school relationship as low in importance. "Turtles" (Johnson & Johnson, 1991) often feel hopeless and helpless in conflicts, yet maintain a stance (facade) that all is well. In groups comprised primarily of avoiders, conflict continues because, typically, no one is willing to address and resolve it. In such situations, conflict can fester and interfere with effective communication and relationship building over time.

3. In an approach to conflict characterized as an *accommodating conflict management style*, individuals, called "teddy bears" by Johnson and Johnson (1991), believe the relationship is more important than their own personal goals, and thus acquiesce to avoid conflict and maintain harmony. Their common interpersonal style is cooperative and unassertive.

4. Compromising styles of conflict management are characterized by a balance of assertiveness and cooperativeness. Persons who espouse this interpersoanl style consider both maintenance of relationships and attention to personal goals as moderately important. They tend to sacrifice some of their own ideas and solutions and demand that others do the same. A "common ground" is pursued, and issues are addressed with an emphasis on the "middle of the road."

5. Individuals who engage in *collaborative styles of conflict management* are both highly assertive and cooperative. They value the importance of relationships as well as their own goals. According to Johnson and Johnson (1991), "owls" (the wise ones!) perceive conflict as an opportunity to seek better solutions and achieve enhanced outcomes. Consistent with our view of home–school collaboration, this style enables parents and teachers to share ideas openly, collectively discuss alternative perspectives, and manage differences constructively. The extent to which parties can address conflicts collaboratively is partly dependent upon the degree of trust present in relationships. The importance of building and strengthening relationships with families throughout a child's educational trajectory, and not only in the face of problems, is again highlighted.

In order for relationships to be characterized as collaborative, family members and educators must be efficacious at behaving both assertively and collaboratively. Research has suggested that teachers with a high degree of self-efficacy are effective at collaborating with parents (Ames, 1993), and parents with a high level of self-efficacy see themselves as effective collaborators in their children's education (Hoover-Dempsey & Sandler, 1997). Educators can support parents' collaboration skills by structuring a dialogue around their concerns, encouraging their input, reinforcing their ideas, and communicating the need for their involvement.

Strategies for Dealing with Conflict

It is often difficult to know the most efficacious way of dealing with tense or conflictual situations. Several strategies have been offered by psychologists and educators; we summarize some specific actions here. The actions reviewed include preserving the relationship, using effective communication skills, problem solving, and employing a mediator.

Preserving the Relationship

Generally speaking, the most important consideration when addressing conflict is to focus on the situation, or issue, and not the individual parent, teacher, or student. It is often natural to lose sight of the problem or issue at hand when issues are emotionally charged and personal. Comments such as "that parent is impossible!" or "That teacher doesn't like my child," personally attack the other party and impede an individual's ability to see alternative perspectives or engage in open dialogue. On the other hand, a focus on the situation recognizes that all parties (parents, teachers, and students) have shared interest, responsibility, and goals for addressing the concern. Retaining that emphasis may compel individuals to participate from a "team" or partnership approach (invoking an "us" orientation) rather than in isolation (leading to an "us vs. them" stance). Likewise, looking for ways to understand the other's perspective and to communicate that understanding will generate opportunities to deescalate potentially conflictual situations and result in positive and productive outcomes.

Using Effective Communication Skills

Communication was discussed extensively in Chapter 4. It is essential that communication remain open, calm, respectful, and genuine. Skills such as active listening, empathizing, using clear verbal and nonverbal messages, paraphrasing, and summarizing are important. Active listening and the use of open-ended questions can be helpful in obtaining information, perspectives, opinions, feelings, and ideas. The use of empathy (i.e., reflecting the feelings behind speakers' messages, such as a parent's underlying frustration or disappointment with his or her child's learning difficulties) can be very instrumental in communicating understanding, which can increase the potential for participants' joining together. Clarity in messages through concreteness (a focus on specific, observable issues) keeps the discussion explicit and minimizes misunderstanding and confusion.

Paraphrasing during conflict is important to convey understanding of feelings and concerns. Summarizing main issues after discussing them helps participants remain focused and move the discussion along in a positive direction. Main concerns, different perspectives, points of agreement and disagreement, and agreed-upon actions or solutions can be summarized.

Welch and Sheridan (1995) discussed the "pause button technique" that encourages communication about the process when tense or unproductive communications begin to emerge. This technique encourages an individual to "postpone the task-oriented focus of the group to request attention to interpersonal conflict or confusion. During this 'time out' or 'pause' from the primary goals of the team, individuals express concerns regarding the manner in which the group is processing information" (p. 130). Essentially, it allows participants to stop, comment on what is being communicated verbally or nonverbally, and request attention to that relationship factor before resuming discussion of the task or problem. For example, when a parent folds his or her arms and rolls his or her eyes, a person on the team may "press the pause button" by commenting that he or she notices that the parent seems unhappy with what is being suggested, and further stating that it will be important to clarify that feeling before moving ahead to make sure that participants agree on the direction that the discussion is going. Once these feelings are aired and understood, the team can resume the task-oriented nature of the discussion.

Problem Solving

Throughout this chapter, proactive problem-solving strategies are offered across several contexts to provide a structure for enhancing opportunities for parents' meaningful dialogue and participation. Conflict situations present one context wherein a structured approach can facilitate a constructive interaction and lead to effective solutions. The steps of consultative problem solving presented earlier in this chapter (i.e., identify and define the problem/concern; analyze conditions surrounding the concern; brainstorm alternative solutions; select the most appropriate solution and develop a specific plan; implement the plan; evaluate outcomes) provide a useful template. When addressing a conflictual situation, the problem-solving steps may focus on the desired outcome or goal (using a conjoint consultation or solution-oriented framework)— using the same approach as systematically resolving issues. The following steps may be useful in conflictual situations:

1. *Identify the desired outcome or goal.* Why are the individual parties coming together, and what can both educators and parents agree on regarding a desired outcome? For example, if a school counselor is concerned about the level of fighting in which a student is engaged, and the parents are concerned that the student's teachers do not do enough to help him work out problems, all can

likely agree upon is that they share a goal of wanting the student to have positive peer relationships at school.

2. *Explore values and perspectives around the goal.* What do parents value about the goal? What do teachers and school personnel believe is important? On which values and perspectives is there agreement, and on which is there disagreement? For example, if parents want their child to learn how to solve problems calmly on his own, and the teachers want to retain peace on the playground, differences of learning and safety arise. It is important to note again that families and schools can share values but disagree on issues or priorities. Oftentimes in schools, in placing efforts on specific details, individuals lose sight of the bigger picture of shared values and mutual goals. A focus on overarching objectives and common values, even in light of different perspectives, can support efforts toward constructive resolution of conflict.

3. *Discuss factors that enhance or impede goal attainment.* Often, there are specific, identifiable factors that can serve to support the attainment of shared goals. These are often resources that are available in the environment but for some reason are overlooked. Likewise, there may be influences that can deter or impede participants' abilities to reach the desired outcome. These variables in the environment can interfere with a solution and may need to be addressed. Whenever possible, identifying ways to enhance the use of facilitators and circumvent or alter deterrents will support goal attainment. For example, the availability of structured social skills lessons in classrooms focusing on problem solving may be a potentially useful resource that can facilitate students' learning appropriate conflict management skills. However, the failure to prompt and encourage use of such skills on the playground, with a concomitant focus on punitive strategies, can deter a child's attempts.

4. *Explore alternatives or options for achieving goal.* Once goals, values, resources, and deterrents are identified, the task of exploring options becomes much more manageable. As with all steps of the problem-solving process, the focus is on what can be done proactively. Considering how the options affect the home and the school systems, and the degree to which they might help achieve the desired outcome, is also necessary. Finally, determining the feasibility of the options (including necessary resources and their availability, such as time, materials, and persons) is an important prerequisite to selecting an alternative.

5. *Developing a plan.* Oftentimes, a main objective for coming together in a formal meeting between parents and educators is to

leave the meeting with some type of mutually determined plan in place. The strategy of identifying concerns concretely, establishing goals, determining resources and deterrents, and exploring alternatives typically leads to a reasonable plan. However, it is also important to realize that it is not always possible for all parties to have all of their wishes met. The process of establishing an open, trustful relationship within which collaborative interactions can operate (those that focus on both shared goals and maintenance of the relationship) will override the proclivity to focus only on personal agendas.

6. *Evaluate movement towards goal.* As with any problem or concern that is addressed by educators and parents, it is important that follow-up occur. Oftentimes, a great deal of energy is spent on the previous steps, a plan is established, but little to no follow-up occurs. This undermines the conflict management process because it precludes the possibility of ensuring adequate resolution of the issue. Engaging in structured evaluation activities also maintains open communication channels and allows for ongoing feedback and input.

Employing a Mediator

Although we believe that the strategies suggested heretofore maximize the potential to manage conflict effectively, some situations present either extremely intense or intractable differences, making the calm resolution of conflict unrealistic (Margolis & Shapiro, 1989). In these cases, a third party may be instrumental in helping parents and educators work through their difficulties. The "mediator" should be a neutral party, from outside of the school, who can help structure the communications, monitor affect, maintain order, and promote peaceful resolution.

SUPPORTING FAMILIES

Successful home learning environments were well described in Chapter 2. Given the strength of correlations between students' opportunities to learn at home and indicators of school performance, Rich (1987) contended that fostering positive home learning environments is the "meat and potatoes" of parent involvement. Epstein (1995) identified home learning activities as the one type of endeavor for which there is empirical support for impacting students' school performance. Deslandes, Royer, Potvin, and

Leclerc (1999) found that involvement in learning activities at home predicts grades and time spent on homework for both general and special education adolescents. Both Clark's (1990) finding that high achieving low income students spend a significant amount of time outside of school engaged in constructive learning activities during the academic year and Entwisle and Alexander's (2000) finding that summer learning opportunities widen the achievement gap over time for students suggests that enhancing learning at home may be a viable way to address equity issues for students. Furthermore, enhancing learning at home and school is one of the primary objectives of the National Education Goal 8. Toward this end, it is critical that parents be involved in activities that directly focus on student learning (i.e., academic and motivational support for learning), and not just in activities that indirectly support student learning (e.g., volunteering at school, taking parent classes).

Focus on Socialization Experiences

What does it mean to enhance learning at home? Particularly poignant here is the socialization of achievement in poor and minority students. In this book, we have suggested that parents and school personnel are educators, but not all education is schooling. Consistent with systems theory, we have referred to the critical nature of out-of-school and in-school time, the informal education provided by families and the formal education provided by schools, and the necessary home and school inputs for students' school performance. The work of Bempechat, Graham, and Jimenez (1999) is particularly relevant here. In their study of 1,000 fifth- and sixth-grade, successful (i.e., no grades lower than C) low-income students from four ethnic backgrounds, they examined students' attributions for success and failure, math performance, and the role of parents' academic and motivational support for learning, for the purpose of describing messages that socialize students as learners.

They found that the high achievers in this sample, regardless of ethnicity, attribute success to ability and effort in the face of challenge; they attribute failure to lack of effort rather than lack of ability. They also found that students who received the most academic support for learning at home had the lowest math performance. Based on their results, they suggested that (1) unsolicited, intense, frequent help from parents can be interpreted by students as evidence of their own low ability; (2) children/youth need encouragement, interest, less direct help, and more motivational support at home (e.g., regulating time, so that schoolwork is a priority); and (3) the issue may be the timing of when parents get involved. If parent involvement at home with learning and schoolwork increases at the point when a child's school performance is poor, parents are placed in a reactive rather than a proactive stance. They also suggest that too much parental support deprives children of the opportunity to learn from mistakes. They advocate the importance of effortful learning, which provides children with the message that learning is a process requiring sustained effort, persistence and diligence in face of challenge; practice and understanding that mistakes are part of the process, and delay of gratification.

In her book, *Against the Odds*, Janine Bempechat (1998) provides much food for thought about working effectively with families. In her attempt to understand the power of messages from parents, she asks (but does not answer) many questions, including the following: How do parents encourage their child's success in school? How do negative attitudes about learning develop? How hard do children have to try to do well in school? How do parents prepare children for the tasks in school? What is the parental understanding of the schooling process? What is the parental understanding of their own roles and responsibilities? She challenges the reader to recognize that poverty does not imply family dysfunction and that different cultures understand the purpose of education, as well as their role, differently. Also, she suggests important lessons for parents and teachers to deliver in the socialization process of students as learners: Set education as the family's top priority; let children try and learn from their mistakes; orient children to the process of learning; maintain high expectations and standards; encourage a healthy self-perception of ability (i.e., awareness of strengths and weaknesses); practice cultural sensitivity; and strengthen home–school partnerships, particularly by providing children with mutual support and consistent messages about the value of education.

Focus on Content and Process

Developing positive family learning environments has been advocated by Kellaghan and his colleagues (1993) as a way to connect with or reach all families, because it may often not be possible for parents to come to school, especially during scheduled times for events. They advocate the use of a home process approach that entails introducing more school-relevant tasks in the home. Specifically, they found that the work habits of the home (routine and priority for schoolwork), academic guidance and support, stimulation to explore and discuss ideas and events, language environment, and academic aspirations and expectations were behaviors and conditions in the home that best predicted school learning. These home process variables parallel school factors that positively influence student achievement (Christenson & Christenson, 1998). There is increasing support for the fact that when home and school share a similar emphasis on motivation and learning, children and youth perform optimally. The corollary is also true: When home and school provide conflicting or inconsistent messages about learning, particularly effortful learning, children are likely to suffer in their school performance (Hansen, 1986). The influence of Vygotsky's (1962) emphasis on optimal environmental conditions for learning has now been broadened to include family learning environments.

The degree to which the home environment is a learning environment is a significant, positive correlate of student success in school. Although social scientists have long known the correlates of learning success, the general public has not. Although we agree with the importance of informing parents about ways to foster academic and motivational support at home, we also believe that how this is done is critical. How we support families to enhance learning at home is different than home support for learning. For example, if parents cannot help due to specific circumstances (e.g., working two jobs), a supportive strategy is to identify, with the parents' help, an individual who serves as a contact with the school and supports the student's learning in out-of-school hours. Furthermore, our actions should not just be directed at what families can do; sharing information on academic and motivational support at school, and the congruence between home and school messages for learning, are equally important.

Possible Practices for Supporting Families

Effective practices for enhancing learning at home and school depend on (1) adopting a proactive stance with respect to information parents and school personnel need, and (2) communicating with, not to, families. Bempechat et al. (1999) have demonstrated that "poor parents, regardless of ethnicity, actively engage in cognitive socialization by assisting their children with schoolwork when performance is low. However, depending on ethnicity, parents bring different approaches to the task of academic socialization, approaches that are no doubt guided by cultural and contextual conceptions of achievement" (p. 155). They remind us that some families provide a family context in which the home process variables are internalized—they may not need to be proffered explicitly.

Examples of possible practices for enhancing consistency in learning at home and school are a well-designed media campaign, home–school–student partnership contracts, workshops, and encouragement of home support for learning by inviting parental assistance.

Media Campaigns

Dorothy Rich (1993), of the Home and School Institute, has repeatedly challenged educators to establish an infrastructure for enhancing student learning. She defined infrastructure as creating new formal relationships between schools and community, and suggested examples that include a media campaign about the critical role played by families, staff development for teachers, parent support groups, involvement of senior citizens and the larger community, and use of home learning activities, particularly the program, MegaSkills (Rich, 1988).

A well-designed, carefully crafted media blitz serves to reinforce the tone that both home and school influences are important for school learning, and that there must be consistency in messages between key socializing agents. It also provides an unambiguous message about ongoing, frequent, and regular home support for learning. Sample practices include a regular "Did You Know?" column in the principal/classroom newsletters; Teachers Involving Parents in Schoolwork (TIPS) sheets specifying parent, teacher, and student roles that accompany some assignments (Epstein, 1987); local newspaper columns with contributions from students, parents, and educators; and availability/dissemination of handouts about presenting concerns for students (see *Helping Children at Home and School: Handouts from Your School Psychologist*; Canter & Carroll, 1998). Variety in presenting home and school influences and user-friendly messages are beneficial for supporting student learning.

Partnership Contracts

Partnership contracts have appeared in the literature under different names, including pledges, compacts, agreements, and contracts. They are not new to educators, who are accustomed to writing behavioral and academic contracts for individual students. The newer dimension may be to implement home–school–student contracts proactively (beginning of the year) and systemwide. Interested readers are encouraged to consult the U.S. Department of Education (1997) publication, *A Compact for Learning*, which contains sample contracts, clearly articulated procedures, and troubleshooting ideas. Materials may be obtained by calling (800–USA–LEARN) or visiting the U.S. Department of Education website (http://www.ed.gov/G2K/community).

The benefits provided by this practice consist of the invitation to parents and students, clarification of roles and responsibilities among the partners, a clear focus on student goals and progress, and a useful tool for communication about students' learning. Issues relate to determining the roles and responsibilities of the partners and developing a system for consistent monitoring of implementation. The use of contracts provides an opportunity to introduce and discuss conditions across home and school that influence student learning in parents', teachers', and students' decision-making process. Both the Parents in Touch program (Warner, 1991) in the Indianapolis school district and Operation Higher Achievement (Walberg, Bole, & Waxman, 1980) found that achievement gains were greatest when contracts were used systemwide and careful monitoring was in place. Finally, the intent and application of contracts to other school practices in working with families is encouraged. For example, although parents sign IEPs for their children, the IEP does not designate specific responsibilities for the family. Is there any reason, if mutually determined, why doing so would be inappropriate?

Workshops

Epstein (1995) suggested, "'Workshop' must mean more than a *meeting* about a topic held at the school building at a particular time. 'Workshop' may also mean making information about a topic available in a variety of forms that can be viewed, heard, or read anywhere, any time, in varied forms" (p. 705). This redefinition alters the far-too-common thinking that workshops are the only standard parent training or course offerings through community education to which school personnel make recommendations to parents, especially when students present with related concerns. Workshops now include information sharing about children and youth and their world of schooling, and can be offered in a variety of formats. Thus, when parents participate in a regularly scheduled workshop (i.e., meeting) and miss a session or are nonattendees at an orientation night, it is more common for schools to have a mechanism for providing them with information (e.g., phone call, home visit, printed material). Also, workshops include specifically designed course offerings, casual parent–educator conversation hours and question–answer sessions, and parent-support-parent groups supervised by school or community professionals.

It is important to organize the extensive database about family learning environments in a user-friendly and doable format. One possibility is to work with a small group of interested parents to develop "M&M" workshop offerings. M&M's consist of the following: Be a good role model; motivate your child; monitor your child's school performance; and maintain contact with teachers. Table 5.7 presents some home support ideas from the SAF-T project (Christenson, 1994), categorized under the M&Ms.

Several guidelines may be followed to create connections for student learning in workshops. To empower parents, it is imperative to provide structure as well as flexibility and to incorporate parent sharing of strategies and ideas generated during the meeting time. In addition, workshop facilitators can keep the focus on improving performance of the student in the school setting; invite parent assistance, and sharing with other parents, to solve a concern (e.g., low task-completion rates); and discuss parent-determined topics. Providing support for parents in the way of transportation, food, incentives, varying schedules, and ongoing communication is extremely important to maximize the success of workshops (Goodman, Sutton, & Harkavy, 1995).

An excellent way to make initial contact with families, especially if they have felt alienated from schools, or if their children have had learning and behavior problems across grade levels, is to invite parents to attend a meeting where they will learn about their children's school programming. Consider featuring their children in the explanation. For example, one of us (SLC) implemented parent meetings for parents of middle-school-age children identified with severe emotional/behavioral disabilities. Project personnel invited parents to attend a dinner meeting with teachers to learn about a five-step problem-solving strategy that the students were learning to manage anger and to handle frustration constructively, while striving to meet task demands at school. Several students demonstrated the strategy using different scenarios. Parents asked questions and, at the request of a parent, discussed the relevance of using the strategy to manage anger at home. This

TABLE 5.7. M&Ms: Creating a Learning Environment

Be a good role model.

- Complete chores that require learning in front of your child.
- Read.
- Balance a checkbook.
- Write letters.
- Look up information.
- Use a computer.
- Discuss the effort taken to accomplish a personal goal.
- Discuss the value and purpose of education.
- Voice a positive attitude toward the teacher and school.
- Make schoolwork and learning a priority.

Motivate your child.

- Show interest in your child's learning.
- Spotlight success.
- Create a balance of study and play.
- Emphasize effort and ability over just ability.
- Reinforce progress toward a goal, not just perfection (100%).

Monitor your child's performance.

- Create a niche for studying.
- Keep good learning/research resources handy.
- Monitor work/TV schedules.
- Check homework and school papers.
- Call teachers for an update, or if concerned.
- Schedule a conference.

Maintain contact with teachers.

- Meet your child's teachers.
- Determine an appropriate communication system.
- Discuss roles and responsibilities (plan the partnership).
- Ask for suggestions on how to support student learning.

led to a list of parent-desired topics for helping children be more successful at school and at home that project personnel addressed throughout the school year. Clearly, relationship building rather than a school-determined agenda led to the success of this effort, which was measured by the active participation of a high percentage of parents.

Fostering Home Support for Learning

Inviting parental assistance to address a school-based (or school observed) concern is another way to encourage home support for learning and to coordinate learning at home and at school. Parent–educator problem solving (PEPS) is one such example. The purpose of PEPS was to create a partnership between family and school, and to use problem solving as a vehicle for fostering an educative home environment (Christenson, 1995). This family–school meeting emphasizes sharing information and resources to help the student achieve a goal. It is unique because it is characterized by (1) inviting parent assistance and creating an opportunity to explain how the home environment fosters student learning and performance in school, (2) encouraging options for parent support, (3) allowing parents to select ways that work best for them, and (4) focusing future communication on achieving a mutual goal. The facilitator sets a positive tone by maintaining "our" (vs. "your" or "my") goal, skills "we" want to encourage and teach, and clarity of roles and responsibilities in supporting student learning. This structure does not require that parents and educators work exclusively on a common goal. Rather, they can also work independently; the key is that they are engaged in co-communication and have a shared vision about the student's behavior and school performance. An example of the PEPS steps appears in Table 5.8.

PEPS can be helpful as an entree to discuss both homework issues and encourage the use of home learning activities. With traditional homework, the requirement for parents is to monitor/supervise task completion, whereas in home learning activities, including interactive homework, parents are required to be actively involved. Smrekar (1996) preferred the use of home learning activities because parents have little time to monitor traditional homework assignments on a daily basis. Therefore, she suggested that monitoring task completion could be made more realistic for family and school by revamping traditional homework to interactive homework (e.g., family interview, science projects, family biography). Furthermore, she noted that the value of interactive homework assignments lies in encouraging a stimulating family learning environment. In her TIPS process, Epstein (1987) identified the benefit of interactive homework as enhancing communication between parent and child about what the child was learning.

Professionals consulting with families and teachers with respect to the design of homework or home learning programs will want to consider the literacy level of parents, degree of resources available in the homes, and the kind of support families need to be successful, particularly in the secondary grades, when these issues are often more dominant. Scott-Jones (1995a, 1995b) classified

TABLE 5.8. Parent–Educator Problem Solving (PEPS) Steps

Introduction

+ Rapport building
+ Describe school- (or parent-) based concern:
    + Express concerns as learning goals (what the child needs to learn; what we want to teach the child).
    + Invite parent assistance and express interest in working as partners (opportunity to explain the effect of family influences and synergism between home and school on children's learning).

Identification

+ Identify all issues and perspectives related to school-based concern:
    + Gather parent input and reframe as learning goals.
+ Identify mutual learning goals:
    + List and prioritize goals.
    + Select one goal to work on collaboratively.
    + May decide parent and teacher will work independently on some goals.
+ Check for understanding:
    + Restate mutual goal as a discrepancy between actual and desired child behavior/performance.
    + Goal is to establish a common effort to close this discrepancy.
    + Check on other contributing factors relevant to concern.

Selection

+ Generate possibilities for a solution by brainstorming, listing all ideas, and engaging in no evaluation.
+ Select idea(s) from the list.
+ Parent and teacher choice is essential.
+ Provide supportive facilitation: Ask parents and teachers: What resources and/or information would you find helpful for attaining our goal?
+ Mutual decision making for community resource involvement often occurs.

Implementation / evaluation

+ Describe the solution plan.
+ Review roles and responsibilities.
+ Engage in perception checking.
+ Determine an evaluation date.
+ Implement.
+ Identify way to make contact, if necessary (e.g., no phones).
+ Follow-up by a case manager/monitor/facilitator.
+ Evaluate effectiveness of plan.
+ Did the discrepancy close?
    + If not, revise the plan (no blaming).
    + If so, celebrate!

---

various parental roles as valuing, monitoring, helping, and doing. With this breakdown, educators can find a way to affirm all parents' participation as well as consider some parents' overparticipation (i.e., doing the work). For example, if parents cannot help with homework because of literacy or work issues, their value for learning can be demonstrated by helping to find an individual who could assist, or by discussing with students what they are studying. Also, poverty is pervasive in America for many families; therefore, the need to offer resources such as a lending library or checkout system for learning packets at home are examples of how school personnel can be responsive to these family circumstances.

School personnel are finding it beneficial to attend to the kind of support parents need to be successful in implementing homework support programs or home learning activities. Two secondary-level examples in suburban school districts in a metropolitan area in Minnesota illustrate the creativity and commitment of many teachers. A ninth-grade algebra teacher offered monthly curriculum nights to parents of students in one his classes. The purpose was to "teach" parents how to respond to their adolescents' questions about key concepts and procedures introduced in class during the next month. Although both parents and the teacher strongly supported this approach, it has been a challenge to expand the program beyond the offering to one class. Good ideas often require resource support for teachers. The second example focuses on enhancing home learning. An eighth-grade English teacher created a book club for parents and students. Of those involved, many were very enthusiastic. Increased, positive parent–adolescent communication was an unanticipated side effect of this intervention, particularly from the perspective of the parents. One parent noted that she now had something interesting and fun about which to communicate with her daughter.

Creating effective homework and home learning opportunities requires careful attention to the goals and constraints that exist in both home and school environments (Olympia, Sheridan, & Jenson, 1994). Because of the emphasis on enhanced learning at home and at school in Goal 8 and the documented accrued benefits of doing so for students, the challenge is well worth our effort. Problem solving with parents is essential to achieve real parental inclusion. If parents help develop the goals, they are more likely to concur with them, be invested in them, and foster them at home (Eccles & Harold, 1996). Interested readers will find *Sanity Savers for Parents: Tips for Tackling Homework* (Olympia, Jenson, & Hepworth-Neville, 1996) and *Study Buddies: Parent Tutoring Tactics*

(Bowen, Olympia, & Jenson, 1996) to be helpful resources in designing structured, coordinated home programs.

Focus on Student Involvement

Bempechat's (1998) work raises critical questions not only about the unique role played by culture, context, and motivation in preparing children and youth to handle the task demands of school, but also the role of students in family–school partnerships. Although the literature is quite clear conceptually that student learning, development, and success are the reason for creating family–school partnerships (Epstein & Connors, 1995), in practice, the degree to which students are actively included varies remarkably. Weiss and Edwards (1992) have challenged school personnel to view efforts systemically; therefore, students are always included in family–school meetings and conferences. Other problem-solving consultation approaches (e.g., Christenson, 1995; Carlson et al., 1992; Sheridan et al., 1996) tend to recommend, but not require, student involvement. Student attendance at traditional parent–teacher conferences is becoming more common, and, the recent use of student-led conferences provides a very active role for the student and has the unique characteristic of emphasizing the student's personal responsibility for learning (*Education Daily*, 1993). An example of a student led conference format is illustrated in Table 5.9.

Minke (2000) clearly reinforced previously articulated reasons for the central role of students in the family–school partnership (e.g., Epstein & Connors, 1995) when she described the following benefits to having students participate: observing significant adults working together to help, hearing adults share their expectations of students, contributing solutions that increase their investment in the outcome, and witnessing processes and not having to rely on others' interpretations. There seems to be no doubt that strong family–school connections for students do not remove personal responsibility for student learning. Students are the leading actors in their school performance; parents and teachers are the supporting actors. Bempechat (1998) cogently and poignantly cautions educators and families that there is no substitute for a consistent message that time and effort are necessary for optimal learning. Although all students do not attain the same level of achievement, they all can show learning progress with standards and supports from their parents and educators. Her message is direct: Educators need to work effectively with families to under-

TABLE 5.9. Student-Led Conference Format

Introduction

- Student introduces his or her parent(s) to the home-base teacher.
- Student articulates the purpose of the conference: to report student learning progress and performance in school.
- An agenda is provided for the participants.

Academic progress review

- The student explains and illustrates progress in academic subjects using a portfolio system (work samples, progress report, teacher comments).
- Student presents information in the order of his or her daily schedule.
- The home-base teacher takes notes and cues the student to provide specifics for each class.

Behavior review (if an issue)

- Student describes school rules.
- Student explains his or her goal.
- Student explains how he or she is working to achieve the goal.

Parent perspectives

- Comments are solicited from the parent.
- Questions and concerns are addressed.
- Goals may be modified or established.

Summary

- The written summary by the home-base teacher is shared with the parent and student.
- A copy is placed in the student's educational file.

Follow-up

- A different teacher contacts the parent shortly after the conference.

stand the joint purpose of education and to provide students with a consistent, congruent message that allow them to become socialized as learners. Others have challenged us to carry out this action as well (Maehr & Midgley, 1996; Phelan et al., 1998).

HELPING TEACHERS IMPROVE COMMUNICATION AND RELATIONSHIPS WITH PARENTS

Throughout this book, we have emphasized the importance of open, clear communication with families. Consultants working to enhance home–school partnerships have opportunities to facilitate positive communications with families in several ways, including in their own dialogue and information sharing with families, and in helping teachers communicate effectively with parents. They can model effective communication skills and provide guidance on the types of information that are helpful for parents.

Guidelines for effective communication with families were presented in Chapter 4. Essentially, each guideline (e.g., maintain a positive, open orientation; consider tone as well as content; emphasize a "win–win" orientation; keep the focus on the child's performance; underscore the notion of shared responsibility) can be framed into an opportunity for modeling. Interacting with other school personnel allows us to pursue opportunities to orient staff in ways to think about, communicate with, and involve families.

The strategies for attaining relationship goals in conjoint behavioral consultation, discussed earlier in this chapter, and in Table 5.6, provide examples of what consultants can do to promote a positive communication style about families in schools. For example, using words such as "us" and "we" connotes shared responsibilities and may suggest to teachers a different way of thinking about the relationship. Modeling effective listening skills with parents is also useful. When parents express a concern or a problem, school and community consultants can acknowledge the concern, ask for clarification, and emphasize a willingness to work together. This is more productive than taking a defensive stance, refuting the concern, or arguing about the accuracy of the issue. Throughout the interaction, comments such as "I like your suggestion" and "I see your point" suggest that the educator is taking the perspective of the parent in a concrete way.

Reframing, also described in Chapter 4, is a useful communication strategy when working with teachers and parents. For example, a teacher's negative interpretations of families (such as a teacher's interpretation of a parent as "nosey") can be reframed (e.g., into a constructive interpretation, focusing on the parent's interest in his or her child's school day) to retain a positive orientation and encourage perspective taking. The notion of similarities across settings can also be enhanced by pointing out the similarity of examples provided by parents and teachers. Likewise, consultants can provide observations that concerns expressed by parents and teachers, even when presented in a different way, based on the different home and school contexts, are highly congruent. Finally, reinforcing both parents and teachers for their efforts at working together is essential. It not only provides the sincere message that such efforts are important and worthwhile but it also encourages continued partnerships over time.

Various nonverbal strategies can be used to promote a partnership orientation with families. When in meetings with parents, seating arrangements can be important. For example, if parents and teachers sit next to each other, at a 90 degree angle, there are opportunities for both eye contact and closeness. As a facilitator of meetings, "shared eye contact" allows for glances between the parent and teacher when one or the other is talking, in contrast to gazing at only the speaker, which may leave the other party "out" when he or she is not talking. This also conveys the notion that what one person communicates about his or her setting or observations is also relevant to the other party.

A friendly, positive tone with families was emphasized by McWilliam et al. (1998) in their description of family–centered practice (see Chapter 3). This can be communicated to families through enthusiastic, encouraging, and genuine interactions. Optimistic, realistic, shared messages can convey positive connotations about the child, the family, and the relationship between the home and school systems. Positive notes home, or phone calls, can go a long way in fostering a sense of commitment to the student and to ongoing communications with the family (rather than communications that occur only when problems arise). Ensuring that parents know how to reach their child's teacher and others in the school (and vice versa) is yet another strategy that conveys a deep concern for communication and reciprocal information sharing. Likewise, it connotes the fact that parents have access to a resource in the school when they need it.

There will be times when teachers or other school staff must contact a parent with a concern. Effective strategies for communicating difficult information are essential. For example, a teacher may need to express concern about a child's lack of progress in an academic subject area. Or a playground volunteer may need to call a parent about a fight during recess that involved their child. Guidance and training in constructive (vs. confrontive) and helpful (vs. hurtful) communication strategies can assist staff in dealing with potentially negative encounters. Suggestions of such positive communication strategies that can be provided to teachers include the following:

- Always start with a positive message.
- Convey the desire to work together to help the child.

- ◆ Use good communication skills to promote cohesion.
  - ◆ Use common language, and refrain from speaking "above" the parent.
  - ◆ Use the parent's own words when possible.
  - ◆ Listen quietly to what the parent says, verbalizing initially only to convey understanding (such as through "mm-hmm," "OK," or other similar, minimal encouragers).
- ◆ Express the fact that the parent's input and perspective are very important.
- ◆ Respect that the family members are experts, that they are doing the best they can, and that they want what is best for their child.
- ◆ Clearly describe expectations for school behavior and ask the parents if they agree and can support the expectations.
- ◆ Keep in mind the responsibilities of each person.
- ◆ Avoid giving advice as much as possible.
- ◆ Ask the parent for help.
- ◆ Thank the parent for listening, caring, and helping.

These and related key communication tips are illustrated in a scenario in Appendix D, in which Cathryn Peterson, seventh-grade teacher at FAIR (Fine Arts Interdisciplinary Resource) School, describes her orientation to contacting and communicating with families.

Several additional opportunities exist for teachers to create positive communication channels with families. These include "Back to School" nights held several times throughout the year, handwritten invitations by students to invite their parents to be involved in school and learning activities, asking parents more than once for their involvement (rather than only once), written letters to parents in their native language, and the creation of bidirectional newsletters or other communication channels (e.g., weekly folders, phone trees).

CONCLUDING REMARKS

In this chapter, we have described seven broad actions to be taken to create essential connections between families and schools, and individual families and school personnel. We consider these and similar actions to be critical for promoting shared responsibility for children's learning. We contend that these actions are applicable to all families and schools, and on the behalf of all children. We recognize that "buy-in" for families outside the social mainstream is more complex and challenging (Comer et al., 1996). However, we also believe that if educators change their traditionally oriented practices with families to those that are characterized by inclusion and dialogue, disconnected families *and* educators will be able to form positive, realistic connections to socialize and support learners. Actions for connecting with uninvolved families are not necessarily qualitatively different. Rather, they may require more time, multiple efforts, and a variety of approaches. They may be more frequent and persistent, such as asking for help repeatedly over time, and not just once.

Responses from different families will also differ—some may participate readily and consistently; others may appear to be more sporadic in their responsiveness. An important message is that the effects of educators' efforts to form meaningful connections with families is relative. Establishing a relationship and promoting a positive home–school link even one time, in relation to one issue or objective, is a start. For some families, it may represent a first experience of the school as an inviting and welcoming place. To us, this is a major success that can be nourished and built upon throughout the remainder of the educational life of the child.

QUESTIONS TO CONSIDER

1. In a suburban middle school, low-task completion rates were common, particularly for seventh and eighth graders. The school had a homework policy, albeit one that was implemented inconsistently. Based on parent, student, and teacher input, homework policies were changed to begin a process for providing students with a consistent message about schoolwork in general and homework in particular. The family–school team garnered student, family, and school perspectives. The following is an example of communication to families and educators:

You told us homework is a problem. We agree.

Shared goal: To have students complete meaningful homework assignments on time and to hand the work in at the required time.

- ◆ Parents said: We do not know when our children have homework. We ask, but we often hear: "I did it at school or we didn't have any."

   - ◆ Teachers have agreed to assign homework every night, Monday– Thursday.

- Parents said: Sometimes the homework "bunches up." Some nights the homework is really light; other nights, my child has a lot of homework in every subject.

  - Teachers have agreed to rotate homework so that class periods 1, 2, and 3 assign homework on Monday and Wednesday, and class periods 4, 5, and 6 assign homework on Tuesday and Thursday. Homework is not to exceed 30 minutes per class. Parents and students have agreed to indicate when homework takes longer than expected.

- Parents said: I do not know what our role is. Are we to monitor work completion, help with homework, or quiz our children on the material?

  - Teachers have requested students to complete the assignments on their own. They appreciate it when parents support homework completion by helping their child structure a consistent time and place for homework, and monitoring work completion, but they have requested that parents avoid correcting the work or assisting extensively with assignments, unless specified by the teacher.

Action plan: To implement the new procedures and to evaluate the plan after 6 weeks. If you have comments to share, please contact Mr. Bennett at 768-6200, ext. 3.

Ask yourself:

- In what ways is the notion of parents and teachers as co-problem solvers evident in this case scenario?
- How is shared responsibility for learning and goal attainment demonstrated?
- What is the role of the student in this situation?
- What types of information do parents and teachers need to work together to successfully address homework problems?
- In what ways can this information be attained and shared?

2. Obtain copies of reports, memos, newsletters, or other communications that are sent home from your school. Consider the following:

   - What language is used to communicate information to parents? Does it convey an open and inviting tone, or one-way information sharing?
   - What family roles and responsibilities are implied? Are roles for participation implicit, explicit, or absent?
   - What opportunities for family input or interaction are present?
   - How can the communication be changed to promote a shared responsibility and partnership for learning (see Table 5.1 for ideas)?

Epilogue

♦

In this book, we have argued that the constructive family–school relationship is a concept, not a program or model. We believe educators must set a tone for positive connections between schools and families. Because parents and teachers both underestimate their place and piece in the puzzle, we suggest that the tone must underscore that both are essential to engaging students as learners and promoting successful school experiences. We have suggested that actions taken are affected by the degree to which the essential nature of "family and schools as partners" is clearly articulated. Ideally, schools have both a mission and policies that (1) embrace the importance of family–school relationships for promoting children's learning; (2) reflect the significance of families and contributions of schools to children's development; and (3) place family–school relationships front and center in their overall structure and organization. Similarly, families ideally have values for engaging in meaningful ways with school personnel and supporting and nurturing their children's education and development.

We have argued that it is time to "raise the bar" for children's performance in school, and for homes and schools to work together to enhance student achievement. Roles for families vary; in fact, they range from interest in their child's education and performance to interest in how the school (or district) functions and the achievement of students districtwide. Families have many options, some of which allow them to be involved in education through in-school (e.g., volunteering) or out-of-school experiences (e.g., providing a structured time for homework or talking about their child's school day) and opportunities. Other options for partnerships allow parents truly to be included (e.g., shared decision making with school personnel). Because of perceived differences in the conception of parental roles related to children's schooling, we have argued that the purpose for family and school working as partners must be explicit. Raising the bar, at a minimum, involves halting blame between families and schools for children's performance; establishing a shared, common perspective of children's educational experiences and performance; increasing shared responsibility for children's educational performance; and striving for balance by considering needs of families, educators, and students in decision making. Continual contact between home and school is foundational not only to prevent miscommunication but also to achieve "two-way learning." The latter provides the mechanism for parents and school personnel to learn from each other about the student, and how each system interacts with the student. It provides a mechanism for designing mutual support between family and school.

As a concept, constructive family–school relationships can take many forms; however, they consist of specific characteristics. Regardless of the particular family–school–student context, we believe that the probability for positive connections to exist among the players is highest when educators expect that families will be involved, invite active family participation, include families in decisions for their children, and are open to options for family involvement. In other words, school personnel do not set the agenda for family involvement or establish the role for family participation when the child is having academic or social difficulties. We have encouraged school personnel to question the effectiveness of their current outreach strategies, ask for assistance to address educational concerns, and seek advice from families about the kinds of information and support desired. As explained in previous chapters, we contend that school practices must provide families with access, voice, and ownership. And we favor actions that place parents and educators in a proactive rather than reactive stance with regard to children's school performance and behavior.

In that vein, we offered four components (approach, attitudes, atmosphere, actions) that reflect critical process variables for establishing school–family connections for children's learning. In Chapter 2, we described the necessary approach as one in which school personnel adopt an orientation based on systems theory, whereby family and school contexts are considered essential for socializing and supporting children as learners. In Chapter 3, we described the benefits of attitudes that are solution-oriented, proactive, and directed toward establishing a connection between home and school. In Chapter 4, we described how an inviting, welcoming, and communication-rich atmosphere is of central importance for creating a "climate of participation" (Batey, 1996) for families and between parents and educators. In Chapter 5, we explicated actions that raise the bar by asking parents to become involved and to take some responsibility for their children's education. The use of school-based practices that focus on shared responsibility represents a significant behavioral change for educators and can only be implemented successfully with input from school personnel and parents. Establishing shared responsibility for students' educational performance is contingent upon educators expecting and inviting parent involvement, but not mandating how parents (collectively or individually) should be involved. Shared goals, shared contributions, and shared accountability equate to the concept of shared responsibility as described in this book. Clearly, the four components are similar in that they maintain a mesosystemic focus for school practices, and specifically, a focus on the intersection of school and family with respect to school performance and behavior for children and adolescents. Also, we acknowledge the interrelationship of the components, and we speculate that the process for optimal school–family connections for children's learning attends to all components.

Our emphasis on process for developing school–family connections for student success, rather than a set of "best" activities, has been intentional. Also, each school community must decide what works in its context. Quite simply, the rights, roles and responsibilities, and resources for family, school, and students vary remarkably across educational contexts. The components have been explicated and are presented in their entirety as an "Inventory for Creating School–Family Connections" in Appendix E, so that school personnel and families can easily reproduce it.

Given the contextual nature of establishing constructive school–family connections for children's learning, we have chosen not to prescribe exactly what the inventory is or how it should be used. Rather, we believe it has several potential uses. For example, we envision that it could be useful as a needs assessment, a checklist for consideration by the family–school action team, or an organizational framework for staff development. A school is not just curriculum, tests, and graduation requirements. Learning is not just dependent upon what the students do. Both need good relationships between individuals to reflect optimal educational outcomes. Parents need to portray a positive attitude toward school and learning. Educators need to believe they can be successful with all students. Students need to complete work and persist in the face of challenges. Ideally, parents, educators, and students understand their roles and responsibilities, and have opportunities to dialogue and act collaboratively. We recognize that not all conditions in schools reflect a common effort toward shared goals. However, we believe school personnel can stimulate a new compact among families, educators, and students. We offer the inventory as a guide for discussing and creating the necessary positive connections for children's and adolescent's learning.

In 1999, a secondary-level English teacher in a class on collaborative family–school relationships taught by one of us (SLC) wrote:

> "The ideas of parents and teachers as co-teachers of the child; the importance of parents and teachers as both having a 'real' voice in the education of the child; the significance of continuous, sustained communication between parents and teachers; the importance of interdependence and cooperation in effective partnerships; the ability to recognize differences, not as deficits, but as opportunities to learn from one another; and the vital importance of a warm, inviting school and classroom climate are exciting. It seems that when these ideas are implemented in school, both parents and teachers feel empowered and partnerships are enhanced. I see these implications as truly part of a larger culture of a school. Ultimately, they need to be supported by administration but can be accomplished in the classroom. As I was reading, I was generating ideas for how I could turn some of these ideas into action in my classroom. Am I on the right track?

> ◆ Interactive homework (interviews, parents telling oral stories and students creating the written version; book clubs with child and family adult members; writing stories/poems together).
> ◆ Ask for parents to read student work and provide written comments and feedback on the student's writing development.
> ◆ Ask parents upfront, at the beginning of the year, what they need from me, and have them evaluate my performance in meeting these expectations.
> ◆ Communicate with parents what I and their child need from them in order to enhance student success.
> ◆ Assist parents in becoming involved in the school (e.g., don't just ask once, invite twice).

- ◆ Implement parent suggestions when possible and ask parents to be active participants in the implementation.
- ◆ Have students create handwritten invitations to invite/inform parents participation in school and learning activities.
- ◆ Create a student newspaper and have students write articles with other family members for submission, or have a parent column.
- ◆ Include students as much as possible, and communicate with parents and students immediately in the fall, or, if possible, before the beginning of the year.
- ◆ If necessary, provide initial letters to parents in their native language (Spanish, Hmong, etc.)."

Our response to this teacher is a resounding "yes!" As illustrated by one teacher's comments, we believe there is much interest on the part of families and schools to reduce the social and physical distance that exists in many schools and to form partnerships. To accomplish this, however, we recognize that time, trust, and tools for the partnership, such as leadership, administrative support, and staff development, are critical.

Schools can promote connections in the messages that are conveyed to families about partnerships. They can communicate clearly in their actions and words a desire for parents' active participation and ways that this can be achieved. They can also foster connections by communicating information to families about what happens at school, both in terms of macroissues (including school policies and events) and microissues (including activities in their child's classroom and requirements for homework). For meaningful connections to occur, families need information on the "what, why, how, and when" they can be involved. And schools need feedback on the feasibility and reality of the "what, why, how, and when." We have advocated that school personnel act in ways to preserve the relationship with parents. In particular, we have highlighted process, because we have encouraged educators to not be so focused on solutions for student concerns that they forget *the interaction process that can yield a sound product.* Clearly, educators want to solve students' concerns, but we believe that for them to expect that it will necessarily be resolved quickly, or their way, is shortsighted. Student referrals are increasingly complex and often involve multiple years of assessment and intervention.

The process of relationship building with families must start early and continue across an academic year, and across a child's entire academic experience. There are certainly challenges associated with this continuous, cumulative approach to family involvement. Numerous teachers are involved with each family, and the child and family undergo various developmental changes over the course of a child's academic lifespan. Policies and strategies within schools and districts that recognize the importance of ongoing family involvement and support can encourage the development of constructive, positive relationships. It is our hope that school psychologists will take the initiative to raise the bar for students' performance in school by heeding John Fantuzzo's (1999) advice to make the word "partner" a verb.

♦♦♦

NASP Position Statement on Home–School Collaboration: Establishing Partnerships to Enhance Educational Outcomes

♦

The National Association of School Psychologists is committed to increasing the academic, behavioral, and social competence of all students through effective home–school partnerships. Such partnerships involve collaboration among families, educators and community members to support students' educational and mental health needs. Unlike traditional "parent involvement" activities that emphasize passive support roles for parents, family–school collaboration involves families and educators actively working together to develop shared goals and plans that support the success of all students.

BENEFITS OF COLLABORATION

When families are involved in education, there are significant benefits for students, educators, and families. Students demonstrate more positive

Note. "Parent" is defined as any adult who fulfills a parenting role for a child; it should not be interpreted to mean only birth parents. "Educators" is used to emphasize that collaboration involves the entire school community, not just teachers.

attitudes toward school and learning, higher achievement and test scores, increased homework completion, and improved school attendance. Teachers report greater job satisfaction and higher evaluation ratings from parents and administrators. Parents experience better understanding of schools and improved communication with their children. Although it cannot be shown that family participation causes these benefits, these positive outcomes have been documented across families from diverse ethnic and socioeconomic backgrounds.

CHALLENGES OF COLLABORATION

Despite these many benefits, family-school collaboration is very difficult to attain. Families and educators often differ in their expectations, goals, and communication patterns, sometimes leading to frustration and misunderstanding among students, families, and educators. When these differences are not recognized and addressed, a lack of communication between home and school further divides and separates the two most vital support systems available to the student. Open communication is essential in order for educators and families to understand and respect each other's perspectives.

ESTABLISHING EFFECTIVE PARTNERSHIPS

The Role of Schools

Working together toward shared goals with shared power is the essential characteristic of effective home–school collaboration. The process requires ongoing planning, development, and evaluation. It also requires the allocation of adequate resources to assist families and teachers in fulfilling their partnership roles. Schools must take the lead in providing opportunities for collaborative partnerships to be developed and sustained through:

Providing a Positive Environment

It is the school's responsibility to provide a welcoming environment for all families. The school must send consistent messages to families that their contributions to forming effective partnerships are valued. Efforts are made to work collaboratively with all families, including those whose primary language is not English and those with limited literacy skills.

Supporting the Efforts of Families and Educators

Family participation increases when such participation is promoted by the school. Schools can encourage collaboration by eliciting and understanding families' perspectives and expectations. Multiple options for participation should be made available, with the recognition that individual families will support their children in different ways. Schools can foster an open dialogue between home and school and should provide opportunities for families to have decision-making roles in school governance. Resources must be provided by the school to support the collaborative efforts of families and educators (e.g., release time for teachers to meet with families in the community, development of a family support room in the school).

Increasing the Understanding of Diversity

Families come in many shapes and sizes with multiple perspectives, expectations, and communication styles. Schools need to provide education to staff and families that encourages understanding and celebration of diverse family forms, cultures, and ethnicities. When schools and families make the effort to understand and educate each other, they often find more similarities than differences. Collaboration is based in the assumption that families, children, and educators are doing the best they can; efforts are made to understand others' behavior and intentions rather than judge them as right or wrong.

Promoting a view of education as a shared responsibility: Home–school collaboration is not an activity; it is a process that guides the development of goals and plans. When collaboration is characterized by open communication, mutually agreed-upon goals, and joint decision making, education becomes a shared responsibility. Together, families and educators can discuss expectations for student achievement and their respective roles in helping students meet these expectations; they can develop programs to promote effective home–school–community partnerships that support positive academic, behavioral, and social competencies in all students; and they can engage in efforts to increase mutual respect, understanding, caring, and flexibility among families and the school community. When problems arise, they are addressed jointly by families, students, and educators in a respectful, solution-focused manner.

The Role of Families

Child rearing is both complex and difficult. Individual families face multiple challenges with unique sets of resources, skills, and preferences.

Therefore, it is unrealistic and potentially damaging to family–school relationships to take a "one size fits all" approach to collaboration. Roles for families should be broadly conceived, but individually applied. That is, educators and families should work together to develop an array of opportunities for families to participate meaningfully in their children's education. Such opportunities should be offered with the knowledge that families will differ in their choices; these differences must be understood to reflect individual families' needs and preferences. Potential avenues for family participation may include, but are not limited to:

- ◆ Active involvement in school decisions and governance
- ◆ Participation at school as volunteers and committee members
- ◆ Encouragement of leisure reading with their children
- ◆ Participation in school functions, athletics, and other extracurricular activities
- ◆ Monitoring homework completion
- ◆ Regular communication with school personnel about their child's progress
- ◆ Frequent communication with their children about academic and behavioral expectations and progress
- ◆ Participation as fully informed, decision-making members of problem-solving teams (e.g., IEP teams)
- ◆ Participation in adult educational opportunities offered by the school
- ◆ Active support of the school through communication, sharing resources and seeking partnership with educators

The Role of the School Psychologist

NASP encourages school psychologists to take part in national, state, and local efforts to define parent involvement in education as true collaborative partnerships among homes, schools, and communities. School psychologists need to advocate for increased home–school collaboration and identify strategies to encourage family participation by:

- ◆ Establishing school-based teams consisting of parents, educators, and community members that assess needs, develop priorities and plans, and implement joint efforts to improve educational outcomes for students
- ◆ Serving as a liaison to support communication among homes, schools, and communities
- ◆ Ensuring the meaningful participation of families in special education processes by providing decision-making opportunities for

families in assessment, intervention, and program planning activities

◆ Providing direct service to families regarding strategies that promote academic, behavioral, and social success across environments

◆ Working with administrators to ensure that sufficient resources are allocated to family–school collaboration efforts

◆ Pursuing and promoting continuing education on topics such as family interventions, multicultural issues, models of home–school collaboration, and parent education

SUMMARY

Home–school collaboration leads to improved student achievement, better behavior, better attendance, higher self-concept, and more positive attitudes toward school and learning. Successful home–school collaboration is dependent upon educators, families, and community members working together to understand each others' perspectives and to develop shared goals. NASP is committed to supporting collaboration among families, educators, and community members to promote positive educational outcomes for all children and youth.

♦♦♦

Checklist for Quality Indicators of the Six National Standards for Parent/Family Involvement

♦

STANDARD I: COMMUNICATING

Successful programs:

- ♦ Use a variety of communication tools on a regular basis, seeking to facilitate two-way interaction through each type of medium.
- ♦ Establish opportunities for parents and educators to share partnering information such as student strengths and learning preferences.
- ♦ Provide clear information regarding course expectations and offerings, student placement, school activities, student services, and optional programs.
- ♦ Mail report cards and regular progress reports to parents. Provide support services and follow-up conferences as needed.
- ♦ Disseminate information on school reforms, policies, discipline procedures, assessment tools, and school goals, and include parents in any related decision-making process.
- ♦ Conduct conferences with parents at least twice a year, with follow-up as needed. These should accommodate the varied schedules of parents, language barriers, and the need for child care.

- Encourage immediate contact between parents and teachers when concerns arise.
- Distribute student work for parental comment and review on a regular basis.
- Translate communications to assist non-English-speaking parents.
- Communicate with parents regarding positive student behavior and achievement, not just regarding misbehavior or failure.
- Provide opportunities for parents to communicate with principals and other administrative staff.
- Promote informal activities at which parents, staff, and community members can interact.
- Provide staff development regarding effective communication techniques and the importance of regular two-way communication between the school and the family.

STANDARD II: PARENTING

Successful programs:

- Communicate the importance of positive relationships between parents and their children.
- Link parents to programs and resources within the community that provide support services to families.
- Reach out to all families, not just those who attend parent meetings.
- Establish policies that support and respect family responsibilities, recognizing the variety of parenting traditions and practices within the community's cultural and religious diversity.
- Provide an accessible parent/family information and resource center to support parents and families with training, resources, and other services.
- Encourage staff members to demonstrate respect for families and the family's primary role in the rearing of children to become responsible adults.

STANDARD III: STUDENT LEARNING

Successful programs:

- Seek and encourage parental participation in decision making that affects students.

- Inform parents of the expectations for students in each subject at each grade level.
- Provide information regarding how parents can foster learning at home, give appropriate assistance, monitor homework, and give feedback to teachers.
- Regularly assign interactive homework that will require students to discuss and interact with their parents about what they are learning in class.
- Sponsor workshops or distribute information to assist parents in understanding how students can improve skills, get help when needed, meet class expectations, and perform well on assessments.
- Involve parents in setting student goals each year and in planning for postsecondary education and careers. Encourage the development of a personalized education plan for each student, where parents are full partners.
- Provide opportunities for staff members to learn and share successful approaches to engaging parents in their child's education.

STANDARD IV: VOLUNTEERING

Successful programs:

- Ensure that office staff greetings, signage near the entrances, and any other interaction with parents create a climate in which parents feel valued and welcome.
- Survey parents regarding their interests, talents, and availability, and then coordinate the parent resources with those that exist within the school and among the faculty.
- Ensure that parents who are unable to volunteer in the school building are given the options for helping in other ways, at home or place of employment.
- Organize an easy, accessible program for utilizing parent volunteers, providing ample training on volunteer procedures and school protocol.
- Develop a system for contacting all parents to assist as the year progresses.
- Design opportunities for those with limited time and resources to participate by addressing child care, transportation, work schedule needs, and so forth.
- Show appreciation for parents' participation, and value their diverse contributions.

- Educate and assist staff members in creating an inviting climate and effectively utilizing volunteer resources.
- Ensure that volunteer activities are meaningful and built on volunteer interests and abilities.

STANDARD V: SCHOOL DECISION MAKING AND ADVOCACY

Successful programs:

- Provide understandable, accessible, and well-publicized processes for influencing decisions, raising issues or concerns, appealing decisions, and resolving problems.
- Encourage the formation of PTAs or other parent groups to identify and respond to issues of interest to parents.
- Include parents on all decision-making and advisory committees, and ensure adequate training for such areas as policy, curriculum, budget, school reform initiatives, safety, and personnel. Where site governance bodies exist, give equal representation to parents.
- Provide parents with current information regarding school policies, practices, and both student and school performance data.
- Enable parents to participate as partners when setting school goals, developing or evaluating programs and policies, or responding to performance data.
- Encourage and facilitate active parent participation in the decisions that affect students, such as student placement, course selection, and individual personalized education plans.
- Treat parental concerns with respect and demonstrate genuine interest in developing solutions.
- Promote parent participation on school district, state, and national committees and issues.
- Provide training for staff and parents on collaborative partnering and shared decision making.

STANDARD VI: COLLABORATING WITH COMMUNITY

Successful programs:

- Distribute information regarding cultural, recreational, academic, health, social, and other resources that serve families within the community.

- Develop partnerships with local business and service groups to advance student learning and assist schools and families.
- Encourage employers to adopt policies and practices that promote and support adult participation in children's education.
- Foster student participation in community service.
- Involve community members in school volunteer programs.
- Disseminate information to the school community, including those without school-age children, regarding school programs and performance.
- Collaborate with community agencies to provide family support services and adult learning opportunities, enabling parents to more fully participate in activities that support education.
- Inform staff members of the resources available in the community and strategies for utilizing those resources.

APPENDIX C

♦♦♦

Selected Examples from the "Partner Up" Newsletter

♦

EXAMPLE 1

ABC's of Home Learning

Schools are not the only places where children learn. The time your children spend at home is full of opportunities for learning. How can you help your children learn at home? It's as simple as A . . . B . . . C!

A. Show **A**ffection to your children. Children who are loved are not afraid make mistakes.
B. **B**e aware of how your children are doing in school.
C. Be **C**onsistent. Set rules and consequences that your children can understand.
D. **D**iscuss your children's day at school with them everyday.
E. Set high **E**xpectations for your children and talk about them together.
F. Have a regular "**F**amily time" together each week when evening comes.
G. Help your children set long-term **G**oals. Teach your children to defray immediate gratification to meet their goals.
H. Set a regular time to do **H**omework everyday.
I. Stay **I**nformed about school policies and rules.
J. Give your children small **J**obs that they can do around the house.
K. **K**eep your children's favorite schoolwork and hang it on the refrigerator.

L. Listen to your children. Talk to them about their questions or fears.
M. Monitor and discuss what your children watch on TV.
N. Notify your children's teachers of important changes going on at home.
O. Give your children many Opportunities to learn throughout the day. Make learning a part of trips to the grocery store, making dinner, family outings, and so on.
P. Form a Partnership with your children's school. Work with teachers to help your children be successful learners.
Q. Set aside a Quiet area for studying and reading.
R. Read to your children—or have your children read to you— every day.
S. Create a study Space for doing schoolwork.
T. Talk to your children's teachers about how your children are doing in school. Share your concerns, too.
U. Use community resources. Find out what services are available to your and your children.
V. Visit your children's classroom to see what they are learning.
W. Help your children learn a new Word every day.
X. Strive for eXcellence in your children's education!
Y. Emphasize learning all Year 'round!
Z. Zoos, museums, and parks are inexpensive and great places to learn. The Como Zoo in St. Paul is free!

In a partnership, both parents and teachers contribute to students' school performance. Learners benefit from school and home learning environments.

EXAMPLE 2

What Parents Can Do

- ◆ Structure home and family time: Establish a daily routine and positive work habits.
- ◆ Support your children and their efforts at schoolwork: Talk with and listen to your children about school activities, homework, and friends.
- ◆ Expect your children to be active learners at school: Show your children that you value education and praise them for working hard and improving.

- Create an environment for learning at home: Read, write, and provide learning opportunities.
- Become active in your children's education at home or at school.

What Educators Can Do

- Provide appropriate instruction and practice opportunities for students.
- Send home activities or share ideas to assist children's schoolwork.
- Communicate with parents.

What We Both Can Do

- Contact each other if there are questions or concerns.
- Attend "Partner Up" activities on Thursday evenings.

EXAMPLE 3

We know parents want their children to be successful, happy students. Several researchers have talked to parents about their children's performance in school. These studies have reached the same conclusion: Parents want to know how to help their children be more successful in school. One important, fun way is to make your home environment a learning environment. Parents have many teachable moments. For example, cooking together can teach math and chemistry. Recycling teaches about care for the environment. While riding in the car, students can retell a story from reading, and parents can ask questions.

What Parents Can Do to Make Their Home a Learning Home

Structure

- Have daily routines for chores, meals, homework, and bedtime.
- Read or talk to your kids before they fall asleep or at the dinner table.
- Create a quiet place and time for children to study or read.

Support

- Encourage curiosity by trying to answer your children's questions.
- Praise your children for trying to do new things.

- Give your children a smile or word of encouragement just as they are leaving for school, or place a positive note to your children in their lunch or backpack.

Expectations

- Expect your children to learn and work hard by completing all schoolwork.

Environment

- Expect your children to take care of their own things.
- Have books and magazines in your house.
- Practice math every day by talking about dates, time, and money.
- Go places with your children ... like libraries, museums, plays, sporting events, and on walks ... And have fun!

Richard Riley, U.S. Secretary of Education and Director of the Initiative on Family Involvement Partnership, provides the following ideas for families:

- Find time to learn together with your children.
- Commit yourself and your children to challenging standards—help children reach their full potential.
- Limit TV viewing to no more than 2 hours on school nights.
- Read together. It's the starting point of all learning.
- Encourage your children to take the tougher courses at school, and check their homework every day.
- Make sure your children go to school every day and support community efforts to keep children safe and off the streets late at night.
- Set a good example for your children, and talk directly to them about the dangers of drugs and alcohol, and the values you want them to have. Listen to them, too.

We believe the best ideas come from parents. Please tell us your good ideas. We would like to share them with other families. Together, our kids will learn more!

♦♦♦

A Teacher's Perspective on Communicating with Families

♦

Cathryn Peterson, seventh-grade teacher at FAIR School, was asked to describe her approach to communicating with families. Specifically, she was asked why she contacts parents, for what reasons, when, and how. The comments provided by this most adept teacher represent several principles of effective communication and partnership skills, including the following:

- The student and his or her learning are at the center of all communications.
- Communication remains at the level of the issue and do not become personal.
- Concerns, not problems, are described.
- Parents are expert and critical to the success of the school's efforts.
- Contact is made early, before the concerns escalate.
- Positive messages are conveyed at the beginning of and throughout the contact.
- The communication is constructive and not punitive for the child.
- The home and school are supportive, but the child is ultimately responsible for performance.
- Perspective taking is encouraged.
- Good listening skills are important.
- Follow-up contacts are made.

Note. This material was reprinted with permission from Cathryn Peterson.

Before I begin, there is one assumption that drives all of my dealings with parents. I believe that parents are my most important assets as a teacher. In addition, there are two things that I always think about when contacting a parent. First, I believe that all parents do what they believe is best for their child. . . . We may not agree with their opinion or action, but they do their best. Second, and perhaps most importantly, I try to think about how I would want a teacher or adult to handle the situation if this were my child (how would I want to be treated, and how would I want my child to be treated?).

Why Do I Contact Parents?

I contact parents if I have a concern that the student and I cannot resolve without the help of the parent or when the student has made improvement or done something to be proud of. The issue may be academic or behavioral.

For What Reasons Do I Contact Parents?

The following is a list of some of the reasons that I make calls home:

> *Concerns:*
>
> *Insubordination, disrespectful behavior*
> *Excessive tardiness*
> *Missing assignments*
> *Lack of participation*
> *Ability concerns*
> *Achieving lower than a C (I don't have to do too many of these, since I often tell the students that I will be calling in one week if they have a D or NC. It's amazing how the late work comes in.)*
>
> *Positives:*
>
> *Improvements in any of the above areas*
> *Helping another student*
> *Outstanding work*
> *Effort*
> *Any random act of kindness that I witness in or out of class*

When Do I Contact Parents?

I contact parents after the student and I have worked together to resolve the issue and have not been successful, but prior to an administrative referral. If I am calling about a concern, I tell the student that I will be call-

ing the parent. I don't want this to be negative; I want them to know that I am calling to ask for additional help. I also tell the student that I will follow up with the parent as the situation improves.

If I am making a positive phone call, I love to leave messages that the parents will hear after a long day at work. Sometimes I send postcards to the student and/or parent documenting the achievement, too.

How Do I Contact Parents?

If I am calling a parent about a concern, I always start the conversation by introducing myself. I then let the parents know that I am calling because I need their help. I tell them that I believe they know their child better than me, explain the situation, and ask for any ideas they might have to help us resolve the problem. In addition, I find something positive that their child has done in the past and explain that this is what I am trying to achieve all of the time. Parents are very receptive to this. I have yet to have a parent say "You should know . . . you're the expert." Instead, most parents are not defensive, share what has worked in the past, and often begin to tell me about their child's other interests or behaviors at home. Often, I find that parents are struggling with similar issues at home. This turns into a great conversation of sharing ideas. I also tell parents that I am most concerned that their child is learning and that if the strategy or assignment I have given isn't working, I am willing to try something else.

The key to my success in dealing with parents is that I view them as partners who are experts. If I am willing to listen to them first, they are then willing to listen to my ideas. In addition, when I talk to parents about their child, I focus on the behavior that needs to change, rather than attacking the child. I also make a point of telling the parent that I will keep in contact with them about the child's progress. I love to make follow-up phone calls and say "Thank you, your ideas worked!"

Remember, I said the child always knows that I am going to call the parent. The next day, I find the student before he or she comes to class and talk further about the situation. This helps to clear the air if the child has left angry. The child can then come to class knowing that I am not upset and I want to work with him or her. However, if the problem continues, I will often say to the child, "Do we need to call _____?" using the parent's first name. This is less embarrassing for the child and also reminds the child that I know his or her mom or dad.

These phone calls often result in a parent–teacher meeting with all of the student's teachers. We usually invite the student and ask him or her to play an active role. We want the student to know we are having the meeting because we want to help. This allows the teachers and parents to clearly express their expectations and need, and the child to express his or her needs and desires. The meeting should be short, positive, and focused on the behavior or issue. The goal is to have the child leave feeling good and have some tangible ideas about how to improve and be successful.

If I am making a positive phone call home, I often just leave a message where I introduce myself and say, "I just wanted to let you know what your child did today." I briefly describe what happened and tell parents to have a great evening. These phone calls are fun to make. Since I don't usually tell the child that I am going to do this, I often have a happy student the next day saying "Thanks!" It is a nice surprise for the student, too.

APPENDIX E

♦♦♦

Inventory for Creating School–Family Connections

♦

The goal of creating constructive family–school relationships is to engage students as learners. Family and school—out-of and in-school influences—provide different but complementary opportunities for children to learn. Ideally, schools and families interact as partners to achieve the goal of enhancing students' learning and development (i.e., members of a school community that work together to achieve a common mission).

The "four A's" provide a heuristic aid to conceptualize the key elements or conditions that enhance productive school–family relationships: approach, attitude, atmosphere, and actions. Various indicators for each of the four A's are listed. Each indicator can be considered an objective that contributes to the overall goal of creating constructive school–family connections for children's learning.

This inventory was designed to provide a structure for educators, parents, and other individuals in the school community as they dialogue about ways to promote positive connections for children's learning in their school context. Respondents are asked to judge the degree to which each objective stated below has been accomplished in their school community. The following 5-point scale may be useful for sharing perspectives across family and school environments:

1: Not at all/never
2: In some situations/infrequently

3: Variable/sometimes but not usually
4: In most situations/usually
5. Completely/always

APPROACH

To what extent are the following conditions present in our school community?

1. Mutually shared goals across home and school for children's learning.

    1 2 3 4 5

2. Belief that parental involvement in school is paramount.

    1 2 3 4 5

3. Belief that working together as partners will benefit the child's learning and development, with mutually supported roles and actions to achieve this goal.

    1 2 3 4 5

4. Recognition of the value of both in- and out-of-school learning opportunities for children's learning and school progress.

    1 2 3 4 5

5. Recognition that the nature and quality of the family–school relationship influence (positively or negatively) children's school performance.

    1 2 3 4 5

6. Expectation that families will be involved, and recognition that such involvement can mean different things to different families.

    1 2 3 4 5

7. Expectation that teachers and school personnel will seek ways to invite parents to share in the educational process for their children, recognizing that this may "look different" to different families.

    1 2 3 4 5

8. Presence of a mission statement that promotes the importance and expectation of school–family connections for children's learning.

    1 2 3 4 5

ATTITUDES

To what extent are the following conditions present in our school community?

1. Attempts to understand the needs, ideas, opinions, and perspectives of families and educators.

   1   2   3   4   5

2. A nonblaming, no-fault problem-solving stance in interactions with families.

   1   2   3   4   5

3. Willingness to share perspectives across home and school.

   1   2   3   4   5

4. Perception of family involvement as essential (i.e., bringing a critical element to the team that is otherwise unavailable) rather than simply desirable.

   1   2   3   4   5

5. A positive attitude that focuses on school, family, and child strengths, rather than only on problems or deficits.

   1   2   3   4   5

6. Willingness to co-construct the whole picture about children by discussing, exploring, and understanding different perspectives.

   1   2   3   4   5

7. Willingness to listen to and respond to concerns across home and school—viewing different perspectives as a way to better understand students' needs, and viewing parents' and educators' concerns as a way to offer mutual support.

   1   2   3   4   5

8. Mutual respect across home and school (i.e., respect for family members by school personnel, and respect for school personnel by family members).

   1   2   3   4   5

9. Understanding that barriers for positive family–school relationships (i.e., constraints of each system) exist for parents and educators.

   1   2   3   4   5

ATMOSPHERE

To what extent are the following conditions present in our school community?

1. Recognition of the value, and active solicitation, of family input regarding important decisions about their child.

    1   2   3   4   5

2. Use of family and school input to promote positive outcomes for students.

    1   2   3   4   5

3. A welcoming, respectful, inclusive, positive, supportive climate and atmosphere for *all* children and families.

    1   2   3   4   5

4. A variety of communication strategies to reach all parents in a manner that is sensitive or responsive to family background (e.g., language, skills, knowledge level), easy to understand, and "jargon-free."

    1   2   3   4   5

5. A variety of communication strategies to share information and/or monitor children's performance.

    1   2   3   4   5

6. Parental and school trust in each other (including motives, objectives, and communications).

    1   2   3   4   5

7. Mechanisms for listening to and responding to concerns across home and school.

    1   2   3   4   5

8. Meaningful ways and flexible options for parents and students to be involved.

    1   2   3   4   5

9. Opportunities for parents and school personnel to learn from one another (e.g., cross-cultural communication opportunities).

    1   2   3   4   5

ACTIONS

To what extent are the following conditions present in our school community?

1. Information is provided to families about school policies and practices, parents' and students' rights vis-à-vis education, and ways to foster students' engagement with learning.

    1   2   3   4   5

2. Opportunities or mechanisms are provided for home and school to plan jointly and collaborate to resolve a shared concern or to improve learning experiences for students.

    1   2   3   4   5

3. A process exists for creating mutually supportive roles for families and educators.

    1   2   3   4   5

4. Supports and resources exist for creating and maintaining partnerships.

    1   2   3   4   5

5. Policies and practices support a coordinated, collaborative approach (i.e., shared responsibility) for home and school.

    1   2   3   4   5

6. Parents and school personnel (i.e., partners) routinely review the availability, accessibility, and flexibility of family–school roles and responsibilities for fostering children's/adolescents' learning and school engagement.

    1   2   3   4   5

References

♦

Adams, K. S., & Christenson, S. L. (1998). Differences in parent and teacher trust levels: Implications for creating collaborative family–school relationships. *Special Services in the Schools, 14*(1/2), 1–22.

Adams, K., & Christenson, S. L. (2000). Trust and the family–school relationship: Examination of parent–teacher differences in elementary and secondary grades. *Journal of School Psychology, 38*(5), 477–497.

Allport, G. W. (1954). *The nature of prejudice.* Reading, MA: Addison-Wesley.

Ames, C. (1993). How school-to-home communications influence parent beliefs and perceptions. *Equity and Choice, 9*(3), 44–49.

August, G. J., Anderson, D., & Bloomquist, M. L. (1992). Competence enhancement training for children: An integrated child, parent, and school approach. In S. L. Christenson & J. C. Conoley (Eds.), *Home–school collaboration: Enhancing children's academic and social competence* (pp. 175–192). Silver Spring, MD: National Association of School Psychologists.

Baker, D. P., & Stevenson, D. L. (1986). Mothers' strategies for children's school achievement: Managing the transition to high school. *Sociology of Education, 59*, 156–166.

Barton, P. E., & Coley, R. J. (1992). *America's smallest school: The family.* Princeton, NJ: Educational Testing Service.

Bastiani, J. (1996). Working together: A brief reassessment of educational partnership principles and current practice. *Families as Educators,* pp. 4–10.

Batey, C. S. (1996). *Parents are lifesavers: A handbook for parent involvement in schools.* Thousand Oaks, CA: Corwin Press.

Becher, R. M. (1984). *Parent involvement: A review of research and principles for successful practice.* Urbana, IL: ERIC Clearinghouse on Elementary and Early Childhood Education. (ERIC Document Reproduction Service No. ED 247–032)

Bell, N. (1985). Teachers' perceptions of school climate linked to rate of parent participation. *Community Education Journal,* p. 27.

Bempechat, J. (1998). *Against the odds: How "at-risk" students EXCEED expectations.* San Francisco: Jossey-Bass.

Bempechat, J., Graham, S. E., & Jimenez, N. V. (1999). The socialization of achievement in poor and minority students: A comparative study. *Journal of Cross-Cultural Psychology, 30*(2), 139–158.

Bernigner, J. M., & Rodriguez, R. C. (1989). The principal as a catalyst in parental involvement. *Momentum, 20*(2), 32–34.

Bickel, W. E. (1999). The implications of the effective schools literature for school restructuring. In C. R. Reynolds & T. B. Gutkin (Eds.), *The handbook of school psychology* (3rd ed., pp. 959–983). New York: Wiley.

Binns, K., Steinberg, A., & Amorosi, S. (1997). *The Metropolitan Life Survey of the American Teacher 1998: Building family–school partnerships: Views of teachers and students*. New York: Louis Harris & Associates.

Birch, D. A. (1994). Involving families in school health education: Implications for professional preparation. *Journal of School Health, 64*(7), 296–299.

Bloom, B. S. (1985). *Developing talents in young people*. New York: Ballantine Books.

Booth, A., & Dunn, J. F. (Eds.). (1996). *Family–school links: How do they affect educational outcomes?* Mahwah, NJ: Erlbaum.

Bowen, J., Olympia, D., & Jenson, W. (1996). *Study buddies: Parent tutoring tactics*. Longmont, CO: Sopris West.

Bronfenbrenner, U. (1974). *Is early intervention effective: A report on longitudinal evaluations of preschool programs* (Vol. 2). Washington, DC: U.S. Department of Health, Education, and Welfare.

Bronfenbrenner, U. (1979). *The ecology of human development*. Cambridge, MA: Harvard University Press.

Bronfenbrenner, U. (1991). What do families do?: Part 1. *Teaching Thinking and Problem Solving, 13*(4), 1, 3–5.

Bronfenbrenner, U. (1992). Ecological systems theory. In R. Vasta (Ed.), *Annals of child development: Six theories of child development: Revised formulations and current issues* (pp. 187–249). London: Jessica Kingsley.

Brophy, J. E., & Good, T. L. (1986). Teacher behavior and student achievement. In M. L. Wittrock (Ed.), *Handbook of research on teaching* (3rd ed., pp. 328–375). New York: Macmillan.

Brown, D. (1997). Implications of cultural values for cross-cultural consultation with families. *Journal of Counseling and Development, 76*, 29–35.

Canter, A., & Carroll, S. (Eds.). (1998). *Helping children at home and school: Handouts from your school psychologist*. Bethesda, MD: National Association of School Psychologists.

Canter, L., & Canter, M. (1991). *Parents on your side: A comprehensive parent involvement program for teachers*. Santa Monica, CA: Author (Lee Canter & Associates, PO Box 2113, Santa Monica, CA 90407–2113; 800–262–4347).

Carlson, C. I., Hickman, J., & Horton, C. B. (1992). From blame to solutions: Solution-oriented family–school consultation. In S. L. Christenson & J. C. Conoley (Eds.), *Home–school collaboration: Enhancing children's academic and social competence* (pp. 193–213). Silver Spring, MD: National Association of School Psychologists.

Carlyon, P., Carlyon, W., & McCarthy, A. R. (1998). Family and community involvement in school health. In E. Marx & S. F. Wooley (Eds.), *Health is academic: A guide to coordinated school health programs* (pp. 67–95). New York: Teachers College Press.

Carter, J. L. (1994). Moving from principles to practice: Implementing a family–focused approach in schools and community services. *Equity and Choice, 10*(3), 4–9.

Chavkin, N. F. (Ed.). (1993). *Families and schools in a pluralistic society.* Albany: State University of New York Press.

Chrispeels, J. A. (1987). The family as an educational resource. *Community Education Journal,* pp. 10–17.

Christenson, S. L. (1994). *Schools and Families Together (SAF-T): Training of school psychologists to increase school success for students with disabilities* (Grant No. H029-F0069). Washington, DC: U.S. Department of Education, Office of Special Education Programs.

Christenson, S. L. (1995). Supporting home–school collaboration. In A. Thomas & J. Grimes (Eds.), *Best practices in school psychology III* (pp. 253–267). Washington, DC: National Association of School Psychologists.

Christenson, S. L. (2000). Families and schools: Rights, responsibilities, resources, and relationship. In R. C. Pianta & M. J. Cox (Eds.), *The transition to kindergarten* (pp. 143–177). Baltimore, MD: Brookes.

Christenson, S., Abery, B., & Weinberg, R. A. (1986). An alternative model for the delivery of psychology in the school community. In S. N. Elliott & J. C. Witt (Eds.), *The delivery of psychological services in schools: Concepts, processes, and issues* (pp. 349–391). Hillsdale, NJ: Erlbaum.

Christenson, S. L., & Buerkle, K. (1999). Families as educational partners for children's school success: Suggestions for school psychologists. In C. Reynolds & T. B. Gutkin (Eds.), *The handbook of school psychology* (3rd ed., pp. 709–744). New York: Wiley.

Christenson, S. L., & Christenson, C. J. (1998). *Family, school, and community influences on children's learning: A literature review* (Report No. 1). Live and Learn Project. Minneapolis: University of Minnesota Extension Service.

Christenson, S. L., & Conoley, J. C. (Eds.). (1992). *Home–school collaboration: Enhancing children's academic and social competence.* Silver Spring, MD: National Association of School Psychologists.

Christenson, S. L., & Hirsch, J. (1998). Facilitating partnerships and conflict resolution between families and schools. In K. C. Stoiber & T. Kratochwill (Eds.), *Handbook of group interventions for children and families* (pp. 307–344). Boston: Allyn & Bacon.

Christenson, S. L., Hurley, C. M., Sheridan, S. M., & Fenstermacher, K. (1997). Parents' and school psychologists' perspectives on parent involvement activities. *School Psychology Review, 26*(1), 111–130.

Christenson, S. L., Rounds, T., & Franklin, M. J. (1992). Home–school collaboration: Effects, issues, and opportunities. In S. L. Christenson & J. C. Conoley (Eds.), *Home–school collaboration: Enhancing children's academic and social competence* (pp. 19–51). Silver Spring, MD: National Association of School Psychologists.

Christenson, S. L., Rounds, T., & Gorney, D. (1992). Family factors and student achievement: An avenue to increase students' success. *School Psychology Quarterly, 7*(3), 178–206.

Clark, R. M. (1983). *Family life and school achievement.* Chicago: University of Chicago Press.

Clark, R. M. (1988). Parents as providers of linguistic and social capital: How do the literacy skills of low achievers and high achievers differ, and how do parents influence these differences? *Educational Horizons, 66*(2), 93–95.

Clark, R. M. (1990). Why disadvantaged students succeed: What happens outside school is critical. *Public Welfare,* pp. 17–23.

Clark, R. M. (1993). Homework-focused parenting practices that positively affect student achievement. In N. F. Chavkin (Ed.), *Families and schools in a pluralistic society* (pp. 85–105). Albany: State University of New York Press.

Coleman, J. (1987, August–September). Families and schools. *Educational Researcher,* pp. 32–38.

Collins, C. H., Moles, O., & Cross, M. (1982). *The home–school connections: Selected partnership programs in large cities.* Boston, MA: Institute for Responsive Education.

Comer, J. P. (1988). Educating poor minority children. *Scientific American, 259*(5), 2–8.

Comer, J. P. (1995). *School power: Implications of an intervention project.* New York: Free Press.

Comer, J. P., & Haynes, N. M. (1991). Parent involvement in schools: An ecological approach. *Elementary School Journal, 91*(3), 271–278.

Comer, J. P., Haynes, N. M., Joyner, E. T., & Ben-Avie, M. (1996). *Rallying the whole village: The Comer process for reforming education.* New York: Teachers College Press.

Conley, D. (1991). What is restructuring?: Educators adapt to a changing world. *Equity and Choice, 7*(2–3), 46–55.

Connors, L. J., & Epstein, J. L. (1994). *Talking stock: Views of teachers, parents, and students on school, family, and community partnerships in high school.* (Report No. 25). Baltimore, MD: Center on Families, Communities, Schools, and Children's Learning, Johns Hopkins University.

Conoley, J. C. (1987). Schools and families: Theoretical and practical bridges. *Professional School Psychology, 2*(3), 191–203.

Corrigan, D., & Bishop, R. L. (1997, July). Creating family-centered integrated services systems and interprofessional programs to implement them. *Social Work and Education, 19*(3), 149–163.

Dauber, S. L., & Epstein, J. L. (1993). Parents' attitudes and practices of involvement in inner city elementary and middle schools. In N. F. Chavkin (Eds.), *Families and schools in a pluralistic society* (pp. 53–72). Albany: State University of New York Press.

Davies, D. (1987). Parent involvement in the public schools: Opportunities for administrators. *Education and Urban Society, 19,* 147–163.

Davies, D. (1988). Low-income parents and the schools: A research report and a plan for action. *Equity and Choice, 4*(3), 51–59.

Davies, D. (1991). Schools reaching out: Family, school, and community partnerships for student success. *Phi Delta Kappan, 72*(5) 376–382.

Davies, D. (1993). Benefits and barriers to parent involvement: From Portugal to Boston to Liverpool. In N. F. Chavkin (Ed.), *Families and schools in a pluralistic society* (pp. 53–72). Albany: State University of New York Press.

Davies, D., Burch, P., & Johnson, V. (1992, February). *A portrait of schools reaching out: Report of a survey of practices and policies of family–community–school collaboration* (No. 1). Baltimore, MD: Center on Families, Communities, Schools, and Children's Learning, Johns Hopkins University.

Davison, M. L. (1998). *Yearbook: The status of Pre-K–12 education in Minnesota—1998.* Minneapolis: University of Minnesota, Office of Educational Accountability, College of Education and Human Development.

Delgado-Gaitan, C. (1991). Involving parents in the schools: A process of empowerment. *American Journal of Education, 100*(1), 20–46.

Delpit, L. (1995). *Other people's children: Cultural conflict the classroom*. New York: New Press.

Deslandes, R., Royer, E., Potvin, P., & Leclerc, D. (1999). Patterns of home and school partnerships for general and special education students at the secondary level. *Exceptional Children, 65*(4), 496–506.

de Shazer, S. (1982). *Patterns of brief family therapy*. New York: Guilford Press.

de Shazer, S. (1988). *Clues: Investigating solutions in brief therapy*. New York: Norton.

Doherty, W. J., & Peskay, V. E. (1992). Family systems and the school. In S. L. Christenson & J. C. Conoley (Eds.), *Home–school collaboration: Enhancing children's academic and social competence* (pp. 1–18). Silver Spring, MD: National Association of School Psychologists.

Dunst, C. J., Johanson, C., Rounds, T., Trivette, C. M., & Hamby, D. (1992). Characteristics of parent–professional partnerships. In S. L. Christenson & J. C. Conoley (Eds.), *Home–school collaboration: Enhancing children's academic and social competence* (pp. 157–174). Silver Spring, MD: National Association of School Psychologists.

Dunst, C. J., & Trivette, C. M. (1987). Enabling and empowering families: Conceptual and intervention issues. *School Psychology Review, 16*, 443–456.

Eagle, E. (1989, April). *Socioeconomic status, family structure, and parental involvement: The correlates of achievement*. Paper presented at the annual meeting of the American Educational Research Association, San Francisco. (ERIC Document Reproduction Service No. ED 307 332)

Eccles, J. L., & Harold, R. D. (1996) Family involvement in children's and adolescents' schooling. In A. Booth & J. F. Dunn (Eds.), *Family–school links: How do they affect educational outcomes?* (pp. 3–34). Mahwah, NJ: Erlbaum.

Edmonds, R. R. (1979). Some schools do and some schools can. *Social Policy, 9*, 28–32.

Education Daily. (1993, June). Parents heart students' progress from their own lips. pp. 5–6.

Educational Communications. (1997). *Who's who among America's teachers: Teachers blame education woes on parents, students, soft school*. Lake Forest, IL: Author.

Edwards, P. A. (1992). Strategies and techniques for establishing home–school partnerships with minority parents. In A. Barona & E. Garcia (Eds.), *Children at-risk: Poverty, minority status, and other issues in educational equity* (pp. 217–236). Silver Spring, MD: National Association of School Psychologists.

Edwards, P. A., Fear, K. L., & Gallego, M. A. (1995). Role of parents in responding to issues of linguistic and cultural diversity. In E. E. Garcia, B. McLaughlin, G. Spodek, & O. Saracho (Eds.), *Meeting the challenge of linguistic and cultural diversity in early childhood education* (pp. 141–153). New York: Teachers College Press.

Entwisle, D. R., & Alexander, K. L. (2000). Early schooling and social stritfication. In R. C. Pianta & M. J. Cox (Eds.), *The transition to kindergarten* (pp. 13–38). Baltimore, MD: Brookes.

Entwisle, D., Alexander, K., & Olson, L. (1997). *Children, schools, and inequality.* Boulder, CO: Westview Press.

Epstein, J. L. (1986). Parents' reactions to teacher practices of parent involvement. *Elementary School Journal, 86,* 277–294.

Epstein, J. L. (1987). Toward a theory of family–school connections: Teacher practices and parent involvement. In K. Hurrelmann, F. Kaufmann, & F. Losel (Eds.), *Social interaction: Potential and constraints* (pp. 121–136). New York: deGruyter.

Epstein, J. L. (1989). Building parent–teacher partnerships in inner-city schools. *Family Resource Coalition, 8,* 7.

Epstein, J. (1990). School and family connections: Theory, research, and implications for integrating sociologies of education and family. In D. Unger & M. Sussman (Eds.), *Families in community settings: Interdisciplinary perspectives* (pp. 99–126). New York: Haworth Press.

Epstein, J. L. (1991). Effects on student achievement of teachers' practices of parent involvement. In B. S. Silvern (Ed.), *Advances in reading/language research: Vol. 5. Literacy through family, community, and school interaction* (pp. 261–276). Greenwich, CT: JAI Press.

Epstein, J. L. (1992). School and family partnerships: Leadership roles for school psychologists. In S. C. Christenson & J. C. Conoley (Eds.), *Home–school collaboration: Enhancing children's academic and social competence* (pp. 499–515). Silver Spring, MD: National Association of School Psychologists.

Epstein, J. L. (1995). School/family/community partnerships: Caring for the children we share. *Phi Delta Kappan, 76*(9), 701–712.

Epstein, J. L., & Becker, H. J. (1982). Teacher practices of parent involvement. *Elementary School Journal, 83,* 103–113.

Epstein, J. L., Coates, L., Salinas, K. C., Sanders, M. G., & Simon, B. S. (1997). *School, family, and community partnerships: Your handbook for action.* Thousand Oaks, CA: Corwin Press.

Epstein, J. L., & Connors, L. (1995). School and family partnerships in the middle grades. In B. Rutherford (Ed.), *Creating family/school partnerships* (pp. 137–166). Columbus, OH: National Middle School Association.

Epstein, J. L., & Dauber, S. L. (1991). School programs and teacher practices of parent involvement in inner-city elementary and middle schools. *Elementary School Journal, 91,* 289–305.

Estrada, P., Arsenio, W. F., Hess, R. D., & Holloway, S. (1987). Affective quality of the mother–child relationship: Longitudinal consequences for children's school-relevant, cognitive-functioning. *Developmental Psychology, 23,* 210–215.

Fantuzzo, J. W. (1999, August 24). *Discussant for the symposium: Preventing school failure through the use of nontraditional helpers.* Annual meeting of the American Psychological Association, Boston.

Fantuzzo, J. W., & Mohr, W. K. (2000). Pursuit of wellness in Head Start: Making beneficial connections for children and families. In D. Cicchetti, J. Rapapport, I. Sandler, & R. Weissberg (Eds.), *The promotion of wellness in children and adolescents* (pp. 341–369). Thousand Oaks, CA: Sage.

Fehrmann, P. G., Keith, T. Z., & Reimers, T. M. (1987). Home influences on school learning: Direct and indirect effects of parent involvement on high school grades. *Journal of Educational Research, 80,* 330–337.

References

Finders, M., & Lewis, C. (1994). Why some parents don't come to school. *Educational Leadership, 51,* 50–54.

Fine, M. J. (1990). Facilitating home–school relationships: A family-oriented approach to collaborative consultation. *Journal of Educational and Psychological Consultation, 1,* 169–187.

Fine, M. (1993). [Ap]parent involvement: Reflections on parents, power, and urban public schools. *Teachers College Record, 94,* 682–711.

Fine, M. J., & Carlson, C. (Eds.). (1992). *The handbook of family–school intervention: A systems perspective.* Boston: Allyn & Bacon.

Fisher, R., & Ury, W. (1981). *Getting to yes: Negotiating agreement without giving in.* Boston: Houghton Mifflin.

Friend, M., & Cook, L. (1992). *Interactions: Collaboration skills for school professionals.* New York: Longman.

Fruchter, N., Gullotta, A., & White, J. L. (1992). *New directions in parent involvement.* Washington, DC: Academy for Educational Development.

Fullan, M. (1996). Professional culture and educational change. *School Psychology Review, 25,* 496–500.

Fuller, M. L., & Olsen, G. (1998). *Home–school relations: Working successfully with parents and families.* Boston: Allyn & Bacon.

Galloway, J., & Sheridan, S. M. (1994). Implementing scientific practices through case studies: Examples using home–school interventions and consultation. *Journal of School Psychology, 32,* 385–413.

Garbarino, J. (1982). *Children and families in the social environment.* New York: Aldine.

Goodman, J. F., Sutton, V., & Harkavy, I. (1995). The effectiveness of family workshops in a middle school setting: Respect and caring make the difference. *Phi Delta Kappan, 76*(9), 694–700.

Graue, M. E., Weinstein, T., & Walberg, H. J. (1983). School-based home instruction and learning: A quantiative synthesis. *Journal of Educational Research, 76*(6), 351–360.

Gresham, F. M. (1989). Assessment of treatment integrity in school consultation and prereferral intervention. *School Psychology Review, 18,* 37–50.

Grimes, J., & Tilly, W. D. (1996). Policy and process: Means to lasting educational change. *School Psychology Review, 25,* 465–476.

Grolnick, W. S., Benjet, C., Kurowski, C. O., & Apostoleris, N. H. (1997). Predictors of parent involvement in children's schooling. *Journal of Educational Psychology, 89,* 538–548.

Grolnick, W. S., Ryan, R. M., & Deci, E. L. (1991). Inner resources for school achievement: Motivational mediators of children's perceptions of their parents. *Journal of Educational Psychology, 83,* 508–517.

Grolnick, W. S., & Slowiaczek, M. L. (1994). Parents' involvement in children's schooling: A multidimensional conceptualization and motivational model. *Child Development, 65,* 237–252.

Hansen, D. A., (1986). Family–school articulations: The effects of interaction rule mismatch. *American Educational Research Journal, 23*(4), 643–659.

Harry, B. (1992). *Cultural diversity, families, and the special education system: Communication and empowerment.* New York: Teachers College Press.

Harry, B., Allen, N., & McLaughlin, M. (1995). Communication vs. compliance: African-American parents' involvement in special education. *Exceptional Children, 61*(4), 364–377.

Haynes, N. M., Ben-Avie, M., Squires, D. A., Howley, J. P., Negron, E. N., &

Corbin, J. N. (1996). It takes a village: The SDP school. In J. P. Comer, N. M. Haynes, E. T. Joyner, & M. Ben-Avie (Eds.), *Rallying the whole village: The Comer process for reforming education* (pp. 42–71). New York: Teachers College Press.

Haynes, N. M., Comer, J. P., & Hamilton-Lee, H. M. (1989). School climate enhancement through parental involvement. *Journal of School Psychology, 27,* 87–90.

Heath, S. (1983). *Ways with words: Language, life, and work in communities and classrooms.* Cambridge, UK: Cambridge University Press.

Heller, L. R., & Fantuzzo, J. W. (1993). Reciprocal peer tutoring and parent partnership: Does parent involvement make a difference? *School Psychology Review, 22*(3), 517–534.

Henderson, A. T., & Berla, N. (Eds.). (1994). *A new generation of evidence: The family is critical to student achievement.* Washington, DC: National Committee for Citizens in Education.

Hickman, C. W., Greenwood, G., & Miller, M. D. (1995). High school parent involvement: Relationships with achievement, grade level, SES, and gender. *Journal of Research and Development in Education, 28,* 287–294.

Hoover-Dempsey, K. V., Bassler, O. C., & Brissie, J. S. (1992). Explorations in parent–school relations. *Journal of Education Research, 85,* 287–294.

Hoover-Dempsey, K. V., & Sandler, H. M. (1997). Why do parents become involved in their children's education? *Review of Educational Research, 67,* 3–42.

Jayanthi, M., Sawyer, V., Nelson, J. S., Bursuck, W. D., & Epstein, M. H. (1995). Recommendations for homework–communication problems: From parents, classroom teachers, and special education teachers. *Remedial and Special Education, 16*(4), 212–225.

Johnson, D. W., & Johnson, F. P. (1991). *Joining together: Group therapy and group skills* (4th ed.). Englewood Cliffs, NJ: Prentice-Hall.

Johnson, S. K., & Johnson, C. D. (1994–1995). *Monitoring your student's educational progress: Families and schools together.* Longmont, CO: Sopris West.

Kagan, S. L. (1984). *Parental involvement research: A field in search of itself* (Report No. 8). Boston: Institute for Responsive Education.

Kagan, S. L., & Schraft, C. M. (1982). *When parents and schools come together: Differential outcomes of parent involvement in urban schools.* Boston, MA: Institute for Responsive Education. (ERIC Document Reproduction Service No. ED 281–951)

Keith, T. Z., Keith, P. B., Troutman, G. C., Bickley, P. G., Trivette, P. S., & Singh, K. C. (1993). Does parent involvement affect eighth grade student achievement?: Structural analysis of national data. *School Psychology Review, 22*(3), 472–494.

Kellaghan, T., Sloane, K., Alvarez, B., & Bloom, B. S. (1993). *The home environment and school learning: Promoting parental involvement in the education of children.* San Francisco: Jossey-Bass.

Lareau, A. (1987). Social class differences in family–school relationships: The importance of cultural capital. *Sociology of Education, 60,* 73–85.

Lareau, A. (1989). *Home advantage.* Philadelphia, PA: Falmer Press.

Larson, P. J., & Maag, J. W. (1998). Applying functional assessment in general education classrooms: Issues and recommendations. *Remedial and Special Education, 19,* 338–349.

Lazar, L., & Darlington, R. B. (1978). *Summary: Lasting effects after preschool.* Ithaca, NY: Cornell University Consortium for Longitudinal Studies. (ERIC Document Reproduction Service No. ED 175–523)

Leitch, M. L., & Tangri, S. S. (1988). Barriers to home–school collaboration. *Educational Horizons, 66,* 70–74.

Lewis, A. C., & Henderson, A. T. (1997). *Urgent message: Families crucial to school reform.* Washington, DC: Center for Law and Education.

Lindle, J. C. (1989). What do parents want from principals and teachers? *Educational Leadership, 47*(2), 12–14.

Liontos, L. B. (1992). *At-risk families and schools: Becoming partners.* Eugene, OR: ERIC Clearinghouse on Educational Management, College of Education, University of Oregon.

Lombana, J. H. (1983). *Home–school partnerships: Guidelines and strategies for educators.* New York: Grune & Stratton.

Lombard, T. J. (1979). Family-oriented emphasis for school psychologists: A needed orientation for training and professional practice. *Professional Psychology, 10,* 687–696.

Lynch, E. W., & Hanson, M. J. (1998). *Developing cross-cultural competence: A guide to working with children and their families* (2nd ed.). Baltimore: Brookes.

Macfarlane, E. C. (1995). *Boost family involvement: How to make your program succeed under the new Title I guidelines.* Bloomington, IN: EDINFO Press.

Maehr, M. L., & Midgley, C. (1996). *Transforming school cultures.* Boulder, CO: Westview Press.

Maher, C. A., & Illback, R. J. (1985). Implementing school psychological service programs: Description and application of the DURABLE approach. *Journal of School Psychology, 23,* 81–89.

Malatchi, A. (1997). Family partnerships, belonging, and diversity. In L. A. Power-deFur & F. P. Orelove (Eds.), *Inclusive education: Practical implementation of the least restrictive environment* (pp. 91–115). Gaithersburg, MD: Aspen.

Malmgren, D. (1994). More than help with homework. In A family plan: Involving parents in education: 10 ideas that work. Framing the debate: A special commentary report. *Education Week,* pp. 29–33.

Margolis, H., & Brannigan, G. G. (1990). Strategies for resolving parent–school conflict. *Reading, Writing, and Learning Disabilities, 6,* 1–23.

Margolis, H., & Shapiro, A. (1989). Systematically resolving parental conflict with the goal–output–process–input procedure. *High School Journal, 71,* 88–96.

Marjoribanks, K. (1988). Perceptions of family environments, educational and occupational outcomes: Social-status differences. *Perceptual and Motor Skills, 66,* 3–9.

Marx, E., & Wooley, S. F. (Eds.). (1998). *Health is academic: A guide to coordinated school health programs.* New York: Teachers College Press.

McAfee, O. (1993). Communication: The key to effective partnerships. In R. C. Burns (Eds.), *Parents and schools: From visitors to partners* (pp. 21–34). Washington, DC: National Education Association.

McWilliam, R. A., Harbin, G. L., Porter, P., Vandiviere, P., Mittal, M., & Munn, D. (1995). *An evaluation of family-centered coordinated Part H services in North Carolina: Part 1—Family-centered service provision.*

Chapel Hill: University of North Carolina, Frank Porter Graham Child Development Center.

McWilliam, R. A., Lang, L., Vandiviere, P., Angell, R., Collins, L., & Underdown, G. (1995). Satisfaction and struggles: Family perceptions of early intervention services. *Journal of Early Intervention, 19,* 43–60.

McWilliam, R. A., Tocci, L., & Harbin, G. L. (1998). Family-centered services: Service providers' discourse and behavior. *Topics in Early Childhood Special Education, 18,* 206–221.

Merseth, K. K., Schorr, L. B., & Elmore, R. F. (1999, September). Schools, community-based interventions, and children's learning and development: What's the connect? *The CEIC Review, 8*(2), 6–7, 17.

Metropolitan Life Survey of the American Teacher. (1987). *Strengthening links between home and school.* New York: Louis Harris & Associates.

Milne, A. M. (1989). Family structure and the achievement of children. In W. J. Weston (Ed.), *Education and the American family* (pp. 32–65). New York: New York University Press.

Minke, K. M. (2000). Preventing school problems and promoting school success through family–school community collaboration. In K. M. Minke & G. C. Bear (Eds.), *Preventing school problems—promoting school success: Strategies and programs that work* (pp. 377–420). Bethesda, MD: National Association of School Psychologists.

Mitrsomwang, S., & Hawley, W. (1993). *Cultural adaptation and the effects of family values and behavior on the academic achievement and persistence of Indochinese students.* Final report (No. R117E00045) to OERI. Washington, DC: U.S. Department of Education.

Moles, O. (1992). *Schools and families together: Helping children learn more at home.* Washington, DC: Office of Research, Office of Education Research Improvement, U.S. Department of Education, 20208.

Moles, O. C. (1993). *Building school-family partnerships for learning: Workshops for urban educators.* Washington, DC: Office of Educational Research and Improvement (OERI), U.S. Department of Education.

Mostert, M. P. (1998). *Interprofessional collaboration in schools.* Boston: Allyn & Bacon.

National Association of School Psychologists. (1992). *Position statement on home–school collaboration: Establishing partnerships to enhance outcomes* (Rev. 1999). Bethesda, MD: Author.

National Association of State Boards of Education. (1992). *Partners in educational improvement: Schools, parents, and community.* Alexandria, VA: Author.

National Center for Education Statistics. (1998). *Parent involvement in children's education: Efforts by public elementary schools.* Washington, DC: U.S. Department of Education.

National Coalition for Parent Involvement in Education. (1990). *Developing family / school partnerships: Guidelines for schools and school districts.* Washington, DC: National Education Association.

National Council on Disability. (1995, May). *Improving the implementation of the Individuals with Disabilities Act: Making schools work for all of America's children.* Washington, DC: Author.

National Education Goals Panel. (1999). *The National Education Goals Report: Building a nation of learners.* Washington, DC: U.S. Government Printing Office. (Online at http://www.negp.gov/page3–1.htm)

National PTA. (1998). *National standards for parent/family involvement programs*. Chicago: Author.

National PTA. (2000). *Building successful partnerships: A guide for developing parent and family involvement programs*. Bloomington, IN: National Education Service.

Nobles, W. W. (1985). *Africanity and the black family: The development of a theoretical model*. Oakland, CA: Black Family Institute.

Norman, J. M., & Smith, E. P. (1997). Families and schools, islands unto themselves: Opportunities to construct bridges. *Family Futures, 1*, 5–7.

O'Hanlon, W. H., & Weiner-Davis, M. (1989). *In search of solutions: A new direction in psychotherapy*. New York: Norton.

Olympia, D., Jenson, W., & Hepworth-Neville, M. (1996). *Sanity savers for parents: Tips for tackling homework*. Longmont, CO: Sopris West.

Olympia, D., Sheridan, S. M., & Jenson, W. R. (1994). Homework: A natural means of home–school collaboration. *School Psychology Quarterly, 9*, 60–80.

O'Neill, R. E., Horner, R. H., Albin, R. W., Sprague, J. R., Storey, K., & Newton, J. S. (1997). *Functional assessment and program development for problem behavior: A practical handbook* (2nd ed.). Pacific Grove, CA: Brooks/Cole.

Ooms, T., & Hara, S. (1991). *The family–school partnership: A critical component of school reform*. Washington, DC: Family Impact Seminar, American Association of Marriage and Family Therapy.

Osher, T. (1997, July). IDEA reauthorized—role for families enhanced. *Claiming Children*, pp. 1–8.

Palanki, A., & Burch, P. (1995, July). *In our hands: A multi-site parent–teacher action research project* (Research Report No. 30). Baltimore, MD: Center on Families, Communities, Schools, and Children's Learning, Johns Hopkins University.

Peng, S. S., & Lee, R. M. (1992, April). *Home variables, parent–child activities, and academic achievement: A study of 1988 eighth graders*. Paper presented at the annual meeting of the American Educational Research Association, San Francisco.

Phelan, P., Davidson, A. L., & Yu, H. C. (1998). *Adolescents' worlds: Negotiating family, peers, and school*. New York: Teachers College Press.

Phillips, V., & McCullough, L. (1990). Consultation-based programming: Instituting the collaborative ethic. *Exceptional Children, 56*, 291–304.

Phinney, J. S. (1996). When we talk about American ethnic groups, what do we mean? *American Psychologist, 51*(9), 918–927.

Pianta, R., & Walsh, D. B. (1996). *High-risk children in schools: Constructing sustaining relationships*. New York: Routledge.

Powell, D. R. (1992). *Families and young children's school readiness*. Paper prepared for the National Center for Educational Statistics, Office of Educational Research and Improvement, Washington, DC.

Power, T. J., & Bartholomew, K. L. (1985). Getting uncaught in the middle: A case study in family–school system consultation. *School Psychology Review, 14*, 222–229.

Power, T. J., & Bartholomew, K. L. (1987). Family–school relationship patterns: An ecological assessment. *School Psychology Review, 16*, 498–512.

Procidano, M. E., & Fisher, C. B. (1992). *Contemporary families: A handbook for school professionals*. New York: Teachers College Press.

Public Agenda. (1999). *Playing their parts: Parents and teachers talk about parent involvement in public schools*. New York: Author.

Rafaelle, L. M., & Knoff, H. M. (1999). Improving home–school collaboration with disadvantaged families: Organizational principles, perspectives, and approaches. *School Psychology Review, 28,* 448–466.

Ramey, C. T., & Ramey, S. L. (1998). Early intervention and early experience. *American Psychologist, 53*(2), 109–120.

Rappaport, J. (1981). In praise of paradox: A social policy of empowerment over prevention. *American Journal of Community Psychology, 9,* 1–25.

Reid, J. B., & Patterson, G. R. (1992). Early prevention and intervention with conduct problems: A social interactional model for the integration of research and practice. In G. Stoner, M. R. Shinn, & H. M. Walker (Eds.), *Interventions for achievement and behavior problems* (pp. 715–739). Silver Spring, MD: National Association of School Psychologists.

Resnick, M. D., Bearman, P. S., Blum, R. W., Bauman, K. E., Harris, K. M., Jones, J., Tabor, J., Beuhring, T., Sieving, R. E., Shew, M., Ireland, M., Bearinger, L. H., & Udry, J. (1997). Protecting adolescents from harm: Findings from the National Longitudinal Study on Adolescent Health. *Journal of the American Medical Association, 278*(10), 823–832.

Rich, D. (1987). *Schools and families: Issues and actions.* Washington, DC: National Education Association.

Rich, D. (1988). *MegaSkills: How families can help children succeed in school and beyond.* Boston: Houghton Mifflin.

Rich, D. (1993). Building the bridge to reach minority parents: Education infrastructure supporting success for children. In N. F. Chavkin (Ed.), *Families and schools in a pluralistic society* (pp. 235–244). Albany: State University of New York Press.

Rimm-Kaufmann, S. E., & Pianta, R. C. (1999). Patterns of family–school contact in preschool and kindergarten. *School Psychology Review, 28*(3), 426–438.

Rioux, J. W., & Berla, N. (1993). *Innovations in parent and family involvement.* Princeton Junction, NJ: Eye on Education.

Rumberger, R. W. (1995). Dropping out of middle school: A multilevel analysis of students and schools. *American Educational Research Journal, 32*(3), 583–625.

Rutherford, B., Billig, S. H., & Kettering, J. (1995). A review of the research and practice literature on parent and community involvement. In B. Rutherford (Ed.), *Creating family / school partnerships* (pp. 1–73). Columbus, OH: National Middle School Association.

Ryan, B. A., Adams, G. R., Gullotta, T. P., Weissberg, R. P., & Hampton, R. L. (Eds.). (1995). *The family–school connections: Theory, research, and practice.* Thousand Oaks, CA: Sage.

Sattes, B. (1985). *Parent involvement: A review of the literature* (Report No. 21). Charleston, WV: Appalachia Educational Laboratory.

Scott-Jones, D. (1987). Mother-as-teacher in the families of high- and low-achieving low-income black first-graders. *Journal of Negro Education, 56,* 21–34.

Scott-Jones, D. (1995a). Activities in the home that support school learning in middle grades. In B. Rutherford (Ed.), *Creating family / school partnerships* (pp. 167–190). Columbus, OH: National Middle School Association.

Scott-Jones, D. (1995b). Parent-child interactions and school achievement. In B. A. Ryan, G. R. Adams, T. P. Gullotta, R. P. Weissberg, & R. L. Hampton (Eds.), *The family–school connection: Theory, research, and practice* (pp. 75–107). Thousand Oaks, CA: Sage.

SEARCH Institute. (1994). Connecting schools and families. *SOURCE, 10*(3), 1–3.

Seeley, D. S. (1985). *Education through partnership.* Washington, DC: American Enterprise Institute for Public Policy Research.

Seeley, D. S. (1989). A new paradigm for parent involvement. *Educational Leadership, 47*(2), 46–48.

Sheridan, S. M. (1997). Conceptual and empirical bases of conjoint behavioral consultation. *School Psychology Quarterly, 12,* 119–133.

Sheridan, S. M., & Colton, D. L. (1994). Conjoint behavioral consultation: A review and case study. *Journal of Educational and Psychological Consultation, 5,* 211–228.

Sheridan, S. M., Cowan, R. J., & Eagle, J. W. (2000). Partnering with parents in educational programming for students with special needs. In C. Telzrow & M. Tankersley (Eds.), *IDEA Amendments of 1997: Practice guidelines for school-based teams* (pp. 307–349). Bethesda, MD: National Association of School Psychologists.

Sheridan, S. M., & Kratochwill, T. R. (1992). Behavioral parent–teacher consultation: Conceptual and research considerations. *Journal of School Psychology, 30,* 117–139.

Sheridan, S. M., Kratochwill, T. R., & Bergan, J. R. (1996). *Conjoint behavioral consultation: A procedural manual.* New York: Plenum Press.

Sheridan, S. M., Kratochwill, T. R., & Elliott, S. N. (1990). Behavioral consultation with parents and teachers: Delivering treatment for socially withdrawn children at home and school. *School Psychology Review, 19,* 33–52.

Sinclair, M., Lam, S. F., Christenson, S. L., & Evelo, D. (1993). Action research in middle schools. *Equity and Choice, 10*(1), 23–24.

Skoglund, B. (Ed.). (1999). Building family involvement vital to student success. *Connections, 4*(1), 1, 4–5.

Sloane, K. D. (1991). *Home support for successful learning.* In S. B. Silvern (Ed.), *Advances in reading/language research: Vol. 5. Literacy through family, community, and school interaction* (pp. 153–172). Greenwich, CT: JAI Press.

Smith, E. P., Connell, C. M., Wright, G., Sizer, M., Norman, J. M., Hurley, A., & Walker, S. N. (1997). An ecological model of home, school, and community partnerships: Implications for research and practice. *Journal of Educational and Psychological Consultation, 8,* 339–360.

Smrekar, C. (1996). *The impact of school choice and community (in the interest of families and schools).* Albany: State University of New York Press.

Steinberg, L., Mounts, N. S., Lamborn, S. D., & Dornbusch, S. M. (1991). Authoritative parenting and adolescent adjustment across varied ecological niches. *Journal of Research on Adolescence, 1*(1), 19–36.

Stevenson, D., & Baker, D. (1987). The family–school relation and the child's school performance. *Child Development, 58,* 1348–1357.

Strong families, strong schools: Building community partnerships for learning. (1994). Washington, DC: U.S. Department of Education, Government Printing Office.

Swap, S. (1990). *Schools reaching out and success for all children: Two case studies.* Boston: Institute for Responsive Education.

Swap, S. M. (1993). *Developing home–school partnerships: From concepts to practice.* New York: Teachers College Press.

Swick, K. J. (1988). Parental efficacy and involvement: Influences on children. *Childhood Education, 65,* 37–38.

Swick, K. J., & McKnight, S. (1989). Characteristics of kindergarten teachers who promote parent involvement. *Early Childhood Research Quarterly, 4,* 19–29.

Tagiuri, R. (1968). The concept of organizational climate. In R. Tagiuri & G. H. Litwin (Eds.), *Organizational climate: Exploration of a concept* (pp. 10–32). Cambridge, MA: Harvard University Press.

Taverne, A., & Sheridan, S. M. (1995). Parent training in interactive book reading: An investigation of its effects with families at-risk. *School Psychology Quarterly, 10,* 41–64.

Thomas, K. W., & Kilmann, R. H. (1974). *Thomas–Kilmann conflict mode instrument.* Tuxedo, NY: Xicom.

Thorp, E. K. (1997). Increasing opportunities for partnerships with culturally and linguistically diverse families. *Intervention in School and Clinic, 32,* 261–269.

Tilly, W. D., Knoster, T. P., & Ikeda, M. J. (2000). Functional behavioral assessment: Strategies for positive behavior support. In C. F. Telzrow & M. Tankersley (Eds.), *IDEA amendments of 1997: Practice guidelines for school-based teams* (pp. 151–197). Bethesda, MD: National Association of School Psychologists.

Turnbull, A. P., & Turnbull, H. R. III (1997). *Families, professionals, and exceptionality: A special partnership* (3rd ed.). Columbus: Merrill.

U.S. Congress. (1999, March 12). IDEA: Rules and regulations. *Federal Register, 64,* 12406–12672. Washington, DC: Author.

U.S. Department of Education. (1997). *A compact for learning: An action handbook for school–family–community partnerships.* Washington, DC: U.S. Department of Education Partnership for Family Involvement in Education. (Online at www.ed.gov)

Victor, J. B., Halvorson, C. F., Jr., & Wampler, K. S. (1988). Family–school context: Parent and teacher agreement on temperament. *Journal of Consulting and Clinical Psychology, 56,* 573–577.

Vosler-Hunter, R. W. (1989). *Changing roles, changing relationships: Parent–professional collaboration on behalf of children with emotional disabilities.* Portland, OR: Portland State University, Research and Training Center on Family Support and Children's Mental Health.

Vygotsky, L. (1962). *Thought and language* (E. Hanfmann & G. Vakar, Eds., & Trans.). Cambridge, MA: MIT Press.

Wahler, R. G., & Fox, J. J. (1981). Setting events in applied behavioral analysis: Toward a conceptual and methodological expansion. *Journal of Applied Behavioral Analysis, 14,* 327–338.

Walberg, H. J. (1984). Families as partners in educational productivity. *Phi Delta Kappan, 65,* 397–400.

Walberg, H. J., Bole, R. J., & Waxman, H. C. (1980). School-based socialization and reading achievement in the inner city. *Psychology in the Schools, 17,* 500–514.

Wang, M. C., Haertl G. D., & Walberg, H. J. (1997). Fostering educational resilience in inner-city schools. In R. P. Weissberg, O. Reyes, & H. J. Walberg (Eds.), *Urban children and youth* (pp. 135–142). Thousand Oaks, CA: Sage.

Warner, I. (1991). Parents in touch: District leadership for parent involvement. *Phi Delta Kappan, 65,* 397–400.

Webster, M. (1981). *Webster's new collegiate dictionary.* Springfield, MA: Merriam.

Webster-Stratton, C. (1993). Strategies for helping school-age children with oppositional defiant and conduct disorders: The importance of home–school partnerships. *School Psychology Review, 22,* 437–457.

Weiss, H. M., & Edwards, M. E. (1992). The family–school collaboration project: Systemic interventions for school improvement. In S. L. Christenson & J. C. Conoley (Eds.), *Home–school collaboration: Enhancing children's academic and social competence* (pp. 215–243). Silver Spring, MD: National Association of School Psychologists.

Weissberg, R. P., & Greenberg, M. T. (1998). School and community competence–enhancement and prevention programs. In W. Damon (Series Ed.) & I. E. Sigel & K. A. Renninger (Vol. Eds.), *Handbook of child psychology: Vol. 4. Child psychology in practice* (5th ed., pp. 877–954). New York: Wiley.

Welch, M., & Sheridan, S. M. (1995). *Educational partnerships: Serving students at risk.* San Antonio, TX: Harcourt Brace.

White, K. R. (1982). The relationship between socioeconomic status and academic achievement. *Psychological Bulletin, 91,* 461–481.

Williams, D. L., Jr., & & Chavkin, N. F. (1989). Essential elements of strong parent involvement programs. *Educational Leadership, 47*(4), 18–20.

Wright, G., & Smith, E. P. (1998). Home, school, and community partnerships: Integrating issues of race, culture, and social class. *Clinical Child and Family Psychology Review, 1,* 145–162.

Wynn, J., Meyer, S., & Richards-Schuster, K. (1999, September). Furthering education: The relationship of schools and other organizations. *The CEIC Review, 8*(2), 8–9,17–19.

Yeaton, W. H., & Sechrest, L. (1981). Critical dimensions in the choice and maintenance of successful treatment: Strength, integrity, and effectiveness. *Journal of Consulting and Clinical Psychology, 49,* 156–167.

Young, E. (1992). *Seven blind mice.* New York: Philomel Books.

Ysseldyke, J., & Christenson, S. L. (1993). *The Instructional Environment Scale—II.* Longmont, CO: Sopris West.

Zellman, G. L., & Waterman, J. M. (1998). Understanding the impact of parent school involvement on children's educational outcomes. *Journal of Educational Research, 91*(6), 370–380.

Zill, N., & Nord, C. W. (1994). *Running in place: How American families are faring in a changing economy and an individualistic society.* Washington, DC: Child Trends.

Index

♦